77.62 (eet) Batfield 567 (Sheffin)

ORIGINAL NARRATIVES
OF EARLY AMERICAN HISTORY

REPRODUCED UNDER THE AUSPICES OF THE
AMERICAN HISTORICAL ASSOCIATION

GENERAL EDITOR, J. FRANKLIN JAMESON, Ph.D., LL.D., LITT.D.

DIRECTOR OF THE DEPARTMENT OF HISTORICAL RESEARCH IN THE
CARNEGIE INSTITUTION OF WASHINGTON

———————

ORIGINAL NARRATIVES
OF EARLY AMERICAN HISTORY

No. 10

VOYAGES OF

SAMUEL DE CHAMPLAIN

1604—1618

EDITED BY

W. L. GRANT, M.A. (Oxon.)

BEIT LECTURER ON COLONIAL HISTORY IN THE UNIVERSITY
OF OXFORD

New York

BARNES & NOBLE, INC.

CONTENTS

VOYAGES OF SAMUEL DE CHAMPLAIN

Edited by W. L. Grant, A.M.

CONTENTS

NOTE

CHAMPLAIN'S narrative, as Mr. Grant has explained in his Introduction, is not solely one of the fundamental bases for the history of New France, but also, by reason of his explorations of the New England coast and his incursions into the Iroquois country, of high importance for that of the United States. A series, however, which aims primarily to illustrate the latter may properly omit the story of his later years, subsequent to 1618, the interest of which is chiefly Canadian. This volume presents the texts of the *Voyages* of 1613 and the *Voyages et Descouvertures* of 1619, as given in the excellent translation by Dr. Charles Pomeroy Otis, in the second and third volumes of the late Dr. Edmund F. Slafter's *Voyages of Samuel de Champlain*, published in three volumes by the Prince Society. Cordial thanks are due to Dr. Slafter and to the Council of the Prince Society for the permission to use this version.

It is proper to say that certain pages, which in the original occur in the *Voyages* of 1613 between the address to the Queen Mother and the "Privilege," have been omitted. They contain, first, a poem of sixteen stanzas upon Champlain's voyages, addressed to the French nation, and signed "L'Ange Paris" [iensis]; secondly, a poem of seven stanzas, "to Monsieur de Champlain, upon his book and his marine charts," signed Motin; and thirdly, a summary of the chapters, which in the present volume is replaced by the table of contents.

J. F. J.

THE VOYAGES OF SAMUEL DE CHAMPLAIN

INTRODUCTION

SAMUEL DE CHAMPLAIN was born about the year 1567 in the town of Brouage in the province of Saintonge. Now a quiet little village in the department of Charente Inférieure,[1] in the days when Catholic and Huguenot were at each other's throats all through France, the harbor of Brouage and its proximity to the Huguenot stronghold of La Rochelle made it a stirring and important place, several times taken and retaken during the youth of Champlain. A devout Catholic, but a fervent Royalist, he rallied to the side of Henry IV., and fought with credit both on sea and land during the confused years of foreign and domestic warfare which were terminated by the peace of Vervins in 1598. But from the first his love had been for the sea, and soon after the peace he entered the service of the King of Spain, and in January, 1599, set sail for the West Indies, as captain of the *St. Julian*, a stout ship of five hundred tons. Till March, 1601, he remained in the neighborhood of the Caribbean Sea, visiting Mexico, Cartagena, Havana, and the other Spanish colonies on the main land and among the Antilles. On his return he wrote a short account of his travels entitled *Brief Discours des Choses plus remarquables que Sammuel Champlain de Brouage a reconneues aux Indes Occidentalles au voiage qu'il en a faict en icelles en l'année 1599 et en l'année 1601, comme ensuite.*

This first production of his pen is illustrated by Champlain himself with sixty-two maps and pictures, which, though drawn with the most delightful disregard of perspective and of tech-

[1] An interesting account of Brouage by D. R. Jack, with excellent illustrations, appeared in *Acadiensis*, IV. 226–233.

nique, are not without a rude vigor and fidelity. His keen eye
and his exceptional opportunities enabled him to bring back to
France a store of information on the flora, fauna, mines and
system of government of those rich colonies which Spain so
grimly endeavored to conceal from prying eyes. Among other
interesting suggestions is one as to the commercial value of a
trans-Isthmian canal, "by which the voyage to the South Sea
would be shortened by more than fifteen hundred leagues."
The value of his report brought him into favor with Henry IV.,
who knew and loved a man; he was assigned a small pension,
and it was probably at this time that he was raised to the rank
of the untitled nobility.

For a brief period after his return, Champlain dangled in
the ante-chambers of the Louvre, but was soon swept into the
current of a movement which was to absorb his life. Since the
expedition of Jacques Cartier, in 1534, a series of voyages had
been made from the seaports of France to the banks of Newfoundland and the Gulf of St. Lawrence in quest of fish and of
fur. Especially from the ports of Normandy and Brittany,
but also from those of the west and southwest, brown-sailed
fishing-smacks braved the Atlantic in search of cod. In 1578
Anthony Parkhurst was "informed that there are above 100
saile of Spaniards that come to take Cod" off Newfoundland,
"besides 20 or 30 more that come from Biskaie to kill Whale
for Traine; . . . of Portugals there are not lightly above 50
saile, . . . Of the French nation and Britons [Bretons]
are about one hundred and fiftie sailes," of English only fifty
sail.[1]

With peace came thoughts of larger enterprizes, of the West
or North West Passage to the Orient for which the English
mariners had been searching in vain, of colonies whose mineral
wealth should exceed that of Mexico and of Peru, of savage

[1] Hakluyt, *Principall Navigations*, ed. 1903, VIII. 10, 11.

tribes brought beneath the easy yoke of the Church. Of the various attempts to realize these high thoughts, the first which concerns us is that of Aymar de Chastes, governor of Dieppe, a grey-haired veteran of the civil wars, and one of the most unselfish and single-hearted of the gallant band, good Catholics and true Frenchmen, who had clung to Henry of Navarre in his darkest hours. In 1603 he proposed to the now triumphant monarch a plan for setting up in the new world the Cross of Christ and the fleur-de-lis of France. To aid him in defraying expenses he requested the monopoly of the fur-trade.

This was granted, and de Chastes wisely allayed the indignation of the merchants of the west coast by forming an alliance with several of the more prominent, chief among whom was du Pont Gravé, a merchant of St. Malo who had already made numerous voyages. Champlain was well known to de Chastes, under whom he had served in the royal fleet during the civil wars, and was offered a place in the expedition. The king's consent was obtained, and Champlain was commissioned to bring back to His Majesty "a true report of what should befall." He thus sailed with the position of Geographer Royal. The expedition, consisting of two vessels, one under Pont Gravé, the other under Sieur Prevert of St. Malo, left Honfleur on March 15, 1603, and sailed up the St. Lawrence as far as the present city of Montreal, but could find no trace of the Indian town of Hochelaga, visited by Cartier in 1535. Champlain busied himself with exploring and mapping out both shores of the Gulf of St. Lawrence.

After a prosperous voyage, they returned to France with a valuable cargo of furs, arriving at Havre de Grace on September 20, 1603, to be greeted by the news that de Chastes had died in the previous May. Champlain at once set about preparing for the king a report, illustrated by maps, which was printed with the royal sanction, and published early in 1604 with the title *Des Sauvages: ou Voyage de Samuel Champlain, de*

Brouage, faict en la France Nouvelle, l'an mil six cens trois.

This short treatise, which was dedicated to Charles de Montmorency, the Admiral of France, covers almost the same ground as that gone over by Jacques Cartier in 1534–1535, but gives fuller and more accurate descriptions of the coastline and its harbors, and contains valuable information about the customs and habits of the savages.

The mantle of de Chastes fell upon Pierre de Guast (or de Gua), Sieur de Monts, a Huguenot nobleman, governor of Pons in Saintonge. In spite of the opposition of the king's great minister Sully, who augured much expense and little profit from such fantastic enterprises, he obtained the title of Lieutenant-General in Acadia, with plenary jurisdiction over all the lands in America lying between the fortieth and forty-sixth degrees of latitude, and a ten years' monopoly of the fur-trade. De Monts entered vigorously upon the work of trade and colonization, associated with himself Champlain and Pont Gravé, and early in April, 1604, set sail from Havre de Grace. From this date till 1619 the life of Champlain is contained in his journals, of which this volume is composed. Only a few additional details need here be given. In 1610, while in Paris, he married Hélène Boullé, the daughter of Nicolas Boullé, secretary of the king's chamber. Although the contract was signed, and the greater part of her dowry paid over, the youth of the bride prevented her from accompanying her husband, and she remained for some years longer in the charge of her parents; but in 1620 accompanied Champlain to Quebec.

In 1613 he published his second volume, and in 1619 a continuation, which was reprinted in 1620 and 1627. The translation of these two volumes is given in the following pages.

In 1615–1616 his voyages of exploration came to an end, and for the next twenty years his history is that of the struggling settlement of Quebec. The fur trade grew, and the company is said to have paid an annual dividend of forty per cent. But colonization languished, and in 1627 Quebec contained only two families of permanent settlers. In that year the Cardinal de Richelieu, grand-admiral and virtual ruler of France, determined to make New France more than a high sounding name for a mere trading-post. The old company was dissolved, and a new one formed under the name of "La Compagnie de la Nouvelle France," which received large privileges, and undertook colonization on a large scale. In its organization Champlain was prominent, and he remained in charge of the settlement at Quebec.

War had broken out between England and France, and in 1628 David Kirke, an energetic Franco-Scottish freebooter, who had entered the English service, sailed up the Saint Lawrence, captured the fleet sent out with supplies by the newly founded company, and demanded the surrender of Quebec. Champlain, though almost destitute, put on so bold a face that Kirke withdrew. But in the next year he reappeared; winter had exhausted the scanty supplies of the French; and on July 19, 1629, Champlain surrendered on honorable terms, which were faithfully observed by the English. By the treaty of St. Germain-en-Laye, signed on March 29, 1632, the French possessions in Canada were restored, and in the next year Champlain returned to Quebec, bringing with him two members of the Jesuit order, which for the next hundred years was to be largely responsible for the fortunes of the colony.

In 1632 he published his last work, under the title, *Les Voyages de la Nouvelle France Occidentale, dicte Canada, faits par le Sr de Champlain, Xainctongeois, Capitaine pour le Roy en la Marine du Ponant, et toutes les Descouvertes qu'il a faites en ce Pais depuis l'an 1603 jusques en l'an 1629, Où se voit comme ce Pays a esté premièrement descouvert par les François,* *sous l'Authorité de nos Roys très Chrestiens, jusques au Regne de sa Majesté à present regnante Louis XIII. Roy de France et de Navarre.   A Paris, chez Claude Collet, au Palais, en la Gallerie des Prisonniers, à l'Estoille d'Or, MDCXXXII.   Avec Privilege du Roy.*

This volume is divided into two parts. The first gives a résumé of the voyages of his predecessors, and of his own travels up to 1620.   Many details, and even some important episodes, given in his earlier publications are omitted, and though a few errors are corrected, its interest is much less. The second part brings the history of Quebec and of the St. Lawrence up to 1631, and contains a full account of the English conquest.   It is doubtful how far Champlain is responsible for the form in which this volume appeared.   The absence of any word of praise for the early missionary work of the Re-collets, and the prominence given to the labors of the Jesuits, have rendered it probable in the eyes of some writers that he allowed his journals to be put through the press by a Jesuit editor.   The volume also contains a treatise on navigation by Champlain, a brief work on Christian doctrine translated into the language of the Montagnais by the Jesuit Father Brebeuf, and the Lord's Prayer and Apostles' Creed, translated into the same language by Father Massé.

During the final years of his life, Champlain worked hard at rebuilding and improving the fort and other buildings of Quebec, and at forming alliances for war and trade with various Indian tribes, with whom he sought to make a confederacy for the subjugation of the dreaded Iroquois.   But toil and privation and manifold disappointments had sapped his strength, and in October, 1635, he was compelled to take to his bed.   For over two months he lingered, and then on Christmas Day, 1635, the founder of New France passed quietly to rest, solaced in his last hours by the rites of the Church which he loved so well.   A few days later his body was laid to rest amid the sorrow of all the little community. Pious hands soon raised a chapel over his ashes, but all traces of it have long disappeared, and its site is now occupied by the post-office.

The life of Champlain is primarily connected with the history of Canada. He first planted the lilies of France upon the rock of Quebec, and nursed into existence the colony whose descendants still play so large a part in the Dominion. As such he is of interest to students of American history. For over one hundred years the colony which he founded waged equal war with the British settlements as far south as New York; its cession to England rendered possible American Independence, so long delayed by fear of the northern thunder-cloud. But Champlain is still more intimately connected with the beginnings of the great republic. His voyages of exploration extended to the south of Boston Harbor; more than any other of the early seamen he brought order out of confusion, and gave the first clear account of the shores of New England. To this side of his career insufficient attention has been paid. While the trials of the settlements at Plymouth and Massachusetts Bay are known to every school-boy, the connection of Champlain with the history of the United States has often been disregarded, and he has been considered solely as the founder of Quebec. The exclusive attention paid to the English colonists has glorified Massachusetts at the expense of Maine, and one of the noblest names in the history of exploration has been passed over.

The result has been to give an inadequate view of the character of Champlain. As a colonizer he had in a measure the defects of his military training. The site chosen by de Monts at St. Croix in 1604, largely at the instance of Champlain, however easy of defence as a military station, was most unsuitable for a permanent colony. Equally unsound was his advice to begin settlement not on the ground where Montreal now stands, but on the adjacent islet of St. Helens. Even

Quebec was chosen rather as a fur-trading post than with the thought of founding a great city, and Champlain's ideas of nation-building were less enlightened than those of his contemporary Lescarbot. (See p. 41, *note*.)   But as an explorer his energy, his care, his intelligence, leave nothing to desire. His " three voyages are the first thoroughly intelligible contributions to the cartography of Maine," says General Brown. "Gosnold and Pring had touched the coast; but their brief stay and imperfect and shadowy notes are to the historian tantalizing and only faintly instructive," says Mr. Slafter. But from Cape Canso to Boston Harbor Champlain gives a clear account of the coast-line; his writings were soon known in England and in Spain, and were used by the early cartographers of both nations.

His observations on the manners and customs of the Indians are also valuable, made as they were before contact with the white invader had changed and darkened the character of the red man.   Though without the lively fancy and versatile intelligence of Lescarbot, he had a far wider personal knowledge of the savage tribes, and his account is marked with truth and sincerity.

To his high moral qualities his narrative bears witness. "He is particularly interesting to Americans," says a recent writer, "because he is a Frenchman with those qualities which a wayward English tradition denies to the French — patience, sobriety, calm self-control, and a complete absence of vanity." In him the valor and the religious ardor of a crusader were unsullied by the intolerance and the superstition which marked so many of his contemporaries.

Canada has long honored his worth; from the rock of Quebec his statue looks proudly across the city which he founded to the north-west whose greatness he foresaw; his equal merit as explorer and as geographer has not yet been so fully recognized.

In 1640 the edition of 1632 was reprinted. Not till 1830 was another edition called for. In that year the same work was republished in two volumes by the French government, to give work to printers thrown out of employment by the Revolution of July. In this the text is given without note or comment, and the maps and plates are omitted. In 1870 the Abbé Laverdière published at Quebec, under the patronage of the University of Laval, a complete edition in six volumes of the works of the explorer, which has ever since formed the standard edition of Champlain. It contains all his writings, including the Brief Discourse of his journey to the West Indies in 1599, which had never before been printed, and of which a happy chance had preserved the manuscript. It is, as Mr. Slafter says, "an exact reprint, most carefully done and entirely trustworthy, while its notes are full and exceedingly accurate." It reproduces the drawings of the West India manuscript, and the maps and drawings of the printed editions of the other works, and contains a valuable introduction and appendices. The latter include the text of a letter of Champlain to Richelieu written in August, 1635, and dealing with various important questions of colonial policy (see p. 165).

In 1625 an English translation of the *Sauvages* of 1604 was printed at London by Purchas in his *Pilgrimes*, Vol. IV., pp. 1605–1619.

In 1859 the Brief Discourse of his voyage to the West Indies was translated by Alice Wilmere, edited by Norton Shaw, and published at London by the Hakluyt Society.

In 1878, 1880, and 1882 the Prince Society of Boston published in three volumes a translation of the Journals of 1604, 1613, and 1619 by Charles Pomeroy Otis, with a long introductory memoir and very full historical and geographical notes by the Reverend Edmund F. Slafter. The maps and drawings are well reproduced, as are two portraits of Champlain. The translation is extremely accurate, and has been, with the Society's permission, used in this volume.   In the one or two instances where I have ventured to disagree I have stated my reasons in a footnote.   Mr. Slafter's notes are a model of care and thoroughness.   In some cases, it will be seen, I have transferred them outright, and in others have reproduced his statements in condensed form.

The portion of the *Voyages* of 1632 dealing with events prior to 1617 has been issued in English translation in the "Trail Makers" series in 1906, together with the narrative of the voyage of 1603 reprinted from Purchas, the whole edited by Professor Edward G. Bourne.

There are many lives of Champlain, but for the ordinary reader the best sketch of his career remains that given by Francis Parkman in his *Pioneers of France in the New World*. The chapter by Mr. Slafter in Vol. IV. of the *Narrative and Critical History of America* edited by Mr. Justin Winsor, contains a full bibliography.   I must also acknowledge my indebtedness to "Coasting Voyages in the Gulf of Maine, made in 1604, 1605, and 1606, by Samuel Champlain," a paper by General John M. Brown, published in the *Collections of the Maine Historical Society*, first series, Vol. VII. (1876) and republished separately.   I must also express my thanks to the officials of the British Museum and of the Toronto Public Library for their invariable kindness and courtesy.

W. L. GRANT.

THE VOYAGES OF SIEUR DE CHAMPLAIN

THE VOYAGES OF SIEUR DE CHAMPLAIN

OF SAINTONGE, CAPTAIN IN ORDINARY
TO THE KING IN THE MARINE; OR,

A MOST FAITHFUL JOURNAL OF OBSERVATIONS
made in the exploration of New France, describing not
only the countries, coasts, rivers, ports, and harbors, with
their latitudes and the various deflections of the magnetic
needle, but likewise the religious belief of the inhabitants,
their superstitions, mode of life and warfare; furnished
with numerous illustrations.

Together with two geographical maps: [1] *the first for the purposes*
of navigation, adapted to the compass as used by mari-
ners, which deflects to the north-east; the other in its true
meridian, with longitudes and latitudes, to which is
added the Voyage to the Strait north of Labrador, from
the 53d to the 63d degree of latitude, discovered in 1612
by the English when they were searching for a northerly
course to China.

Paris: Jean Berjon, Rue St. Jean de Beauvais, at the Flying
Horse, and at his store in the Palace, at the Gallery of
the Prisoners. MDCXIII. With authority of the
King. [2]

---

[1] This italic heading is a translation of the title-page of the original
printed book.

TO THE KING[1]

SIRE,

Your Majesty has doubtless full knowledge of the discoveries made in your service in New France, called Canada, through the descriptions, given by certain Captains and Pilots, of the voyages and discoveries made there during the past eighty years. These, however, present nothing so honorable to your Kingdom, or so profitable to the service of your Majesty and your subjects, as will, I doubt not, the maps of the coasts, harbors, rivers, and the situation of the places described in this little treatise, which I make bold to address to your Majesty, and which is entitled a Journal of Voyages and Discoveries, which I have made in connection with Sieur de Monts, your Lieutenant in New France. This I do, feeling myself urged by a just sense of the honor I have received during the last ten years in commissions, not only, Sire, from your Majesty, but also from the late king, Henry the Great, of happy memory, who commissioned me to make the most exact researches and explorations in my power. This I have done, and added, moreover, the maps contained in this little book, where I have set forth in particular the dangers to which one would be liable. The subjects of your Majesty, whom you may be pleased hereafter to employ for the preservation of what has been discovered, will be able to avoid those dangers through the knowledge afforded by the maps contained in this treatise, which will serve as an example in your kingdom for increasing the glory of your Majesty, the welfare of your subjects, and for the honor of the very humble service, for which, to the happy prolongation of your days, is indebted,

SIRE,

Your most humble, most obedient,
and most faithful servant and subject,
CHAMPLAIN.

[1] Louis XIII., born 1601, succeeded 1610, declared of age 1614, died 1643.

TO THE QUEEN REGENT,[1]

MOTHER OF THE KING

MADAME,

Of all the most useful and excellent arts, that of navigation has always seemed to me to occupy the first place. For the more hazardous it is, and the more numerous the perils and losses by which it is attended, so much the more is it esteemed and exalted above all others, being wholly unsuited to the timid and irresolute. By this art we obtain knowledge of different countries, regions, and realms. By it we attract and bring to our own land all kinds of riches, by it the idolatry of paganism is overthrown and Christianity proclaimed throughout all the regions of the earth.[2] This is the art which from my early age has won my love, and induced me to expose myself almost all my life to the impetuous waves of the ocean, and led me to explore the coasts of a part of America, especially of New France, where I have always desired to see the Lily flourish, and also the only religion, catholic, apostolic, and Roman. This I trust now to accomplish with the help of God, assisted by the favor of your Majesty, whom I most humbly entreat to continue to sustain us, in order that all may succeed to the honor of God, the welfare of France, and the splendor of your reign, for the grandeur and prosperity of which I will pray God to attend you always with a thousand blessings, and will remain,

MADAME,

Your most humble, most obedient,

and most faithful servant and subject,

CHAMPLAIN.[3]

[1] Marie de Médicis, 1573–1642, widow of Henry IV., regent 1610–1614.

[2] This double aim characterized to the last the French settlements in North America. New France has been described as "a Jesuit mission, grafted on a fur-trading post." Most of the early settlements were made, however, not so much in view of the fur-trade, as for halting-places on the supposed road to Cathay and the Orient.

[3] This dedication is followed in the original by two poems in honor of

5

EXTRACT FROM THE LICENSE

By letters patent of the KING, given at Paris the ninth of
January, 1613, and in the third year of our reign, by the King
in his Council, PERREAU, and sealed with the simple yellow seal,[1]
it is permitted to JEAN BERJON, printer and bookseller in this
city of Paris, to print, or have printed by whomsoever it
may seem good to him, a book entitled *The Voyages of Samuel
de Champlain of Saintonge, Captain in ordinary for the King
in the Marine, etc.*, for the time and limit of six entire consecutive years, from the day when this book shall have
been printed up to the said time of six years. By the same
letters, in like manner all printers, merchant booksellers, and
any others whatever, are forbidden to print or have printed,
to sell or distribute said book during the aforesaid time,
without the special consent of said BERJON, or of him to whom
he shall give permission, on pain of confiscation of so many
of said books as shall be found, and a discretionary fine,
as is more fully set forth in the aforesaid letters.

Champlain, and by a table of contents. The insertion of such poems, sometimes by the author, as in the case of Lescarbot, and sometimes by his friends,
as here, is a frequent characteristic of these early books of travel.

[1] Used for letters patent of a temporary character or validity.

THE VOYAGES OF 1604–1607

BOOK I[1]

THE VOYAGES OF 1604–1607

Chapter 1

The benefits of commerce have induced several princes to seek an easier route for traffic with the people of the East. Several unsuccessful voyages. Determination of the French for this purpose. Undertaking of Sieur de Monts: his commission and its revocation. New commission to Sieur de Monts to enable him to continue his undertaking.

THE inclinations of men differ according to their varied dispositions; and each one in his calling has his particular end in view. Some aim at gain, some at glory, some at the public weal. The greater number are engaged in trade, and especially that which is transacted on the sea. Hence arise the principal support of the people, the opulence and honor of states. This is what raised ancient Rome to the sovereignty and mastery over the entire world, and the Venetians to a grandeur equal to that of powerful kings. It has in all times caused maritime towns to abound in riches, among which

---

[1] Though Book I. is not given in the original a separate title or heading, such as is given to Book II., the distinction between the two is broadly marked in the table of contents of the original. It reads: "Book First, in which are described the discoveries of the coast of Acadia and Florida." Then follows the list of the seventeen chapters of Book I.; then, "Book Second, in which are described the voyages made to the great River St. Laurens by the Sieur de Champlain"; then, the list of its eleven chapters. In other words, the first book describes the voyages of 1604–1607, the second those of 1608–1610 (or 1608–1612, if the second and third voyages, despite their separate headings and their separate series of chapters, be reckoned as parts of Book II.), while that of 1611 is the subject of the "Troisiesme Voyage" and that of 1613 of the "Quatriesme Voyage."

Alexandria and Tyre are distinguished, and numerous others, which fill up the regions of the interior with the objects of beauty and rarity obtained from foreign nations. For this reason, many princes have striven to find a northerly route to China, in order to facilitate commerce with the Orientals, in the belief that this route would be shorter and less dangerous.

In the year 1496, the king of England commissioned John Cabot and his son Sebastian to engage in this search.[1] About the same time, Don Emanuel, king of Portugal, despatched on the same errand Gaspar Cortereal, who returned without attaining his object. Resuming his journeys the year after, he died in the undertaking; as did also his brother Michel, who was prosecuting it perseveringly.[2] In the years 1534 and 1535, Jacques Cartier received a like commission from King Francis I., but was arrested in his course.[3] Six years after, Sieur de Roberval, having renewed it, sent Jean Alfonse of Saintonge farther northward along the coast of Labrador; but he returned as wise as the others.[4] In the years 1576, 1577, and 1578, Sir Martin Frobisher, an English-

---

[1] The first commission was granted by Henry VII. of England to John Cabot and his three sons, Lewis, Sebastian, and Sancius, March 5, 1496. The first voyage, however, was made in 1497. The second commission was granted to John Cabot alone, in 1498.

Sebastian Cabot played a smaller part in these early voyages than popular history relates, and has in large measure usurped the credit due to his father. See C. R. Beazley, *John and Sebastian Cabot* (London, 1898).

[2] Gaspar Cortereal made two voyages, the first in 1500, the second with three vessels in 1501. Two reached home safely, but that on which he himself sailed was lost. This is the less to be regretted as he had tried to carry off the Labrador Indians to sell in the slave-market of Lisbon. His brother Miguel went in search of him in 1502 with three vessels. These reached St. John's, Newfoundland, in June, and separated in search of Gaspar. That bearing Cortereal was never again heard of. The other two reached Portugal in safety. See H. P. Biggar, *Voyages of the Cabots and the Cortereals* (Paris, 1903).

[3] This does less than justice to Cartier, who explored very thoroughly the river and gulf of St. Lawrence as far as Montreal, and whose memoirs greatly assisted subsequent navigators. See Parkman, *Pioneers of France in the New World*. In 1541 he made a third expedition, under the orders of Roberval.

[4] Roberval's voyage was made in 1542. See Hakluyt for this, and for the subsequent English voyages.

man, made three voyages along the northern coasts.[1]   Seven
years later, Humphrey Gilbert, also an Englishman, set out
with five ships, but suffered shipwreck on Sable Island, where
three of his vessels were lost.[2]   In the same and two following years, John Davis, an Englishman, made three voyages
for the same object; penetrating to the 72d degree, as far as
a strait which is called at the present day by his name.   After
him, Captain Georges made also a voyage in 1590, but in consequence of the ice was compelled to return without having
made any discovery.[3]   The Hollanders, on their part, had
no more precise knowledge in the direction of Nova Zembla.

So many voyages and discoveries without result, and attended with so much hardship and expense, have caused us
French in late years to attempt a permanent settlement in
those lands which we call New France, in the hope of thus
realizing more easily this object; since the voyage in search
of the desired passage commences on the other side of the
ocean, and is made along the coast of this region.   These
considerations had induced the Marquis de la Roche, in 1598,
to take a commission from the king for making a settlement
in the above region.   With this object, he landed men and
supplies on Sable Island; but, as the conditions which had
been accorded to him by his Majesty were not fulfilled, he

[1] Frobisher's voyages were partially in search of the Northwest Passage,
partially in the hope of finding gold.   He was unsuccessful in both objects.
On all these voyages, consult Winsor's *Narrative and Critical History of
America.*

[2] Gilbert's voyage to colonize Newfoundland was made in 1583.   He
went down in a storm on the return voyage to England, some days after
leaving Sable Island.   See Froude, "England's Forgotten Worthies," in his
Short Studies on Great Subjects, or the report of the voyage written by Master
Edward Haies, in the volume of this series entitled *Early English and French
Voyages, chiefly from Hakluyt.*   Davis's first voyage took place in 1585.

[3] There may have been a voyage by a Captain Georges, which for some
unknown reason was never reported; or, what is more likely, Champlain may
refer to the voyage of Captain George Waymouth, undertaken in 1602 for the
East India Company, which was defeated by the icebergs he encountered
and the mutiny of his men.   It was not uncommon to omit part of a name
at that period, and Champlain may have mistaken the date, as the report of
Waymouth's voyage was not printed till after Champlain wrote.   (Slafter.)

was obliged to abandon his undertaking, and leave his men there.[1]   A year after, Captain Chauvin accepted another commission to transport settlers to the same region; but, as this was shortly after revoked, he prosecuted the matter no farther.[2]

After the above, notwithstanding all these accidents and disappointments, Sieur de Monts desired to attempt what had been given up in despair, and requested a commission for this purpose of his Majesty, being satisfied that the previous enterprises had failed because the undertakers of them had not received assistance, who had not succeeded, in one nor even two years' time, in making the acquaintance of the regions and people there, nor in finding harbors adapted for a settlement.   He proposed to his Majesty a means for covering these expenses, without drawing any thing from the royal revenues; viz., by granting to him the monopoly of the fur-trade in this land.   This having been granted to him, he made great and excessive outlays, and carried out with him a large number of men of various vocations.   Upon his arrival, he caused the necessary number of habitations for his followers to be constructed.   This expenditure he continued for three consecutive years, after which, in consequence of the jealousy and annoyance of certain Basque merchants, together with some from Brittany, the monopoly which had been granted to him was revoked by the Council to the great injury and loss of Sieur de Monts, who, in consequence of this revocation, was compelled to abandon his entire undertaking, sacrificing his labors and the outfit for his settlement.

But since a report had been made to the king on the fertility of the soil by him, and by me on the feasibility of dis-

---

[1] De la Roche's crew were a set of jail-birds.   He landed some forty of them temporarily on Sable Island, and went on to find a site for a permanent settlement.   A storm carried him back to France, where he was imprisoned by an old enemy.   The convicts quarrelled and slew each other till only twelve remained, who were brought back to France in 1603, and pardoned by Henry IV. in pity for their sufferings.

[2] Chauvin made two voyages in 1599 and 1600, in company with **Pont** Gravé (see Introduction).

covering the passage to China, without the inconveniences of the ice of the north or the heats of the torrid zone, through which our sailors pass twice in going and twice in returning, with inconceivable hardships and risks, his Majesty directed Sieur de Monts to make a new outfit, and send men to continue what he had commenced. This he did. And, in view of the uncertainty of his commission,[1] he chose a new spot for his settlement, in order to deprive jealous persons of any such distrust as they had previously conceived. He was also influenced by the hope of greater advantages in case of settling in the interior, where the people are civilized, and where it is easier to plant the Christian faith and establish such order as is necessary for the protection of a country, than along the seashore, where the savages generally dwell. From this course, he believed the king would derive an inestimable profit; for it is easy to suppose that Europeans will seek out this advantage rather than those of a jealous and intractable disposition to be found on the shores, and the barbarous tribes.

Chapter 2

Description of Sable Island; Cape Breton; La Hève; Port au Mouton; Port Cape Nègre; Sable Bay and Cape; Cormorant Island; Cape Fourchu; Long Island; Bay of Saint Mary; Port Saint Margaret; and of all noteworthy objects along this coast.

Sieur de Monts, by virtue of his commission[2] having published in all the ports and harbors of this kingdom the prohibition against the violation of the monopoly of the fur-trade accorded him by his Majesty, gathered together about one

---

[1] This refers to the commission of 1608, granted after the revocation of that of 1603. See its text in book II., chap. I., below.

[2] This commission was issued on November 8, 1603, and is given by Lescarbot, *Histoire de la Nouvelle France*, book IV.; in English translation by Williamson, *History of Maine*, I. 651, and Murdoch, *History of Nova Scotia*, I. 21; and in both French and English in Baird, *Huguenot Emigration*, I. 341.

hundred and twenty artisans, whom he embarked in two vessels: one of a hundred and twenty tons, commanded by Sieur de Pont Gravé; another, of a hundred and fifty tons, in which he embarked himself, together with several noblemen.

We set out from Havre de Grâce April 7, 1604, and Pont Gravé April 10, to rendezvous at Canseau,[1] twenty leagues [2] from Cape Breton.[3]   But, after we were in mid-ocean, Sieur de Monts changed his plan, and directed his course towards Port Mouton,[4] it being more southerly and also more favorable for landing than Canseau.

On May 1, we sighted Sable Island, where we ran a risk of being lost in consequence of the error of our pilots, who were deceived in their calculation, which they made forty leagues ahead of where we were.

This island is thirty leagues distant north and south from Cape Breton, and in length is about fifteen leagues.[5]   It contains a small lake.   The island is very sandy, and there are no trees at all of considerable size, only copse and herbage, which serve as pasturage for the bullocks and cows, which the Portuguese carried there more than sixty years ago, and which were very serviceable to the party of the Marquis de la Roche.   The latter, during their sojourn of several years there, captured a large number of very fine black foxes, whose

---

[1] The harbor of Canso on the northeast coast of Nova Scotia.   The name is also given to an island in the neighborhood, and to the strait separating the island of Cape Breton from Nova Scotia.

[2] The league (Fr. *lieue*) varied in length in different localities and at different dates.   In Champlain and Lescarbot it is roughly equivalent to two English miles.

[3] This cape, which later gave its name to the whole island, probably took its name from the fishermen of Brittany, who frequented the region in search of cod since about 1504.   Others suppose it to have been named by the Basque fishermen in memory of Cape Breton on the southwest coast of France, north of Bayonne.

[4] Still so called.   It derives its name from a sheep (*mouton*) which on this voyage fell overboard and was drowned.

[5] It is now about twenty miles in length by one in breadth, and owing to the action of wind and wave tends to decrease in size, in spite of the efforts of the Canadian government.   Its long record of disastrous wrecks has won it the name of "the graveyard of the Atlantic."

skins they carefully preserved. There are many sea-wolves [1] there, with the skins of which they clothed themselves since they had exhausted their own stock of garments. By order of the Parliamentary Court of Rouen, a vessel was sent there to recover them. The directors of the enterprise caught codfish near the island, the neighborhood of which abounds in shoals.

On the 8th of the same month, we sighted Cap de la Hève,[2] to the east of which is a bay, containing several islands covered with fir-trees. On the main land are oaks, elms, and birches. It joins the coast of La Cadie at the latitude of 44° 5′, and at 16° 15′ of the deflection of the magnetic needle,[3] distant east-north-east eighty-five leagues from Cape Breton, of which we shall speak hereafter.

On the 12th of May, we entered another port, five leagues from Cap de la Hève, where we captured a vessel engaged in the fur-trade in violation of the king's prohibition. The master's name was Rossignol, whose name the port retained,[4] which is in latitude 44° 15′.

On the 13th of May, we arrived at a very fine harbor, where there are two little streams, called Port au Mouton, which is seven leagues distant from that of Rossignol. The land is very stony, and covered with copse and heath. There are a great many rabbits, and a quantity of game in consequence of the ponds there.

As soon as we had disembarked, each one commenced making huts after his fashion, on a point at the entrance of

[1] *I.e.*, seals.

[2] Still so called from Cap de la Hève in Normandy, a little north of Havre de Grâce, their point of embarkation. The harbor is that now called Palmerston Bay at the mouth of Petit River, in about 44° 15′. Many of the latitudes and longitudes given by Champlain are only approximately correct.

[3] Before the invention of the chronometer, longitudes could not be accurately determined. Champlain's practice is to give the declination of the needle from the true north, as a means of obtaining the longitude. His explanation of his system may be seen in the Prince Society's edition, III. 219–224.

[4] Now Liverpool. A lake in the interior still bears the name of Rossignol.

the harbor near two fresh-water ponds. Sieur de Monts at the same time despatched a shallop, in which he sent one of us, with some savages as guides, as bearers of letters, along the coast of La Cadie, to search for Pont Gravé, who had a portion of the necessary supplies for our winter sojourn. The latter was found at the Bay of All-Isles,[1] very anxious about us (for he knew nothing of the change of plan); and the letters were handed to him. As soon as he had read them, he returned to his ship at Canseau, where he seized some Basque vessels engaged in the fur-trade, notwithstanding the prohibition of his Majesty, and sent their masters to Sieur de Monts, who meanwhile charged me to reconnoitre the coast and the harbors suitable for the secure reception of our vessel.

With the purpose of carrying out his wishes, I set out from Port Mouton on the 19th of May, in a barque of eight tons, accompanied by Sieur Ralleau, his secretary, and ten men. Advancing along the coast, we entered a harbor very convenient for vessels, at the end of which is a small river, extending very far into the main land. This I called the Port of Cape Negro, from a rock whose distant view resembles a negro, which rises out of the water near a cape passed by us the same day, four leagues off and ten from Port Mouton. This cape is very dangerous, on account of the rocks running out into the sea. The shores which I saw, up to that point, are very low, and covered with such wood as that seen at the Cap de la Hève; and the islands are all filled with game. Going farther on, we passed the night at Sable Bay,[2] where vessels can anchor without any danger.

The next day we went to Cape Sable, also very dangerous, in consequence of certain rocks and reefs extending almost a league into the sea. It is two leagues from Sable Bay, where we had spent the night before. Thence we went

[1] It was the bay, or rather the waters, that stretch along the shores of Halifax County, between Owl's Head and Liscomb River. (Slafter.)

[2] Near Cape Sable Island, at what is now known as Barrington Harbor. (Laverdière.) The reader should be warned not to confuse Sable Island, lying some one hundred miles off the coast, with Cape Sable Island, at the southeast extremity of Nova Scotia.

to Cormorant Island,[1] a league distant, so called from the infinite number of cormorants found there, of whose eggs we collected a cask full. From this island, we sailed westerly about six leagues, crossing a bay, which makes up to the north two or three leagues. Then we fell in with several islands[2] distant two or three leagues from the main land; and, as well as I could judge, some of them were two leagues in extent, others three, and others were still smaller. Most of them are very dangerous for large vessels to approach, on account of the tides and the rocks on a level with the water. These islands are filled with pines, firs, birches, and aspens. A little farther out, there are four more. In one, we saw so great a quantity of birds, called penguins,[3] that we killed them easily with sticks. On another, we found the shore completely covered with sea-wolves, of which we captured as many as we wished. At the two others there is such an abundance of birds of different sorts that one could not imagine it, if he had not seen them. There are cormorants, three kinds of duck, geese, *marmettes ?*, bustards, sea-parrots, snipe, vultures, and other birds of prey; gulls, sea-larks of two or three kinds; herons, large sea-gulls, curlews, sea-magpies, divers, ospreys, *appoils ?*, ravens, cranes, and other sorts which I am not acquainted with, and which also make their nests here. We named these Sea-Wolf Islands. They are in latitude 43° 30$'$, distant from four to five leagues from the main land, or Cape Sable. After spending pleasantly some time there in hunting (and not without capturing much game), we set out and reached a cape, which we christened Port Fourchu[4] from its being fork-shaped, distant from five to six leagues from the Sea-Wolf Islands. This harbor is very convenient for vessels at its entrance; but its remoter part is entirely dry at low tide, except the channel of a little

---

[1] Probably Hope Island.   [2] The Tusket or Tousquet Islands.

[3] The great auk, now extinct. Champlain gave to the birds, beasts, and flowers of North America the names of the European varieties most closely resembling them.

[4] Still so called.

stream, completely bordered by meadows, which make this spot very pleasant. There is good codfishing near the harbor. Departing from there, we sailed north ten or twelve leagues without finding any harbor for our vessels, but a number of very fine inlets or shores, where the soil seems to be well adapted for cultivation. The woods are exceedingly fine here, but there are few pines and firs. This coast is clear, without islands, rocks, or shoals; so that, in our judgment, vessels can securely go there. Being distant quarter of a league from the coast, we went to an island called Long Island, lying north-north-east and south-south-west, which makes an opening into the great Baye Françoise,[1] so named by Sieur de Monts.

This island is six leagues long, and nearly a league broad in some places, in others only quarter of a league. It is covered with an abundance of wood, such as pines and birch. All the coast is bordered by very dangerous rocks; and there is no place at all favorable for vessels, only little inlets for shallops at the extremity of the island, and three or four small rocky islands, where the savages capture many sea-wolves. There are strong tides, especially at the little passage of the island, which is very dangerous for vessels running the risk of passing through it.

From Long Island passage, we sailed north-east two leagues, when we found a cove where vessels can anchor in safety, and which is quarter of a league or thereabouts in circuit. The bottom is all mire, and the surrounding land is bordered by very high rocks. In this place there is a very good silver mine, according to the report of the miner, Master Simon, who accompanied me. Some leagues farther on, there is a little stream called River Boulay[2] where the tide rises half a league into the land, at the mouth of which vessels of a hundred tons can easily ride at anchor. Quarter of a league from here there is a good harbor for vessels, where we found an iron

---

[1] The Bay of Fundy. Early English maps call it Argall's Bay, after the captor of Port Royal in 1614. The origin of its present name is doubtful.
[2] Now known as Sandy Cove.

mine, which our miner estimated would yield fifty per cent.[1] Advancing three leagues farther on to the north-east, we saw another very good iron mine, near which is a river surrounded by beautiful and attractive meadows. The neighboring soil is red as blood. Some leagues farther on there is still another river, dry at low tide, except in its very small channel, and which extends near to Port Royal. At the extremity of this bay is a channel, also dry at low tide, surrounding which are a number of pastures and good pieces of land for cultivation, where there are nevertheless great numbers of fine trees of all the kinds previously mentioned. The distance from Long Island to the end of this bay may be some six leagues. The entire coast of the mines is very high, intersected by capes, which appear round, extending out a short distance. On the other side of the bay, on the south-east, the land is low and good, where there is a very good harbor, having a bank at its entrance over which it is necessary to pass. On this bar there is a fathom and a half of water at low tide; but after passing it you find three, with good bottoms. Between the two points of the harbor there is a pebbly islet, covered at full tide. This place extends half a league inland. The tide falls here three fathoms, and there are many shell-fish, such as muscles, cockles, and sea-snails. The soil is as good as any that I have seen. I named this harbor Saint Margaret.[2] This entire south-east coast is much lower than that of the mines, which is only a league and a half from the coast of Saint Margaret, being separated by the breadth of the bay, which is three leagues at its entrance. I took the altitude at this place, and found the latitude 45° 30′, and a little more, the deflection of the magnetic needle being 17° 16′.

After having explored as particularly as I could the coasts, ports, and harbors, I returned, without advancing any farther, to Long Island passage, whence I went back outside of all the islands in order to observe whether there was any danger at

---

[1] This and the above mentioned silver-mine afterwards proved of little value. Lescarbot, book IV., ch. III.

[2] Now Weymouth Harbor.

all on the water side. But we found none whatever, except
there were some rocks about half a league from Sea-Wolf
Islands, which, however, can be easily avoided, since the sea
breaks over them. Continuing our voyage, we were overtaken
by a violent wind, which obliged us to run our barque ashore,
where we were in danger of losing her, which would have
caused us extreme perplexity. The tempest having ceased,
we resumed the sea, and the next day reached Port Mouton,
where Sieur de Monts was awaiting us from day to day, thinking only of our long stay, and whether some accident had not
befallen us. I made a report to him of our voyage and where
our vessels might go in safety. Meanwhile, I observed very
particularly that place which is in latitude 44°.

The next day Sieur de Monts gave orders to weigh anchor
and proceed to the Bay of Saint Mary, a place which we
had found to be suitable for our vessel to remain in, until we
should be able to find one more advantageous. Coasting
along, we passed near Cape Sable and the Sea-Wolf Islands,
whither Sieur de Monts decided to go in a shallop, and see
some islands of which we had made a report to him, as also
of the countless number of birds found there. Accordingly,
he set out, accompanied by Sieur de Poutrincourt,[1] and several
other noblemen, with the intention of going to Penguin
Island, where we had previously killed with sticks a large
number of these birds. Being somewhat distant from our
ship, it was not in our power to reach it, and still less to
reach our vessel; for the tide was so strong that we were
compelled to put in at a little island to pass the night, where
there was much game. I killed there some river-birds, which
were very acceptable to us, especially as we had taken only a
few biscuit, expecting to return the same day. The next
day we reached Cape Fourchu, distant half a league from there.

---

[1] This nobleman was granted by de Monts the seigneury of Port Royal
(see p. 44) and endeavored to found a colony there. He became embroiled
with the Jesuits, and his attempt proved a failure. He was killed in France
in 1615 during the civil war which followed the death of Henry IV. See
Lescarbot, *Histoire de la Nouvelle France*, books IV. and V.

Coasting along, we found our vessel in the Bay of Saint Mary. Our company were very anxious about us for two days, fearing lest some misfortune had befallen us; but, when they saw us all safe, they were much rejoiced.

Two or three days after our arrival, one of our priests, named Messire Aubry from Paris, got lost so completely in the woods while going after his sword, which he had forgotten, that he could not find the vessel. And he was thus seventeen days without anything to subsist upon except some sour and bitter plants like the sorrel, and some small fruit of little substance large as currants,[1] which creep upon the ground. Being at his wits' end, without hope of ever seeing us again, weak and feeble, he found himself on the shore of Baye Françoise, thus named by Sieur de Monts, near Long Island, where his strength gave out, when one of our shallops out fishing discovered him. Not being able to shout to them, he made a sign with a pole, on the end of which he had put his hat, that they should go and get him. This they did at once, and brought him off. Sieur de Monts had caused a search to be made not only by his own men, but also by the savages of those parts, who scoured all the woods, but brought back no intelligence of him. Believing him to be dead, they all saw him coming back in the shallop to their great delight.[2] A long time was needed to restore him to his usual strength.

[1] The partridge-berry, with its scarlet berries. (Slafter.)
[2] De Monts was the more glad to see him, as a Protestant with whom he had quarrelled lay under suspicion of having murdered him.

Chapter 3

Description of Port Royal and the peculiarities of the same. Isle
Haute. Port of Mines. Baye Françoise. The River
St. John, and what we observed between the Port of Mines
and the same. The island called by the savages Manthane.
The river of the Etechemins, and several fine islands there.
St. Croix Island, and other noteworthy objects on this
coast.

Some days after, Sieur de Monts decided to go and examine the coasts of Baye Françoise. For this purpose, he set out
from the vessel on the 16th of May,[1] and we went through the
strait of Long Island. Not having found in St. Mary's Bay
any place in which to fortify ourselves except at the cost of
much time, we accordingly resolved to see whether there might
not be a more favorable one in the other bay. Heading north-
east six leagues, there is a cove where vessels can anchor in
four, five, six, and seven fathoms[2] of water. The bottom is
sandy. This place is only a kind of roadstead.[3] Continuing
two leagues farther on in the same direction, we entered one of
the finest harbors I had seen along all these coasts, in which
two thousand vessels might lie in security. The entrance is
eight hundred paces broad; then you enter a harbor two leagues
long and one broad, which I have named Port Royal.[4] Three

[1] For May read June. It could not have been in May, since Champlain
set out from Port Mouton on his exploring expedition on May 19, which must
have been a month previous to this. (Slafter.) See also p. 37, note 2.

[2] The French fathom (*brasse*) is of five feet in length. The modern
English fathom is six. In earlier times it varied from five to six.

[3] Gulliver's Hole, about two leagues south-west of Digby Strait. (Slafter.)

[4] Now Annapolis Basin. The first settlement was on the north side of
the bay in the present hamlet of Lower Granville, not, as often alleged, at
Annapolis. (Slafter.)

Lescarbot, book iv., ch. iii., refers to this passage, and accuses Champlain
of unjustly claiming credit for the name, whose choice was really due to de
Monts. However, Champlain retains the passage unchanged in his edition of
1632.

rivers empty into it, one of which is very large, extending eastward, and called Rivière de l'Équille,[1] from a little fish of the
size of an *esplan?*, which is caught there in large numbers,
as is also the herring, and several other kinds of fish found in
abundance in their season.   This river is nearly a quarter of a
league broad at its entrance, where there is an island [2] perhaps half a league in circuit, and covered with wood like all the
rest of the country, as pines, firs, spruces, birches, aspens, and
some oaks, although the latter are found in small numbers in
comparison with the other kinds.   There are two entrances to
the above river, one on the north, the other on the south side
of the island.   That on the north is the better, and vessels can
there anchor under shelter of the island in five, six, seven, eight,
and nine fathoms.   But it is necessary to be on one's guard
against some shallows near the island on the one side, and the
main land on the other, very dangerous, if one does not know
the channel.

   We ascended the river some fourteen or fifteen leagues,
where the tide rises, and it is not navigable much farther.
It has there a breadth of sixty paces, and about a fathom and
a half of water.   The country bordering the river is filled with
numerous oaks, ashes, and other trees.   Between the mouth of
the river and the point to which we ascended there are many
meadows, which are flooded at the spring tides, many little
streams traversing them from one side to the other, through
which shallops and boats can go at full tide.   This place was
the most favorable and agreeable for a settlement that we had
seen.   There is another island [3] within the port, distant nearly
two leagues from the former.   At this point is another little
stream, extending a considerable distance inland, which we

   The present Annapolis occupies the site of a French fort established later
by d'Aulnay de Charnisé.   See Parkman, *The Old Regime in Canada*, vol. I.
   [1] Its name was soon after changed to Rivière du Dauphin.   It is now the
Annapolis River.
   [2] Lescarbot calls it Biencourville.   It is now called Goat Island.   (Laverdière.)
   [3] Bear Island, a name perhaps derived from the French name of Ile
d'Hébert, or d'Imbert.   (Laverdière.)

named Rivière St. Antoine.[1]   Its mouth is distant from the
end of the Bay of St. Mary some four leagues through the woods.
The remaining river is only a small stream filled with rocks,
which cannot be ascended at all on account of the small amount
of water, and which has been named Rocky Brook.[2]   This
place is in latitude [3] 45°; and 17° 8′ of the deflection of the
magnetic needle.

After having explored this harbor, we set out to advance
farther on in Baye Françoise, and see whether we could not
find the copper mine, which had been discovered the year
before.   Heading north-east, and sailing eight or ten leagues
along the coast of Port Royal,[4] we crossed a part of the bay
some five or six leagues in extent, when we arrived at a place
which we called the Cape of Two Bays;[5] and we passed by
an island [6] a league distant therefrom, a league also in circuit,
rising up forty or forty-five fathoms.[7]   It is wholly surrounded
by great rocks, except in one place, which is sloping, at the
foot of which slope there is a pond of salt water, coming from
under a pebbly point, having the form of a spur.   The surface of the island is flat, covered with trees, and containing
a fine spring of water.   In this place is a copper mine.   Thence
we proceeded to a harbor a league and a half distant, where we
supposed the copper mine was, which a certain Prevert[8] of
St. Malo had discovered by aid of the savages of the country.
This port is in latitude 45° 40′, and is dry at low tide.[9]   In
order to enter it, it is necessary to place beacons, and mark
out a sand-bank at the entrance, which borders a channel
that extends along the main land.   Then you enter a bay nearly

---

[1] Bear River.

[2] On modern maps called Moose Brook, and sometimes Deep Brook.
(Slafter.)

[3] 44° 39′ 30″.

[4] I. e., along the Bay of Fundy, nearly parallel to the basin of Port Royal.
(Slafter.)

[5] Cape Chignecto.   [6] Isle Haute.   [7] *Toise* = six feet.

[8] Captain of one of the two ships sent out by de Chastes in 1603.

[9] Advocate's Harbor.   The tides, which here rise to a height of forty
feet, have since Champlain's time carried away the sand bank which he
mentions, and made other changes in the topography.

a league in length, and half a league in breadth. In some
places, the bottom is oozy and sandy, where vessels may get
aground. The sea falls and rises there to the extent of four
or five fathoms. We landed to see whether we could find the
mines which Prevert had reported to us. Having gone about
a quarter of a league along certain mountains, we found none,
nor did we recognize any resemblance to the description of the
harbor he had given us. Accordingly, he had not himself been
there, but probably two or three of his men had been
there, guided by some savages, partly by land and partly by
little streams, while he awaited them in his shallop at the
mouth of a little river in the Bay of St. Lawrence.[1] These
men, upon their return, brought him several small pieces of
copper, which he showed us when he returned from his voyage.
Nevertheless, we found in this harbor two mines of what
seemed to be copper, according to the report of our miner,
who considered it very good, although it was not native
copper.

The head of the Baye Françoise, which we crossed, is
fifteen leagues inland. All the land which we have seen in
coasting along from the little passage of Long Island is rocky,
and there is no place except Port Royal where vessels can lie
in safety. The land is covered with pines and birches, and,
in my opinion, is not very good.

On the 20th of May,[2] we set out from the Port of Mines
to seek a place adapted for a permanent stay, in order to lose
no time, purposing afterwards to return, and see if we could
discover the mine of pure copper which Prevert's men had
found by aid of the savages. We sailed west two leagues as far
as the cape of the two bays, then north five or six leagues;
and we crossed the other bay,[3] where we thought the copper
mine was, of which we have already spoken: inasmuch as

[1] Most early geographers distinguished between the Bay and the Gulf
of St. Lawrence.   The Bay of St. Lawrence included the southern portion
of the gulf, from Cape Rosier to Canso, including Prince Edward Island,
Cape Breton, and the Magdalen Islands. (Laverdière.)
[2] June, see p. 34, note 1.
[3] Chignecto Bay, later called Beaubassin by the French.

there are there two rivers,[1] the one coming from the direction
of Cape Breton, and the other from Gaspé or Tregatté,[2] near
the great river St. Lawrence. Sailing west some six leagues,
we arrived at a little river,[3] at the mouth of which is rather a
low cape, extending out into the sea; and a short distance inland there is a mountain,[4] having the shape of a cardinal's hat.
In this place we found an iron mine. There is anchorage here
only for shallops. Four leagues west-south-west is a rocky
point [5] extending out a short distance into the water, where
there are strong tides which are very dangerous. Near the
point we saw a cove about half a league in extent, in which
we found another iron mine, also very good. Four leagues
farther on is a fine bay running up into the main land,[6] at
the extremity of which there are three islands and a rock, two
of which are a league from the cape towards the west, and the
other is at the mouth of the largest and deepest river we had
yet seen, which we named the river St. John, because it was
on this saint's day that we arrived there.[7] By the savages it is
called Ouygoudy.[8] This river is dangerous, if one does not
observe carefully certain points and rocks on the two sides.
It is narrow at its entrance, and then becomes broader.
A certain point being passed, it becomes narrower again, and
forms a kind of fall between two large cliffs, where the water
runs so rapidly that a piece of wood thrown in is drawn under
and not seen again. But by waiting till high tide you can
pass this fall very easily.[9] Then it expands again to the extent of about a league in some places, where there are three
islands. We did not explore it farther up. But Ralleau,
secretary of Sieur de Monts, went there some time after to see

[1] Cumberland Basin, and the Petitcodiac River, New Brunswick.
(Slafter.)

[2] Tracadie.   [3] Quaco River.   [4] Porcupine Mountain.
[5] McCoy's Head.   [6] The Bay of St. John, N.B.

[7] *I.e.*, June 24, the feast-day of St. John Baptist. Another proof that
May, pp. 34 and 37, is a misprint.

[8] In reality this was the name which the Indians applied to the camp-
ing-ground on Navy Island, rather than to the river.

[9] The fall at the mouth of the St. John can in fact only be passed at about
half tide. The waters of the river at low tide are about twelve feet higher

a savage named Secondon,[1] chief of this river, who reported
that it was beautiful, large, and extensive, with many meadows
and fine trees, as oaks, beeches, walnut-trees, and also wild
grape-vines.   The inhabitants of the country go by this river
to Tadoussac, on the great river St. Lawrence, making but
a short portage on the journey.   From the river St. John to
Tadoussac is sixty-five leagues.[2]   At its mouth, which is in
latitude 45° 40′, there is an iron mine.

From the river St. John we went to four islands,[3] on one
of which we landed, and found great numbers of birds called
magpies, of which we captured many small ones, which are
as good as pigeons.   Sieur de Poutrincourt came near getting
lost here, but he came back to our barque at last, when we
had already gone to search for him about the island, which is
three leagues distant from the main land.   Farther west
are other islands; among them one six leagues in length,
called by the savages Manthane,[4] south of which there are
among the islands several good harbors for vessels.   From
the Magpie Islands we proceeded to a river on the main land
called the river of the Etechemins,[5] a tribe of savages so
called in their country.   We passed by so many islands that
we could not ascertain their number, which were very fine.
Some were two leagues in extent, others three, others more
or less.   All of these islands are in a bay,[6] having, in my
estimation, a circuit of more than fifteen leagues.   There

than the waters of the sea.   At high tide the waters of the sea are about five
feet higher than the waters of the river.   Consequently, at low tide there is a
fall outward, and at high tide there is a fall inward, at neither of which times
can the fall be passed.   (Slafter.)

Twice at each tide, for about twenty minutes, the waters are level, and
ships can sail through the gorge.

[1] Lescarbot spells it Chkoudun.

[2] From the mouth of the St. John to Tadoussac is in direct line about
two hundred and forty miles, but by the winding course of the St. John it
would be much greater.

[3] These are now called the Wolves, near the mouth of Passamaquoddy
Bay.   (Slafter.)

[4] The Grand Manan, or Menane.

[5] The St. Croix River, sometimes called the Schoodic.

[6] Passamaquoddy Bay.

are many good places capable of containing any number of vessels, and abounding in fish in the season, such as codfish, salmon, bass, herring, halibut, and other kinds in great numbers. Sailing west-north-west three leagues through the islands, we entered a river almost half a league in breadth at its mouth, sailing up which a league or two we found two islands: one very small near the western bank; and the other in the middle, having a circumference of perhaps eight or nine hundred paces, with rocky sides three or four fathoms high all around, except in one small place, where there is a sandy point and clayey earth adapted for making brick and other useful articles. There is another place affording a shelter for vessels from eighty to a hundred tons, but it is dry at low tide. The island is covered with firs, birches, maples, and oaks. It is by nature very well situated, except in one place, where for about forty paces it is lower than elsewhere: this, however, is easily fortified, the banks of the main land being distant on both sides some nine hundred to a thousand paces. Vessels could pass up the river only at the mercy of the cannon on this island, and we deemed the location the most advantageous, not only on account of its situation and good soil, but also on account of the intercourse which we proposed with the savages of these coasts and of the interior, as we should be in the midst of them. We hoped to pacify them in the course of time and put an end to the wars which they carry on with one another, so as to derive service from them in future, and convert them to the Christian faith. This place was named by Sieur de Monts the Island of St. Croix.[1] Farther on, there is a great bay, in

---

[1] *I.e.*, Holy Cross; on account of the physical configuration which he goes on to describe.

The island has of recent years commonly been called Dochet Island, but at the celebration of the three-hundredth anniversary of its settlement it was resolved that it be henceforth called St. Croix Island. See the Maine Historical Society's well-illustrated volume, *Tercentenary of De Monts' Settlement at St. Croix Island, June 25, 1904* (Portland, 1905).

In 1796 and 1797 the vexed question between the British and American boundary commissioners, appointed in virtue of the Jay Treaty of 1794, as to which river was really the Saint Croix, was set at rest by the dis-

which are two islands, one high and the other flat; also three rivers, two of moderate size, one extending towards the east, the other towards the north, and the third of large size, towards the west.[1] The latter is that of the Etechemins, of which we spoke before. Two leagues up this there is a waterfall, around which the savages carry their canoes some five hundred paces by land, and then re-enter the river. Passing afterwards from the river a short distance overland, one reaches the rivers Norumbegue [2] and St. John. But the falls are impassable for vessels, as there are only rocks and but four or five feet of water. In May and June, so great a number of herring and bass are caught there that vessels could be loaded with them. The soil is of the finest sort, and there are fifteen or twenty acres of cleared land, where Sieur de Monts had some wheat sown, which flourished finely. The savages come here some-times five or six weeks during the fishing season. All the rest of the country consists of very dense forests. If the land were cleared up, grain would flourish excellently. This place is in latitude 45° 20′, and 17° 32′ of the deflection of the magnetic needle.[3]

covery of the outlines of De Monts' original fortifications. See Moore's *International Arbitrations*, ch. i., and Ganong's illustrated monograph on Dochet Island in the *Transactions of the Royal Society of Canada*, second series, vol. VIII.

However suitable from a military point of view, or as a trading post, the situation was extremely ill-chosen for a permanent and self-supporting colony. This was clearly seen by Lescarbot, whose ideas on colonization are far in advance of those of his time. "I attach little importance to mines," he says. "The true mine for the settler is waving wheat and grazing cattle."

[1] Warwig Creek from the east, Oak Bay from the north, and the river of the Etechemins, now called the St. Croix, from the west.

[2] The Penobscot, reached by way of the Mattawamkeag. Laverdière supposes the Norumbegue to be the Bay of Fundy.

[3] The true latitude is 45° 8′ N., the present deflection of the needle somewhat more than 18° 30′. (Ganong.)

Chapter 4

Sieur de Monts, finding no other place better adapted for a permanent settlement than the island of St. Croix, fortifies it and builds dwellings. Return of the vessels to France, and of Ralleau, secretary of Sieur de Monts, for the sake of arranging some business affairs.

Not finding any more suitable place than this island, we commenced making a barricade on a little islet a short distance from the main island, which served as a station for placing our cannon. All worked so energetically that in a little while it was put in a state of defence, although the mosquitoes (which are little flies) annoyed us excessively in our work. For there were several of our men whose faces were so swollen by their bites that they could scarcely see. The barricade being finished, Sieur de Monts sent his barque to notify the rest of our party, who were with our vessel in the bay of St. Mary, to come to St. Croix. This was promptly done, and while awaiting them we spent our time very pleasantly.

Some days after, our vessels having arrived and anchored, all disembarked. Then, without losing time, Sieur de Monts proceeded to employ the workmen in building houses for our abode, and allowed me to determine the arrangement of our settlement.[1] After Sieur de Monts had determined the place

---

[1] The following explanation of his plan of the "Habitation de L'Isle Ste. Croix" is given by Champlain:

"*A.* Dwelling of Sieur de Monts. *B.* Public building where we spent our time when it rained. *C.* The storehouse. *D.* Dwelling of the guard. *E.* The blacksmith shop. *F.* Dwelling of the carpenters. *G.* The well. *H.* The oven where the bread was made. *I.* Kitchen. *L.* Gardens. *M.* Other gardens. *N.* Place in the centre where a tree stands. *O.* Palisade. *P.* Dwellings of the Sieurs d'Orville, Champlain, and Champdoré. *Q.* Dwelling of Sieur Boulay, and other artisans. *R.* Dwelling where the Sieurs de Genestou, Sourin, and other artisans lived. *T.* Dwelling of the Sieurs de Beaumont, la Motte Bourioli, and Fougeray. *V.* Dwelling of our curate. *X.* Other gardens. *Y.* The river surrounding the island.*" *Cf.* the map in *Early English and French Voyages*, p. 412. In 1904 a commemorative tablet was set up, to mark the site of the settlement.

for the storehouse, which is nine fathoms long, three wide, and twelve feet high, he adopted the plan for his own house, which he had promptly built by good workmen, and then assigned to each one his location. Straightway, the men began to gather together by fives and sixes, each according to his desire. Then all set to work to clear up the island, to go to the woods, to make the frame-work, to carry earth and other things necessary for the buildings.

While we were building our houses, Sieur de Monts despatched Captain Fouques in the vessel of Rossignol,[1] to find Pont Gravé at Canseau, in order to obtain for our settlement what supplies remained.

Some time after he had set out, there arrived a small barque of eight tons, in which was Du Glas of Honfleur, pilot of Pont Gravé's vessel, bringing the Basque ship-masters, who had been captured by the above Pont Gravé while engaged in the fur-trade, as we have stated. Sieur de Monts received them civilly, and sent them back by the above Du Glas to Pont Gravé, with orders for him to take the vessels he had captured to Rochelle, in order that justice might be done. Meanwhile, work on the houses went on vigorously and without cessation; the carpenters engaged on the storehouse and dwelling of Sieur de Monts, and the others each on his own house, as I was on mine, which I built with the assistance of some servants belonging to Sieur d'Orville and myself. It was forthwith completed, and Sieur de Monts lodged in it until his own was finished. An oven was also made, and a hand-mill for grinding our wheat, the working of which involved much trouble and labor to the most of us, since it was a toilsome operation. Some gardens were afterwards laid out, on the main land as well as on the island. Here many kinds of seeds were planted, which flourished very well on the main land, but not on the island, since there was only sand here, and the whole were burned up when the sun shone, although special pains were taken to water them.

Some days after, Sieur de Monts determined to ascertain

----

[1] *Vide supra*, p. 27.

where the mine of pure copper was which we had searched
for so much.   With this object in view, he despatched me
together with a savage named Messamoüet, who asserted that
he knew the place well.   I set out in a small barque of five
or six tons, with nine sailors.   Some eight leagues from the
island, towards the river St. John, we found a mine of copper
which was not pure, yet good according to the report of the
miner, who said that it would yield eighteen per cent.   Farther
on we found others inferior to this.[1]   When we reached the
place where we supposed that was which we were hunting for,
the savage could not find it, so that it was necessary to come
back, leaving the search for another time.

Upon my return from this trip, Sieur de Monts resolved to
send his vessels back to France, and also Sieur de Poutrincourt,
who had come only for his pleasure, and to explore countries
and places suitable for a colony, which he desired to found; for
which reason he asked Sieur de Monts for Port Royal, which he
gave him in accordance with the power and directions he had received from the king.   He sent back also Ralleau, his secretary,
to arrange some matters concerning the voyage.   They set
out from the island of St. Croix the last day of August, 1604.

Chapter 5

*Of the coast, inhabitants, and river of Norumbegue, and of all
that occurred during the exploration of the latter.*

After the departure of the vessels, Sieur de Monts, without losing time, decided to send persons to make discoveries
along the coast of Norumbegue;[2] and he intrusted me with
this work, which I found very agreeable.

[1] The first mine was no doubt at Beaver Harbor, the others at Red
Head Harbor.

[2] On Norumbegue or Norumbega see *Narrative and Critical History,*
III. 169–218.   It may be roughly identified with New England.   The river
of Norumbega is the Penobscot.   Jean Alfonse (see p. 22) gives a wonderful
description of a great city of the same name at its mouth.   Lescarbot makes
merry at the credulity of those who believed in such travellers' tales, but it is
quite likely that in the time of Alfonse (1542) there may have been a flourishing

In order to execute this commission, I set out from St. Croix on the 2d of September with a patache [1] of seventeen or eighteen tons, twelve sailors, and two savages, to serve us as guides to the places with which they were acquainted. The same day we found the vessels where Sieur de Poutrincourt was, which were anchored at the mouth of the river St. Croix in consequence of bad weather, which place we could not leave before the 5th of the month. Having gone two or three leagues seaward, so dense a fog arose that we at once lost sight of their vessels. Continuing our course along the coast, we made the same day some twenty-five leagues, and passed by a large number of islands, banks, reefs, and rocks, which in places extend more than four leagues out to sea. We called the islands the Ranges, most of which are covered with pines, firs, and other trees of an inferior sort. Among these islands are many fine harbors, but undesirable for a permanent settlement. The same day we passed also near to an island about four or five leagues long, in the neighborhood of which we just escaped being lost on a little rock on a level with the water, which made an opening in our barque near the keel. From this island to the main land on the north, the distance is less than a hundred paces. It is very high, and notched in places, so that there is the appearance to one at sea, as of seven or eight mountains extending along near each other. The summit of the most of them is destitute of trees, as there are only rocks on them. The woods consist of pines, firs, and birches only. I named it Isle des Monts Déserts. [2] The latitude is 44° 30'.

The next day, the 6th of the month, we sailed two leagues, and perceived a smoke in a cove at the foot of the mountains above mentioned. We saw two canoes rowed by savages, which came within musket range to observe us. I sent our two

Indian village, which disappeared as completely as Hochelaga did between the visits of Cartier and of Champlain.

[1] A narrow vessel, used as a despatch boat.

[2] Still known as Mount Desert. In 1613 the Marchioness de Guercheville attempted to found here a colony, called St. Sauveur, which was destroyed by the English under Samuel Argall.

savages in a boat to assure them of our friendship. Their fear of us made them turn back. On the morning of the next day they came alongside of our barque and talked with our savages. I ordered some biscuit, tobacco, and other trifles to be given them. These savages had come beaver-hunting and to catch fish, some of which they gave us. Having made an alliance with them, they guided us to their river of Pentegoüet,[1] so called by them, where they told us was their captain, named Bessabez, chief of this river. I think this river is that which several pilots and historians call Norumbegue, and which most have described as large and extensive, with very many islands, its mouth being in latitude 43°, 43° 30′, according to others in 44°, more or less. With regard to the deflection, I have neither read, nor heard any one say anything. It is related also that there is a large, thickly settled town of savages, who are adroit and skilful, and who have cotton yarn. I am confident that most of those who mention it have not seen it, and speak of it because they have heard persons say so, who knew no more about it than they themselves. I am ready to believe that some may have seen the mouth of it, because there are in reality many islands, and it is, as they say, in latitude 44° at its entrance. But that any one has ever entered it there is no evidence, for then they would have described it in another manner, in order to relieve the minds of many of this doubt.

I will accordingly relate truly what I explored and saw, from the beginning as far as I went.

In the first place, there are at its entrance several islands distant ten or twelve leagues from the main land, which are in latitude 44°, and 18° 40′ of the deflection of the magnetic needle. The Isle des Monts Déserts forms one of the extremities of the mouth, on the east; the other is low land, called by the savages Bedabedec,[2] to the west of the former, the two

---

[1] The Penobscot.

[2] An indefinite region about Rockland and Camden, on the western bank of the Penobscot near its mouth, appears to have been the domain of the Indian chief, Bessabez, and was denominated Bedabedec. The Camden Hills were called the mountains of Bedabedec and Owl's Head was called Bedabedec Point. (Slafter.)

being distant from each other nine or ten leagues. Almost midway between these, out in the ocean, there is another island very high and conspicuous, which on this account I have named Isle Haute.[1] All around there is a vast number of varying extent and breadth, but the largest is that of the Monts Déserts. Fishing as also hunting are very good here; the fish are of various kinds. Some two or three leagues from the point of Bedabedec, as you coast northward along the main land which extends up this river, there are very high elevations of land, which in fair weather are seen twelve or fifteen leagues out at sea.[2] Passing to the south of the Isle Haute, and coasting along the same for a quarter of a league, where there are some reefs out of water, and heading to the west until you open all the mountains northward of this island, you can be sure that, by keeping in sight the eight or nine peaks of the Monts Déserts and Bedabedec, you will cross the river Norumbegue; and in order to enter it you must keep to the north, that is, towards the highest mountains of Bedabedec, where you will see no islands before you, and can enter, sure of having water enough, although you see a great many breakers, islands, and rocks to the east and west of you. For greater security, one should keep the sounding lead in hand. And my observations lead me to conclude that one cannot enter this river in any other place except in small vessels or shallops. For, as I stated above, there are numerous islands, rocks, shoals, banks, and breakers on all sides, so that it is marvellous to behold.

Now to resume our course: as one enters the river, there are beautiful islands, which are very pleasant and contain fine meadows. We proceeded to a place to which the savages guided us, where the river is not more than an eighth of a league broad, and at a distance of some two hundred paces from the western shore there is a rock on a level with the water, of a dangerous character.[3] From here to the Isle Haute, it is fifteen leagues. From this narrow place, where there is the

---

[1] Meaning high island; it is now called Isle au Haut.
[2] The Camden Hills.
[3] This narrow place is just above Castine.

least breadth that we had found, after sailing some seven or eight leagues, we came to a little river [1] near which it was necessary to anchor, as we saw before us a great many rocks which are uncovered at low tide, and since also, if we had desired to sail farther, we could have gone scarcely half a league, in consequence of a fall of water there coming down a slope of seven or eight feet, which I saw as I went there in a canoe with our savages; and we found only water enough for a canoe. But excepting the fall, which is some two hundred paces broad, the river is beautiful, and unobstructed up to the place where we had anchored. I landed to view the country, and, going on a hunting excursion, found it very pleasant so far as I went. The oaks here appear as if they were planted for ornament. I saw only a few firs, but numerous pines on one side of the river; on the other only oaks, and some copse wood which extends far into the interior. And I will state that from the entrance to where we went, about twenty-five leagues, we saw no town, nor village, nor the appearance of there having been one, but one or two cabins of the savages without inhabitants. These were made in the same way as those of the Souriquois,[2] being covered with the bark of trees. So far as we could judge, the savages on this river are few in number, and are called Etechemins. Moreover, they only come to the islands, and that only during some months in summer for fish and game, of which there is a great quantity. They are a people who have no fixed abode, so far as I could observe and learn from them. For they spend the winter now in one place and now in another, according as they find the best hunting, by which they live when urged by their daily needs, without laying up anything for times of scarcity, which are sometimes severe.

Now this river must of necessity be the Norumbegue; for, having coasted along past it as far as the 41° of latitude, we have found no other on the parallel above mentioned, except

[1] The Kenduskeag, near the city of Bangor.

[2] The Souriquois are the Mic-Macs of Nova Scotia. Closely akin to them were the Etechemins, who extended from St. John, N.B., to the neighborhood of Mount Desert. South of these were the Almouchiquois or Armouchiquois (see pp. 61 *et seqq.*).

that of the Quinibequy,[1] which is almost in the same latitude, but not of great extent. Moreover, there cannot be in any other place a river extending far into the interior of the country, since the great river St. Lawrence washes the coast of La Cadie and Norumbegue, and the distance from one to the other by land is not more than forty-five leagues, or sixty at the widest point, as can be seen on my geographical map.

Now I will drop this discussion to return to the savages who had conducted me to the falls of the river Norumbegue, who went to notify Bessabez, their chief, and other savages, who in turn proceeded to another little river to inform their own, named Cabahis, and give him notice of our arrival.

The 16th of the month there came to us some thirty savages on assurances given them by those who had served us as guides. There came also to us the same day the above-named Bessabez with six canoes. As soon as the savages who were on land saw him coming, they all began to sing, dance, and jump, until he had landed. Afterwards, they all seated themselves in a circle on the ground, as is their custom, when they wish to celebrate a festivity, or an harangue is to be made. Cabahis, the other chief, arrived also a little later with twenty or thirty of his companions, who withdrew one side and greatly enjoyed seeing us, as it was the first time they had seen Christians. A little while after, I went on shore with two of my companions and two of our savages who served as interpreters. I directed the men in our barque to approach near the savages, and hold their arms in readiness to do their duty in case they noticed any movement of these people against us. Bessabez, seeing us on land, bade us sit down, and began to smoke with his companions, as they usually do before an address. They presented us with venison and game.

I directed our interpreter to say to our savages that they should cause Bessabez, Cabahis, and their companions to understand that Sieur de Monts had sent me to them to see them, and also their country, and that he desired to preserve friend-

---

[1] The Kennebec.

ship with them and to reconcile them with their enemies,
the Souriquois and Canadians, and moreover that he desired
to inhabit their country and show them how to cultivate it,
in order that they might not continue to lead so miserable a
life as they were doing, and some other words on the same subject.   This our savages interpreted to them, at which they
signified their great satisfaction, saying that no greater good
could come to them than to have our friendship, and that they
desired to live in peace with their enemies, and that we should
dwell in their land, in order that they might in future more
than ever before engage in hunting beavers, and give us a part
of them in return for our providing them with things which they
wanted.   After he had finished his discourse, I presented them
with hatchets, paternosters, caps, knives, and other little knick-
knacks, when we separated from each other.   All the rest of
this day and the following night, until break of day, they did
nothing but dance, sing, and make merry, after which we traded
for a certain number of beavers.   Then each party returned,
Bessabez with his companions on the one side, and we on the
other, highly pleased at having made the acquaintance of this
people.

The 17th of the month I took the altitude, and found the
latitude 45° 25′.[1]   This done, we set out for another river
called Quinibequy, distant from this place thirty-five leagues,
and nearly twenty from Bedabedec.   This nation of savages of
Quinibequy are called Etechemins, as well as those of Norumbegue.

The 18th of the month we passed near a small river where
Cabahis was, who came with us in our barque some twelve
leagues; and having asked him whence came the river Norumbegue, he told me that it passes the fall which I mentioned
above, and that one journeying some distance on it enters
a lake by way of which they come to the river of St. Croix,
by going some distance over land, and then entering the river
of the Etechemins.   Moreover, another river enters the lake,
along which they proceed some days, and afterwards enter

<hr>

[1] Really 44° 46′.

another lake and pass through the midst of it. Reaching the
end of it, they make again a land journey of some distance,
and then enter another little river,[1] which has its mouth a
league from Quebec, which is on the great river St. Lawrence. All these people of Norumbegue are very swarthy,
dressed in beaver-skins and other furs, like the Canadian
and Souriquois savages, and they have the same mode of
life.

The 20th of the month we sailed along the western coast,
and passed the mountains of Bedabedec, when we anchored.
The same day we explored the entrance to the river, where
large vessels can approach; but there are inside some reefs, to
avoid which one must advance with sounding lead in hand.
Our savages left us, as they did not wish to go to Quinibequy, for the savages of that place are great enemies to
them. We sailed some eight leagues along the western coast
to an island ten leagues distant from Quinibequy, where
we were obliged to put in on account of bad weather and
contrary wind. At one point in our course, we passed a large
number of islands and breakers extending some leagues out
to sea, and very dangerous. And in view of the bad weather,
which was so unfavorable to us, we did not sail more than
three or four leagues farther. All these islands and coasts
are covered with extensive woods, of the same sort as that
which I have reported above as existing on the other coasts.
And in consideration of the small quantity of provisions which
we had, we resolved to return to our settlement and wait
until the following year, when we hoped to return and explore more extensively. We accordingly set out on our
return on the 23d of September, and arrived at our settlement on the 2d of October following.

The above is an exact statement of all that I have observed respecting not only the coasts and people, but also the
river of Norumbegue; and there are none of the marvels

---

[1] The Chaudière. Champlain's account, derived from the Indians,
whose language he but imperfectly understood, is not quite correct, as may
be seen by consulting a map.

there which some persons have described.[1]   I am of opinion that this region is as disagreeable in winter as that of our settlement, in which we were greatly deceived.

Chapter 6

Of the Mal de la Terre, a very desperate malady.   How the savages, men and women, spend their time in winter.   And all that occurred at the settlement while we were passing the winter.

When we arrived at the Island of St. Croix, each one had finished his place of abode.   Winter came upon us sooner than we expected, and prevented us from doing many things which we had proposed.   Nevertheless, Sieur de Monts did not fail to have some gardens made on the island.   Many began to clear up the ground, each his own.   I also did so with mine, which was very large, where I planted a quantity of seeds, as also did the others who had any, and they came up very well. But since the island was all sandy, everything dried up almost as soon as the sun shone upon it, and we had no water for irrigation except from the rain, which was infrequent.

Sieur de Monts caused also clearings to be made on the main land for making gardens, and at the falls three leagues from our settlement he had work done and some wheat sown, which came up very well and ripened.   Around our habitation there is, at low tide, a large number of shell-fish, such as cockles,[2] muscles, sea-urchins, and sea-snails, which were very acceptable to all.

The snows began on the 6th of October.   On the 3d of December, we saw ice pass which came from some frozen river.   The cold was sharp, more severe than in France, and

---

[1] Two noteworthy points are that Champlain received no intelligence of any Europeans on the coast, and found no fixed settlements of natives.   The savages lived on the headwaters of the rivers, and along the great carrying-places which constituted a thoroughfare from one end of the Acadian peninsula to the other.   (Gen. Brown.)

[2] Doubtless clams.   (Ganong.)

of much longer duration; and it scarcely rained at all the entire winter. I suppose that is owing to the north and north-west winds passing over high mountains always covered with snow. The latter was from three to four feet deep up to the end of the month of April; lasting much longer, I suppose, than it would if the country were cultivated.

During the winter, many of our company were attacked by a certain malady called the *mal de la terre;*[1] otherwise scurvy, as I have since heard from learned men. There were produced, in the mouths of those who had it, great pieces of superfluous and drivelling flesh (causing extensive putrefaction), which got the upperhand to such an extent that scarcely any thing but liquid could be taken. Their teeth became very loose, and could be pulled out with the fingers without its causing them pain. The superfluous flesh was often cut out, which caused them to eject much blood through the mouth. Afterwards, a violent pain seized their arms and legs, which remained swollen and very hard, all spotted as if with flea-bites; and they could not walk on account of the contraction of the muscles, so that they were almost without strength, and suffered intolerable pains. They experienced pain also in the loins, stomach, and bowels, had a very bad cough, and short breath. In a word, they were in such a condition that the majority of them could not rise nor move, and could not even be raised up on their feet without falling down in a swoon. So that out of seventy-nine, who composed our party, thirty-five died, and more than twenty were on the point of death. The majority of those who remained well also complained of slight pains and short breath. We were unable to find any remedy for these maladies. A *post mortem* examination of several was made to investigate the cause of their disease.

In the case of many, the interior parts were found morti-

[1] Cartier's men had suffered greatly from the same complaint during their stay at Quebec in the winter of 1535–1536, but had found a remedy in a decoction made of the leaves of an evergreen, called by the savages *aneda*, or *anneda* (see p. 60), apparently the white pine. See Cartier's account in *Early English and French Voyages*, of this series, pp. 73–77.

fied, such as the lungs, which were so changed that no natural fluid could be perceived in them. The spleen was serous and swollen. The liver was *legueux ?* [1] and spotted, without its natural color. The *vena cava,* superior and inferior, was filled with thick coagulated and black blood. The gall was tainted. Nevertheless, many arteries, in the middle as well as lower bowels, were found in very good condition. In the case of some, incisions with a razor were made on the thighs where they had purple spots, whence there issued a very black clotted blood. This is what was observed on the bodies of those infected with this malady.

Our surgeons could not help suffering themselves in the same manner as the rest. Those who continued sick were healed by spring, which commences in this country in May. That led us to believe that the change of season restored their health rather than the remedies prescribed.

During this winter, all our liquors froze, except the Spanish wine.[2] Cider was dispensed by the pound. The cause of this loss was that there were no cellars to our storehouse, and that the air which entered by the cracks was sharper than that outside. We were obliged to use very bad water, and drink melted snow, as there were no springs nor brooks; for it was not possible to go to the main land in consequence of the great pieces of ice drifted by the tide, which varies three fathoms between low and high water. Work on the hand-mill was very fatiguing, since the most of us, having slept poorly, and suffering from insufficiency of fuel, which we could not obtain on account of the ice, had scarcely any strength, and also because we ate only salt meat and vegetables during the winter, which produce bad blood. The latter circumstance was, in my opinion, a partial cause of these dreadful maladies. All this produced discontent in Sieur de Monts and others of the settlement.[3]

---

[1] Watery; or perhaps for *ligneux,* fibrous.

[2] *I.e.,* sherry.

[3] Father Biard says, *Jesuit Relations,* ed. Thwaites, III. 52, "Of all Sieur de Monts' people who wintered first at St. Croix, only eleven remained well."

It would be very difficult to ascertain the character of this region without spending a winter in it; for, on arriving here in summer, every thing is very agreeable, in consequence of the woods, fine country, and the many varieties of good fish which are found there. There are six months of winter in this country.

The savages who dwell here are few in number. During the winter, in the deepest snows, they hunt elks and other animals, on which they live most of the time. And, unless the snow is deep, they scarcely get rewarded for their pains, since they cannot capture anything except by a very great effort, which is the reason for their enduring and suffering much. When they do not hunt, they live on a shell-fish, called the cockle. They clothe themselves in winter with good furs of beaver and elk. The women make all the garments, but not so exactly but that you can see the flesh under the arm-pits, because they have not ingenuity enough to fit them better. When they go a hunting, they use a kind of snow-shoe twice as large as those hereabouts, which they attach to the soles of their feet, and walk thus over the snow without sinking in, the women and children as well as the men. They search for the track of animals, which, having found, they follow until they get sight of the creature, when they shoot at it with their bows, or kill it by means of daggers attached to the end of a short pike, which is very easily done, as the animals cannot walk on the snow without sinking in. Then the women and children come up, erect a hut, and they give themselves to feasting. Afterwards, they return in search of other animals, and thus they pass the winter. In the month of March following, some savages came and gave us a portion of their game in exchange for bread and other things which we gave them. This is the mode of life in winter of these people, which seems to me a very miserable one.

We looked for our vessels at the end of April; but, as this passed without their arriving, all began to have an ill-boding, fearing that some accident had befallen them. For this reason, on the 15th of May, Sieur de Monts decided to have a barque of fifteen tons and another of seven fitted up, so that we might go at the end of the month of June to Gaspé in quest of vessels[1] in which to return to France, in case our own should not meanwhile arrive. But God helped us better than we hoped; for, on the 15th of June ensuing, while on guard about 11 o'clock at night, Pont Gravé, captain of one of the vessels of Sieur de Monts, arriving in a shallop, informed us that his ship was anchored six leagues from our settlement, and he was welcomed amid the great joy of all.

The next day the vessel arrived, and anchored near our habitation. Pont Gravé informed us that a vessel from St. Malo, called the St. Éstienne, was following him, bringing us provisions and supplies.

On the 17th of the month, Sieur de Monts decided to go in quest of a place better adapted for an abode, and with a better temperature than our own. With this view, he had the barque made ready, in which he had purposed to go to Gaspé.

Chapter 7

Discovery of the coast of the Almouchiquois as far as the forty-second degree of latitude, and details of this voyage.

On the 18th of June, 1605, Sieur de Monts set out from the Island of St. Croix with some gentlemen, twenty sailors, and a savage named Panounias,[2] together with his wife, whom he was unwilling to leave behind. These we took, in order to serve us as guides to the country of the Almouchiquois,[3] in the hope of exploring and learning more particularly by their aid what the character of this country was, especially since she was a native of it.

[1] These were the ships which came yearly in search of cod.
[2] He was killed by the Almouchiquois, which led to a war (see pp. 111, 113–114).
[3] The Almouchiquois, or Armouchiquois, lived in what is now Massachusetts.

Coasting along inside of Manan, an island three leagues from the main land, we came to the Ranges on the seaward side, at one of which we anchored, where there was a large number of crows, of which our men captured a great many, and we called it the Isle aux Corneilles. Thence we went to the Island of Monts Déserts, at the entrance of the river Norumbegue, as I have before stated, and sailed five or six leagues among many islands. Here there came to us three savages in a canoe from Bedabedec Point, where their captain was; and, after we had had some conversation with them, they returned the same day.

On Friday, the 1st of July, we set out from one of the islands [1] at the mouth of the river, where there is a very good harbor for vessels of a hundred or a hundred and fifty tons. This day we made some twenty-five leagues between Bedabedec Point and many islands and rocks, which we observed as far as the river Quinibequy, at the mouth of which is a very high island, which we called the Tortoise.[2] Between the latter and the main land there are some scattering rocks which are covered at full tide, although the sea is then seen to break over them.[3] Tortoise Island and the river lie south-south-east and north-north-west. As you enter, there are two medium-sized islands forming the entrance, one on one side, the other on the other;[4] and some three hundred paces farther in are two rocks, where there is no wood, but some little grass. We anchored three hundred paces from the entrance in five and six fathoms of water. While in this place, we were overtaken by fogs, on account of which we resolved to enter, in order to see the upper part of the river and the savages who live there; and we set out for this purpose on the 5th of the month. Having made some leagues, our barque came near being lost on a rock which we grazed in passing.[5]

---

[1] The Fox Islands.   [2] Seguin Island.
[3] Ellingwood Rock, Seguin Ledges, and White Ledge. (Slafter.)
[4] Pond Island on the west, and Stage Island on the east; the two rocks referred to in the same sentence are now called the Sugar Loaves. (Slafter.)
[5] It seems nearly certain that the route traversed by the navigators was as follows. Entering the mouth of the Kennebec, they went on a flood-tide

Further on, we met two canoes which had come to hunt birds, which for the most part are moulting at this season, and cannot fly. We addressed these savages by aid of our own, who went to them with his wife, who made them understand the reason of our coming. We made friends with them and with the savages of this river, who served us as guides. Proceeding farther, in order to see their captain, named Manthoumermer, we passed, after we had gone seven or eight leagues, by some islands, straits, and brooks, which extend along the river, where we saw some fine meadows. After we had coasted along an island [1] some four leagues in length, they conducted us to where their chief was [2] with twenty-five or thirty savages, who, as soon as we had anchored, came to us in a canoe, separated a short distance from ten others, in which were those who accompanied him. Coming near our barque, he made an harangue, in which he expressed the pleasure it gave him to see us, and said that he desired to form an alliance with us and to make peace with his enemies through our mediation. He said that, on the next day, he would send to two other captains of savages, who were in the interior, one called Marchin, and the other Sasinou, chief of the river Quinibequy. Sieur de Monts gave them some cakes and peas, with which they were greatly pleased. The next day they guided us down the river another way than that by which we had come, in order to go to a lake; and, passing by some islands, they left, each one of them, an arrow near a cape [3] where all the savages pass, and they believe that if they should not do this some misfortune would befall them, according to the persuasions of the devil. They live in such superstitions, and practise many others of the same sort. Beyond this cape we passed a very narrow waterfall, but only with great difficulty; for, although we had a favorable and fresh wind, and trimmed our sails to receive it as

up Back River and into Hockomock Bay, then southward around the south end of Westport Island, up its east side to Wiscasset, down its west side, around Hockomock Point, and so through the Sasanoa River, Upper Hell Gate and the Kennebec, and into Merrymeeting Bay.

[1] Westport Island.   [2] Wiscasset Harbor.   [3] Hockomock Point.

well as possible, in order to see whether we could not pass it
in that way, we were obliged to attach a hawser to some trees
on shore and all pull on it. In this way, by means of our arms
together with the help of the wind, which was favorable to
us, we succeeded in passing it. The savages accompanying
us carried their canoes by land, being unable to row them.
After going over this fall, we saw some fine meadows. I
was greatly surprised by this fall, since as we descended with
the tide we found it in our favor, but contrary to us when we
came to the fall. But, after we had passed it, it descended as
before, which gave us great satisfaction. Pursuing our route,
we came to the lake,[1] which is from three to four leagues in
length. Here are some islands, and two rivers enter it, the
Quinibequy coming from the north-north-east, and the other
from the north-west, whence were to come Marchin and
Sasinou. Having awaited them all this day, and as they did
not come, we resolved to improve our time. We weighed
anchor accordingly, and there accompanied us two savages
from this lake to serve as guides. The same day we anchored
at the mouth of the river, where we caught a large number of
excellent fish of various sorts. Meanwhile, our savages went
hunting, but did not return. The route by which we descended
this river is much safer and better than that by which we had
gone. Tortoise Island before the mouth of this river is in
latitude 44°; and 19° 12′ of the deflection of the magnetic
needle. They go by this river across the country to Quebec
some fifty leagues, making only one portage of two leagues.
After the portage, you enter another little stream which flows
into the great river St. Lawrence.[2] This river Quinibequy
is very dangerous for vessels half a league from its mouth, on
account of the small amount of water, great tides, rocks and
shoals outside as well as within. But it has a good channel,
if it were well marked out. The land, so far as I have seen it

[1] Merrymeeting Bay, so called from the junction of the Kennebec and the
Androscoggin.
[2] The Chaudière, flowing into the St. Lawrence nearly opposite Quebec,
about three miles above Levis.

along the shores of the river, is very poor, for there are only rocks on all sides. There are a great many small oaks, and very little arable land. Fish abound here, as in the other rivers which I have mentioned. The people live like those in the neighborhood of our settlement; and they told us that the savages, who plant the Indian corn, dwelt very far in the interior, and that they had given up planting it on the coasts on account of the war they had with others, who came and took it away. This is what I have been able to learn about this region, which I think is no better than the others.

On the 8th of the month, we set out from the mouth of this river, not being able to do so sooner on account of the fogs. We made that day some four leagues, and passed a bay,[1] where there are a great many islands. From here large mountains [2] are seen to the west, in which is the dwelling-place of a savage captain called Aneda, who encamps near the river Quinibequy. I was satisfied from this name that it was one of his tribe that had discovered the plant called Aneda, which Jacques Cartier said was so powerful against the malady called scurvy, of which we have already spoken, which harassed his company as well as our own, when they wintered in Canada. The savages have no knowledge at all of this plant, and are not aware of its existence, although the above-mentioned savage has the same name. The following day we made eight leagues. As we passed along the coast, we perceived two columns of smoke which some savages made to attract our attention. We went and anchored in the direction of them behind a small island near the main land,[3] where we saw more than eighty savages running along the shore to see us, dancing and giving expression to their joy. Sieur de Monts sent two men together with our savage to visit them. After they had spoken some time with them, and assured them of our friendship, we left

---

[1] Casco Bay.

[2] The White Mountains of New Hampshire, indicated on numerous early maps, and visible from the sea at this point.

[3] Old Orchard Beach. They anchored inside of Stratton Island.

with them one of our number, and they delivered to us one
of their companions as a hostage. Meanwhile, Sieur de
Monts visited an island, which is very beautiful in view of
what it produces; for it has fine oaks and nut-trees, the soil
cleared up, and many vineyards bearing beautiful grapes in
their season, which were the first we had seen on all these coasts
from the Cap de la Hève. We named it Isle de Bacchus.[1]
It being full tide, we weighed anchor and entered a little river,
which we could not sooner do; for there is a bar, there being at
low tide only half a fathom of water, at full tide a fathom and a
half, and at the highest water two fathoms. On the other side
of the bar there are three, four, five, and six fathoms. When
we had anchored, a large number of savages came to the bank
of the river, and began to dance. Their captain at the time,
whom they called Honemechin, was not with them. He arrived
about two or three hours later with two canoes, when he came
sweeping entirely round our barque. Our savage could understand only a few words, as the language of the Almouchiquois
(for that is the name of this nation) differs entirely from that
of the Souriquois and Etechemins. These people gave signs
of being greatly pleased. Their chief had a good figure, was
young and agile. We sent some articles of merchandise on
shore to barter with them; but they had nothing but their
robes to give in exchange, for they preserve only such furs
as they need for their garments. Sieur de Monts ordered
some provisions to be given to their chief, with which he was
greatly pleased, and came several times to the side of our
boat to see us. These savages shave off the hair far up on
the head, and wear what remains very long, which they comb
and twist behind in various ways very neatly, intertwined
with feathers which they attach to the head. They paint
their faces black and red, like the other savages which we
have seen. They are an agile people, with well-formed bodies. Their weapons are pikes, clubs, bows and arrows, at
the end of which some attach the tail of a fish called the
signoc, others bones, while the arrows of others are entirely

[1] Richmond Island. The oaks, walnuts, and vines have disappeared.

of wood. They till and cultivate the soil, something which we have not hitherto observed. In the place of ploughs, they use an instrument of very hard wood, shaped like a spade. This river is called by the inhabitants of the country Choü-acoet.[1]

The next day Sieur de Monts and I landed to observe their tillage on the bank of the river. We saw their Indian corn, which they raise in gardens. Planting three or four kernels in one place, they then heap up about it a quantity of earth with shells of the signoc before mentioned. Then three feet distant they plant as much more, and thus in succession. With this corn they put in each hill three or four Brazilian beans,[2] which are of different colors. When they grow up, they interlace with the corn, which reaches to the height of from five to six feet; and they keep the ground very free from weeds. We saw there many squashes, and pumpkins, and tobacco, which they likewise cultivate.

The Indian corn which we saw was at that time about two feet high, some of it as high as three. The beans were beginning to flower, as also the pumpkins and squashes. They plant their corn in May, and gather it in September. We saw also a great many nuts, which are small and have several divisions. There were as yet none on the trees, but we found plenty under them, from the preceding year. We saw also many grape-vines, on which there was a remarkably fine berry, from which we made some very good verjuice. We had heretofore seen grapes only on the Island of Bacchus, distant nearly two leagues from this river. Their permanent abode, the tillage, and the fine trees led us to conclude that

[1] From this comes the modern Saco.

[2] *Phaseolus vulgaris*, the kidney-bean. All the plants here named are indigenous to America, though probably brought to New England from farther south. Cartier found tobacco growing as far north as Quebec in 1535. "They fill their bodies full of smoke, till that it commeth out of their mouth and nostrils, even as out of the Tonnell of a chimney. They say that this doth keepe them warme and in health; they never goe without some of it about them. We ourselves have tryed the same smoke, and having put it in our mouthes, it seemed almost as hot as pepper," is his account. *Early English and French Voyages*, p. 68.

the air here is milder and better than that where we passed
the winter, and at the other places we visited on the coast.
But I cannot believe that there is not here a considerable
degree of cold, although it is in latitude 43° 45'.[1] The forests in the interior are very thin, although abounding in oaks,
beeches, ashes, and elms; in wet places there are many wil-
lows. The savages dwell permanently in this place, and have
a large cabin surrounded by palisades made of rather large
trees placed by the side of each other, in which they take
refuge when their enemies make war upon them. They
cover their cabins with oak bark. This place is very pleasant, and as agreeable as any to be seen. The river is very
abundant in fish, and is bordered by meadows. At the
mouth there is a small island [2] adapted for the construction of
a good fortress, where one could be in security.

On Sunday,[3] the 12th of the month, we set out from the
river Choüacoet. After coasting along some six or seven
leagues, a contrary wind arose, which obliged us to anchor
and go ashore,[4] where we saw two meadows, each a league
in length and half a league in breadth. We saw there two
savages, whom at first we took to be the great birds called
bustards, to be found in this country; who, as soon as they
caught sight of us, took flight into the woods, and were not
seen again. From Choüacoet to this place, where we saw
some little birds, which sing like blackbirds, and are black
excepting the ends of the wings, which are orange-colored,[5]
there is a large number of grape-vines and nut-trees. This
coast is sandy, for the most part, all the way from Quinibequy. This day we returned two or three leagues towards
Choüacoet, as far as a cape which we called Island Harbor,[6]
favorable for vessels of a hundred tons, about which are three
islands. Heading north-east a quarter north, one can enter

[1] Champlain's expression is more colloquial and energetic than that of
the translation: "Mais que je croye qu'il n'y face un peu de froit, bien que
ce soit par la hauteur de 43 degrez 3 quarts de latitude, non."

[2] Ram Island.   [3] July 12, 1605, fell on a Tuesday.

[4] Near Wells Neck.   [5] The red-wing blackbird.

[6] Cape Porpoise Harbor.

another harbor [1] near this place, to which there is no approach, although there are islands, except the one where you enter. At the entrance there are some dangerous reefs. There are in these islands so many red currants that one sees for the most part nothing else, and an infinite number of pigeons, of which we took a great quantity. This Island Harbor is in latitude 43° 25'.

On the 15th of the month we made twelve leagues. Coasting along, we perceived a smoke on the shore, which we approached as near as possible, but saw no savage, which led us to believe that they had fled. The sun set, and we could find no harbor for that night, since the coast was flat and sandy. Keeping off, and heading south, in order to find an anchorage, after proceeding about two leagues, we observed a cape [2] on the main land south a quarter south-east of us, some six leagues distant. Two leagues to the east we saw three or four rather high islands, [3] and on the west a large bay. [4] The coast of this bay, reaching as far as the cape, extends inland from where we were perhaps four leagues. It has a breadth of two leagues from north to south, and three at its entrance. Not observing any place favorable for putting in, we resolved to go to the cape above mentioned with short sail, which occupied a portion of the night. Approaching to where there were sixteen fathoms of water, we anchored until daybreak.

On the next day we went to the above-mentioned cape, where there are three islands [5] near the main land, full of wood of different kinds, as at Choüacoet and all along the coast; and still another flat one, where there are breakers, and which

---

[1] Goose Fair Bay.   [2] Cape Ann.

[3] The Isles of Shoals. Nine years later Captain John Smith visited these islands, and called them Smith's Isles.

[4] This bay is nameless on modern maps. It receives the waters of the Merrimac River.

[5] Straitsmouth, Thatcher and Milk Islands, off Cape Ann. They were named by Captain John Smith the "Three Turks' Heads" in memory of three Turks' heads cut off by him at the siege of Caniza, by which he acquired from Sigismundus, prince of Transylvania, their effigies in his shield for his arms. See his *True Travels, Adventures, and Observations* (London, 1629). (Slafter.)

extends a little farther out to sea than the others, on which
there is no wood at all.   We named this place Island Cape,[1]
near which we saw a canoe containing five or six savages, who
came out near our barque, and then went back and danced on
the beach.   Sieur de Monts sent me on shore to observe them,
and to give each one of them a knife and some biscuit, which
caused them to dance again better than before.   This over,
I made them understand, as well as I could, that I desired them
to show me the course of the shore.   After I had drawn with
a crayon the bay, and the Island Cape, where we were, with the
same crayon they drew the outline of another bay,[2] which they
represented as very large; here they placed six pebbles at
equal distances apart, giving me to understand by this that
these signs represented as many chiefs and tribes.   Then they
drew within the first-mentioned bay a river which we had passed,
which has shoals and is very long.[3]   We found in this place a
great many vines, the green grapes on which were a little
larger than peas, also many nut-trees, the nuts on which were
no larger than musket-balls.   The savages told us that all
those inhabiting this country cultivated the land and sowed
seeds like the others, whom we had before seen.   The latitude
of this place is 43° and some minutes.   Sailing half a league
farther, we observed several savages on a rocky point,[4] who
ran along the shore, dancing as they went, to their companions
to inform them of our coming.   After pointing out to us the
direction of their abode, they made a signal with smoke to
show us the place of their settlement.   We anchored near a
little island,[5] and sent our canoe with knives and cakes for
the savages.   From the large number of those we saw, we
concluded that these places were better inhabited than the
others we had seen.

[1] Cape Ann, so called, later, in memory of the queen of James I. of England.

[2] Massachusetts Bay.

[3] The Merrimac, which Champlain had passed unperceived.

[4] Emerson Point, the eastern extremity of Cape Ann.

[5] Thatcher's Island.   The next anchorage was almost certainly in Boston Harbor.

F

After a stay of some two hours for the sake of observing these people, whose canoes are made of birch bark, like those of the Canadians, Souriquois, and Etechemins, we weighed anchor and set sail with a promise of fine weather. Continuing our course to the west-south-west, we saw numerous islands on one side and the other. Having sailed seven or eight leagues, we anchored near an island, whence we observed many smokes along the shore, and many savages running up to see us. Sieur de Monts sent two or three men in a canoe to them, to whom he gave some knives and paternosters to present to them; with which they were greatly pleased, and danced several times in acknowledgment. We could not ascertain the name of their chief, as we did not know their language. All along the shore there is a great deal of land cleared up and planted with Indian corn. The country is very pleasant and agreeable, and there is no lack of fine trees. The canoes of those who live there are made of a single piece, and are very liable to turn over if one is not skilful in managing them. We had not before seen any of this kind. They are made in the following manner. After cutting down, at a cost of much labor and time, the largest and tallest tree they can find, by means of stone hatchets (for they have no others except some few which they received from the savages on the coasts of La Cadie,[1] who obtained them in exchange for furs), they remove the bark, and round off the tree except on one side, where they apply fire gradually along its entire length; and sometimes they put red-hot pebble-stones on top. When the fire is too fierce, they extinguish it with a little water, not entirely, but so that the edge of the boat may not be burnt. It being hollowed out as much as they wish, they scrape it all over with stones, which they use instead of knives. These stones resemble our musket flints.

[1] This is the spelling given in de Monts' commission from Henry IV. in 1603. (Lescarbot, book IV.) Champlain spells it in different ways in different places. Arcadie, Accadie, Acadie, L'Accadie, L'Arcadie, L'Acadie are found in writers of the time, and several Latinized forms terminating in *ia*. It is a common Indian termination probably meaning "place"; *e.g.*, Shubenacadie, Tracadie, Passamaquoddy, etc.

On the next day, the 17th of the month, we weighed anchor to go to a cape we had seen the day before, which seemed to lie on our south-south-west. This day we were able to make only five leagues, and we passed by some islands [1] covered with wood. I observed in the bay all that the savages had described to me at Island Cape. As we continued our course, large numbers came to us in canoes from the islands and main land. We anchored a league from a cape, which we named St. Louis,[2] where we noticed smoke in several places. While in the act of going there, our barque grounded on a rock, where we were in great danger, for, if we had not speedily got it off, it would have overturned in the sea, since the tide was falling all around, and there were five or six fathoms of water. But God preserved us, and we anchored near the above-named cape, when there came to us fifteen or sixteen canoes of savages. In some of them there were fifteen or sixteen, who began to manifest great signs of joy, and made various harangues, which we could not in the least understand. Sieur de Monts sent three or four men on shore in our canoe, not only to get water, but to see their chief, whose name was Honabetha. The latter had a number of knives and other trifles, which Sieur de Monts gave him, when he came alongside to see us, together with some of his companions, who were present both along the shore and in their canoes. We received the chief very cordially, and made him welcome; who, after remaining some time, went back. Those whom we had sent to them brought us some little squashes as big as the fist, which we ate as a salad, like cucumbers, and which we found very good. They brought also some purslane, which grows in large quantities among the Indian corn, and of which they make no more account than of weeds. We saw here a great many little houses, scattered over the fields where they plant their Indian corn.

There is, moreover, in this bay a very broad river, which we named River du Guast.[3]   It stretches, as it seemed to me,

---

[1] The islands in Boston Bay.   [2] Brant Point.
[3] Charles River.   They named it in honor of Pierre du Guast, Sieur de

towards the Iroquois, a nation in open warfare with the Montagnais, who live on the great river St. Lawrence.

Chapter 8

Continuation of the discoveries along the coast of the Almou-chiquois, and what we observed in detail.

The next day we doubled Cap St. Louis, so named by Sieur de Monts, a land rather low, and in latitude 42° 45′. The same day we sailed two leagues along a sandy coast, as we passed along which we saw a great many cabins and gardens. The wind being contrary, we entered a little bay to await a time favorable for proceeding. There came to us two or three canoes, which had just been fishing for cod and other fish, which are found there in large numbers. These they catch with hooks made of a piece of wood, to which they attach a bone in the shape of a spear, and fasten it very securely. The whole has a fang-shape, and the line attached to it is made out of the bark of a tree. They gave me one of their hooks, which I took as a curiosity. In it the bone was fastened on by hemp, like that in France, as it seemed to me, and they told me that they gathered this plant without being obliged to cultivate it; and indicated that it grew to the height of four or five feet. This canoe went back on shore to give notice to their fellow inhabitants, who caused columns of smoke to arise on our account. We saw eighteen or twenty savages, who came to the shore and began to dance. Our canoe landed in order to give them some bagatelles, at which they were greatly pleased. Some of them came to us and begged us to go to their river. We weighed anchor to do so, but were unable to enter on account of the small amount of water, it being low tide, and were accordingly obliged to anchor at the mouth. I went ashore, where I saw many others, who received us very cordially. I made also an examination of the river, but saw only an arm

Monts. Champlain spells it du Gas; Lescarbot sometimes da Gua, and sometimes de Guast; Charlevoix du Guast.

of water extending a short distance inland, where the land is
only in part cleared up. Running into this is merely a brook
not deep enough for boats except at full tide. The circuit
of the bay is about a league. On one side of the entrance
to this bay there is a point which is almost an island, covered
with wood, principally pines, and adjoins sand-banks, which
are very extensive. On the other side, the land is high.
There are two islets in this bay, which are not seen until one
has entered, and around which it is almost entirely dry at low
tide. This place is very conspicuous from the sea, for the
coast is very low, excepting the cape at the entrance to the
bay. We named it the Port du Cap St. Louis,[1] distant
two leagues from the above cape, and ten from the
Island Cape. It is in about the same latitude as Cap St.
Louis.

On the 19th of the month, we set out from this place.
Coasting along in a southerly direction, we sailed four or five
leagues, and passed near a rock on a level with the surface of
the water. As we continued our course, we saw some land
which seemed to us to be islands, but as we came nearer we
found it to be the main land, lying to the north-north-west of
us, and that it was the cape of a large bay,[2] containing more
than eighteen or nineteen leagues in circuit, into which we
had run so far that we had to wear off on the other tack in
order to double the cape which we had seen. The latter we
named Cap Blanc,[3] since it contained sands and downs
which had a white appearance. A favorable wind was of
great assistance to us here, for otherwise we should have been
in danger of being driven upon the coast. This bay is very
safe, provided the land be not approached nearer than a good
league, there being no islands nor rocks except that just

---

[1] Plymouth Harbor, where in 1620 the *Mayflower* cast anchor with the
Pilgrims. It was visited and named by Captain John Smith in 1614. Of the
two islets mentioned above and in other seventeenth-century narratives,
one has since disappeared.

[2] Cape Cod Bay.

[3] Cape Cod, so named by Bartholomew Gosnold in 1602. See *Early
English and French Voyages*, p. 331, note 1.

mentioned, which is near a river that extends some distance inland, which we named St. Suzanne du Cap Blanc,[1] whence across to Cap St. Louis the distance is ten leagues. Cap Blanc is a point of sand, which bends around towards the south some six leagues. This coast is rather high, and consists of sand, which is very conspicuous as one comes from the sea. At a distance of some fifteen or eighteen leagues from land, the depth of the water is thirty, forty, and fifty fathoms, but only ten on nearing the shore, which is unobstructed. There is a large extent of open country along the shore before reaching the woods, which are very attractive and beautiful. We anchored off the coast, and saw some savages, towards whom four of our company proceeded. Making their way upon a sand-bank, they observed something like a bay, and cabins bordering it on all sides. When they were about a league and a half from us, there came to them a savage dancing all over, as they expressed it. He had come down from the high shore, but turned about shortly after to inform his fellow inhabitants of our arrival.

The next day, the 20th of the month, we went to the place which our men had seen, and which we found a very dangerous harbor in consequence of the shoals and banks, where we saw breakers in all directions. It was almost low tide when we entered, and there were only four feet of water in the northern passage; at high tide, there are two fathoms. After we had entered, we found the place very spacious, being perhaps three or four leagues in circuit, entirely surrounded by little houses, around each one of which there was as much land as the occupant needed for his support. A small river enters here, which is very pretty, and in which at low tide there are some three and a half feet of water. There are also two or three brooks bordered by meadows. It would be a very fine place, if the harbor were good. I took the altitude, and found the latitude 42°, and the deflection of the magnetic needle 18° 40′. Many savages, men and women, visited us,

---

[1] Wellfleet Harbor or Herring River. (Slafter.)

and ran up on all sides dancing. We named this place Port
de Mallebarre.[1]

The next day, the 21st of the month, Sieur de Monts determined to go and see their habitation. Nine or ten of
us accompanied him with our arms; the rest remained to
guard the barque. We went about a league along the coast.
Before reaching their cabins, we entered a field planted with
Indian corn in the manner before described. The corn was
in flower, and five and a half feet high. There was some less
advanced, which they plant later. We saw many Brazilian
beans, and many squashes of various sizes, very good for eating; some tobacco, and roots which they cultivate, the latter
having the taste of an artichoke. The woods are filled with
oaks, nut-trees, and beautiful cypresses,[2] which are of a red-
dish color and have a very pleasant odor. There were also
several fields entirely uncultivated, the land being allowed to
remain fallow. When they wish to plant it, they set fire to
the weeds, and then work it over with their wooden spades.
Their cabins are round, and covered with heavy thatch made
of reeds. In the roof there is an opening of about a foot and
a half, whence the smoke from the fire passes out. We asked
them if they had their permanent abode in this place, and
whether there was much snow. But we were unable to ascertain this fully from them, not understanding their language,
although they made an attempt to inform us by signs, by
taking some sand in their hands, spreading it out over the
ground, and indicating that it was of the color of our collars,
and that it reached the depth of a foot. Others made signs
that there was less, and gave us to understand also that the
harbor never froze; but we were unable to ascertain whether
the snow lasted long. I conclude, however, that this region
is of moderate temperature, and the winter not severe. While
we were there, there was a north-east storm, which lasted four
days; the sky being so overcast that the sun hardly shone at
all. It was very cold, and we were obliged to put on our great-

[1] Nauset Harbor, though its outline has changed greatly since 1605.
[2] The red cedar (*Juniperus Virginiana*).

coats, which we had entirely left off.   Yet I think the cold was accidental, as it is often experienced elsewhere out of season.

On the 23d of July, four or five seamen having gone on shore with some kettles to get fresh water, which was to be found in one of the sand-banks a short distance from our barque, some of the savages, coveting them, watched the time when our men went to the spring, and then seized one out of the hands of a sailor, who was the first to dip, and who had no weapons.   One of his companions, starting to run after him, soon returned, as he could not catch him, since he ran much faster than himself.   The other savages, of whom there were a large number, seeing our sailors running to our barque, and at the same time shouting to us to fire at them, took to flight.   At the time there were some of them in our barque, who threw themselves into the sea, only one of whom we were able to seize.   Those on the land who had taken to flight, seeing them swimming, returned straight to the sailor from whom they had taken away the kettle, hurled several arrows at him from behind, and brought him down.   Seeing this, they ran at once to him, and despatched him with their knives.   Meanwhile, haste was made to go on shore, and muskets were fired from our barque: mine, bursting in my hands, came near killing me.   The savages, hearing this discharge of fire-arms, took to flight, and with redoubled speed when they saw that we had landed, for they were afraid when they saw us running after them.   There was no likelihood of our catching them, for they are as swift as horses. We brought in the murdered man, and he was buried some hours later.[1]   Meanwhile, we kept the prisoner bound by the feet and hands on board of our barque, fearing that he might escape.   But Sieur de Monts resolved to let him go, being persuaded that he was not to blame, and that he had no previous knowledge of what had transpired, as also those who, at

---

[1] This sailor was the first white man to be buried on New England soil, save perhaps Thorwald, son of Eric the Red.   See *The Northmen, Columbus and Cabot*, in this series, p. 56.

In spite of this encounter, the relations of the French to the Indians were, in general, much more friendly than those of the more surly British.

the time, were in and about our barque. Some hours later
there came some savages to us, to excuse themselves, indicating by signs and demonstrations that it was not they who
had committed this malicious act, but others farther off in
the interior. We did not wish to harm them, although it
was in our power to avenge ourselves.

All these savages from the Island Cape wear neither robes
nor furs, except very rarely: moreover, their robes are made
of grasses and hemp, scarcely covering the body, and coming down only to their thighs. They have only the sexual
parts concealed with a small piece of leather; so likewise the
women, with whom it comes down a little lower behind than
with the men, all the rest of the body being naked. Whenever the women came to see us, they wore robes which were
open in front. The men cut off the hair on the top of the
head like those at the river Choüacoet. I saw, among other
things, a girl with her hair very neatly dressed, with a skin
colored red, and bordered on the upper part with little shell-
beads. A part of her hair hung down behind, the rest being
braided in various ways. These people paint the face red,
black, and yellow. They have scarcely any beard, and tear it
out as fast as it grows. Their bodies are well-proportioned.
I cannot tell what government they have, but I think that in
this respect they resemble their neighbors, who have none at
all. They know not how to worship or pray; yet, like the
other savages, they have some superstitions, which I shall
describe in their place. As for weapons, they have only pikes,
clubs, bows and arrows. It would seem from their appearance
that they have a good disposition, better than those of the
north, but they are all in fact of no great worth.[1]   Even a
slight intercourse with them gives you at once a knowledge of
them. They are great thieves and, if they cannot lay hold of
any thing with their hands, they try to do so with their feet,
as we have oftentimes learned by experience. I am of opinion
that, if they had any thing to exchange with us, they would not

_____

[1] Lescarbot, while admitting their *penchant* for theft, speaks in much
more kindly terms of the Indians.

give themselves to thieving. They bartered away to us their bows, arrows, and quivers, for pins and buttons; and if they had had any thing else better they would have done the same with it. It is necessary to be on one's guard against this people, and live in a state of distrust of them, yet without letting them perceive it. They gave us a large quantity of tobacco, which they dry and then reduce to powder. When they eat Indian corn, they boil it in earthen pots, which they make in a way different from ours.[1] They bray it also in wooden mortars and reduce it to flour, of which they then make cakes, like the Indians of Peru.

In this place and along the whole coast from Quinibequy, there are a great many *siguenocs*,[2] which is a fish with a shell on its back like the tortoise, yet different, there being in the middle a row of little prickles, of the color of a dead leaf, like the rest of the fish. At the end of this shell, there is another still smaller, bordered by very sharp points. The length of the tail varies according to their size. With the end of it, these people point their arrows, and it contains also a row of prickles like the large shell in which are the eyes. There are eight small feet like those of the crab, and two behind longer and flatter, which they use in swimming. There are also in front two other very small ones with which they eat. When walking, all the feet are concealed excepting the two hindermost, which are slightly visible. Under the small shell there are membranes which swell up, and beat like the throat of a frog, and rest upon each other like the folds of a waistcoat. The largest specimen of this fish that I saw was a foot broad, and a foot and a half long.

We saw also a sea-bird [3] with a black beak, the upper part slightly aquiline, four inches long and in the form of a lancet;

[1] A description of this savage pottery, the manufacture of which was carried on exclusively by the women, is given in Sagard, *Histoire du Canada* (1636, reprinted 1866), book II., ch. XIII.

[2] *Limulus Polyphemus*, the horse-shoe, or king-crab.

[3] *Rhynchops nigra.* It has a variety of local names: black skinner, cut-water, razor-bill, etc. It is frequent in South Carolina and the Gulf States, but is only occasionally seen in New England.

namely, the lower part representing the handle and the upper
the blade, which is thin, sharp on both sides, and shorter by
a third than the other, which circumstance is a matter of
astonishment to many persons, who cannot comprehend how
it is possible for this bird to eat with such a beak. It is of
the size of a pigeon, the wings being very long in proportion
to the body, the tail short, as also the legs, which are red; the
feet being small and flat. The plumage on the upper part is
gray-brown, and on the under part pure white. They go
always in flocks along the sea-shore, like the pigeons with us.

The savages, along all these coasts where we have been, say
that other birds, which are very large, come along when their
corn is ripe. They imitated for us their cry, which resembles
that of the turkey.[1] They showed us their feathers in several
places, with which they feather their arrows, and which they
put on their heads for decoration; and also a kind of hair
which they have under the throat like those we have in France,
and they say that a red crest falls over upon the beak. According to their description, they are as large as a bustard, which is
a kind of goose, having the neck longer and twice as large as
those with us. All these indications led us to conclude that
they were turkeys. We should have been very glad to see
some of these birds, as well as their feathers, for the sake of
greater certainty. Before seeing their feathers, and the little
bunch of hair which they have under the throat, and hearing
their cry imitated, I should have thought that they were certain birds like turkeys, which are found in some places in Peru,
along the sea-shore, eating carrion and other dead things like
crows. But these are not so large; nor do they have so long a
bill, or a cry like that of real turkeys; nor are they good to eat
like those which the Indians say come in flocks in summer, and
at the beginning of winter go away to warmer countries, their
natural dwelling-place.

[1] The wild turkey, long since extirpated in New England, though still
found occasionally in Canada, and frequently in the Southern States.

Chapter 9

Return from the discoveries along the coast of the Almouchiquois.

We had spent more than five weeks in going over three degrees of latitude, and our voyage was limited to six, since we had not taken provisions for a longer time. In consequence of fogs and storms, we had not been able to go farther than Mallebarre, where we waited several days for fair weather, in order to sail. Finding ourselves accordingly pressed by the scantiness of provisions, Sieur de Monts determined to return to the Island of St. Croix, in order to find another place more favorable for our settlement, as we had not been able to do on any of the coasts which we had explored on this voyage.

Accordingly, on the 25th of July, we set out from this harbor, in order to make observations elsewhere. In going out, we came near being lost on the bar at the entrance, from the mistake of our pilots, Cramolet and Champdoré, masters of the barque, who had imperfectly marked out the entrance of the channel on the southern side, where we were to go. Having escaped this danger, we headed north-east for six leagues, until we reached Cap Blanc, sailing on from there to Island Cape, a distance of fifteen leagues, with the same wind. Then we headed east-north-east sixteen leagues, as far as Choüacoet, where we saw the savage chief, Marchin, whom we had expected to see at the Lake Quinibequy. He had the reputation of being one of the valiant ones of his people. He had a fine appearance: all his motions were dignified, savage as he was. Sieur de Monts gave him many presents, with which he was greatly pleased; and, in return, Marchin gave him a young Etechemin boy, whom he had captured in war, and whom we took away with us; and thus we set out, mutually good friends. We headed north-east a quarter east for fifteen leagues, as far as Quinibequy, where we arrived on the 29th of the month, and where we were expecting to find a savage, named Sasinou, of whom I spoke before. Thinking that he would come, we waited some time for him, in order to recover from him an Etechemin young man and girl, whom he was holding as prisoners. While waiting, there came to us a captain called Anassou, who trafficked a little in furs, and with whom we made an alliance. He told us that there was a ship,[1] ten leagues off the harbor, which was engaged in fishing, and that those on her had killed five savages of this river, under cover of friendship. From his description of the men on the vessel, we concluded that they were English, and we named the island where they were La Nef;[2] for, at a distance, it had the appearance of a ship. Finding that the above-mentioned Sasinou did not come, we headed east-south-east, for twenty leagues, to Isle Haute, where we anchored for the night.

On the next day, the 1st of August, we sailed east some twenty leagues to Cap Corneille,[3] where we spent the night. On the 2d of the month, we sailed north-east seven leagues to the mouth of the river St. Croix, on the western shore. Having anchored between the two first islands,[4] Sieur de Monts embarked in a canoe, at a distance of six leagues from the settlement of St. Croix, where we arrived the next day with our barque. We found there Sieur des Antons of St. Malo, who had come in one of the vessels of Sieur de Monts, to bring provisions and also other supplies for those who were to winter in this country.

[1] This was doubtless the *Archangel*, commanded by Captain George Waymouth, though the latter had sailed for England on June 26, new style. See Rosier's *True Relation*, in *Early English and French Voyages*, and especially p. 378. The five savages spoken of were not killed, but kindly treated, and carried off to England, where they gave much information to the celebrated Sir Ferdinando Gorges.

[2] Monhegan.

[3] Meaning Crow Cape; probably a point near Machias, Maine.

[4] Between Campobello and Moose Island, on which is situated the town of Eastport. (Slafter.)

Chapter 10

The dwelling-place on the island of St. Croix transferred to Port Royal, and the reason why.

Sieur de Monts determined to change his location, and make another settlement, in order to avoid the severe cold and the bad winter which we had had in the Island of St. Croix. As we had not, up to that time, found any suitable harbor, and, in view of the short time we had for building houses in which to establish ourselves, we fitted out two barques, and loaded them with the frame-work taken from the houses of St. Croix, in order to transport it to Port Royal, twenty-five leagues distant, where we thought the climate was much more temperate and agreeable. Pont Gravé and I set out for that place; and, having arrived, we looked for a site favorable for our residence, under shelter from the north-west wind, which we dreaded, having been very much harassed by it.

After searching carefully in all directions, we found no place more suitable and better situated than one slightly elevated, about which there are some marshes and good springs of water. This place is opposite the island at the mouth of the river Équille. To the north of us about a league, there is a range of mountains, extending nearly ten leagues in a north-east and south-west direction. The whole country is filled with thick forests, as I mentioned above, except at a point a league and a half up the river, where there are some oaks, although scattering, and many wild vines, which one could easily remove and put the soil under cultivation, notwithstanding it is light and sandy. We had almost resolved to build there; but the consideration that we should have been too far up the harbor and river led us to change our mind.

Recognizing accordingly the site of our habitation[1] as a good one, we began to clear up the ground, which was full of trees, and to erect houses as soon as possible. Each one

[1] See p. 34, note 4.

was busy in this work. After everything had been arranged,
and the majority of the dwellings built, Sieur de Monts determined to return to France, in order to petition his Majesty
to grant him all that might be necessary for his undertaking.
He had desired to leave Sieur d'Orville to command in this
place in his absence. But the climatic malady, *mal de la terre*,
with which he was afflicted would not allow him to gratify
the wish of Sieur de Monts. On this account, a conference
was held with Pont Gravé on the subject, to whom this charge
was offered, which he was happy to accept; and he finished
what little of the habitation remained to be built. I, at the
same time, hoping to have an opportunity to make some new
explorations towards Florida, determined to stay there also,
of which Sieur de Monts approved.

Chapter 11

What took place after the departure of Sieur de Monts, until,
no tidings of what he had promised being received, we
departed from Port Royal to return to France.

As soon as Sieur de Monts had departed, a portion of the
forty or forty-five who remained began to make gardens.
I, also, for the sake of occupying my time, made one, which was
surrounded with ditches full of water, in which I placed some
fine trout, and into which flowed three brooks of very fine running water, from which the greater part of our settlement
was supplied. I made also a little sluice-way towards the
shore, in order to draw off the water when I wished. This spot
was entirely surrounded by meadows, where I constructed a
summer-house, with some fine trees, as a resort for enjoying
the fresh air. I made there, also, a little reservoir for holding
salt-water fish, which we took out as we wanted them. I
took especial pleasure in it, and planted there some seeds which
turned out well. But much work had to be laid out in preparation. We resorted often to this place as a pastime; and it

seemed as if the little birds round about took pleasure in it, for they gathered there in large numbers, warbling and chirping so pleasantly that I think I never heard the like.

The plan of the settlement was ten fathoms long and eight wide, making the distance round thirty-six. On the eastern side is a store-house, occupying the width of it, and a very fine cellar from five to six feet deep. On the northern side are the quarters of Sieur de Monts, handsomely finished. About the back yard are the dwellings of the workmen. At a corner of the western side is a platform, where four cannon were placed; and at the other corner, towards the east, is a palisade shaped like a platform, as can be seen from the accompanying illustration.

Some days after the buildings were completed, I went to the river St. John to find the savage named Secondon, the same that conducted Prevert's party to the copper-mine, which I had already gone in search of with Sieur de Monts, when we were at the Port of Mines, though without success. Having found him, I begged him to go there with us, which he very readily consented to do, and proceeded to show it to us. We found there some little pieces of copper of the thickness of a sou, and others still thicker imbedded in grayish and red rocks. The miner accompanying us, whose name was Master Jacques, a native of Sclavonia, a man very skilful in searching for minerals, made the entire circuit of the hills to see if he could find any gangue,[1] but without success. Yet he found, some steps from where we had taken the pieces of copper before mentioned, something like a mine, which, however, was far from being one. He said that, from the appearance of the soil, it might prove to be good, if it were worked; and that it was not probable that there could be pure copper on the surface of the earth, without there being a large quantity of it underneath. The truth is that, if the water did not

---

[1] The matrix in which an ore is found.   Professor Ganong, *Acadiensis*, IV. 202, thinks the mines alluded to in the next sentences must have been on the New Brunswick shore of the bay, where the map of 1632 has the legend "C. des Mines."

cover the mines twice a day, and if they did not lie in such hard rocks, something might be expected from them.

After making this observation, we returned to our settlement, where we found some of our company sick with the *mal de la terre*, but not so seriously as at the Island of St. Croix; although, out of our number of forty-five, twelve died, including the miner, and five were sick, who recovered the following spring. Our surgeon, named Des Champs, from Honfleur, skilful in his profession, opened some of the bodies, to see whether he might be more successful in discovering the cause of the maladies than our surgeons had been the year before. He found the parts of the body affected in the same manner as those opened at the Island of St. Croix, but could discover no means of curing them, any more than the other surgeons.

On the 20th of December, it began to snow, and some ice passed along before our settlement. The winter was not so sharp as the year before, nor the snow so deep, or of so long duration. Among other incidents, the wind was so violent on the 20th of February, 1605,[1] that it blew over a large number of trees, roots and all, and broke off many others. It was a remarkable sight. The rains were very frequent, which was the cause of the mild winter in comparison with the past one, although it is only twenty-five leagues from Port Royal to St. Croix.

On the first day of March, Pont Gravé ordered a barque of seventeen or eighteen tons to be fitted up, which was ready on the 15th, in order to go on a voyage of discovery along the coast of Florida.[2] With this view, we set out on the 16th following, but were obliged to put in at an island to the south of Manan, having gone that day eighteen leagues. We anchored in a sandy cove, exposed to the sea and the south

[1] 1606. This is probably a slip, rather than an instance of the old custom of commencing the year at Easter; for in ch. xvi., and thenceforward, Champlain counts as do we. (Laverdière.) Up to 1564 in France the civil year began at Easter.

[2] Florida, as the term was then used, extended from the peninsula in definitely to the north.

G

wind.[1]   The latter increased, during the night, to such an
impetuosity that we could not stand by our anchor, and were
compelled, without choice, to go ashore, at the mercy of God
and the waves.   The latter were so heavy and furious that
while we were attaching the buoy to the anchor, so as to cut
the cable at the hawse-hole, it did not give us time, but broke
straightway of itself.   The wind and the sea cast us as the
wave receded upon a little rock, and we awaited only the
moment to see our barque break up, and to save ourselves,
if possible, upon its fragments.   In these desperate straits,
after we had received several waves, there came one so large
and fortunate for us that it carried us over the rock, and threw
us on to a little sandy beach, which insured us for this time
from shipwreck.

The barque being on shore, we began at once to unload
what there was in her, in order to ascertain where the damage was, which was not so great as we expected.   She was
speedily repaired by the diligence of Champdoré, her master.
Having been put in order, she was reloaded; and we waited
for fair weather and until the fury of the sea should abate,
which was not until the end of four days, namely, the 21st of
March, when we set out from this miserable place, and proceeded to Port aux Coquilles,[2] seven or eight leagues distant.
The latter is at the mouth of the river St. Croix, where there
was a large quantity of snow.   We stayed there until the 29th
of the month, in consequence of the fogs and contrary winds,
which are usual at this season, when Pont Gravé determined
to put back to Port Royal, to see in what condition our companions were, whom we had left there sick.   Having arrived
there, Pont Gravé was attacked with illness, which delayed
us until the 8th of April.

On the 9th of the month he embarked, although still in-
disposed, from his desire to see the coast of Florida, and in the
belief that a change of air would restore his health.   The

---

[1] Seal Cove, between the southwest end of Grand Manan and Wood
Island.   The barque was thrown upon the latter.

[2] *I.e.*, Shell Harbor, probably the modern Head Harbor.

same day we anchored and passed the night at the mouth of the harbor, two leagues distant from our settlement.

The next morning before day, Champdoré came to ask Pont Gravé if he wished to have the anchor raised, who replied in the affirmative, if he deemed the weather favorable for setting out. Upon this, Champdoré had the anchor raised at once, and the sail spread to the wind, which was north-north-east, according to his report. The weather was thick and rainy, and the air full of fog, with indications of foul rather than fair weather.

While going out of the mouth of the harbor, we were suddenly carried by the tide out of the passage, and, before perceiving them, were driven upon the rocks on the east-north-east coast.[1] Pont Gravé and I, who were asleep, were awaked by hearing the sailors shouting and exclaiming, "We are lost!" which brought me quickly to my feet, to see what was the matter. Pont Gravé was still ill, which prevented him from rising as quickly as he wished. I was scarcely on deck, when the barque was thrown upon the coast; and the wind, which was north, drove us upon a point. We unfurled the mainsail, turned it to the wind, and hauled it up as high as we could, that it might drive us up as far as possible on the rocks, for fear that the reflux of the sea, which fortunately was falling, would draw us in, when it would have been impossible to save ourselves. At the first blow of our boat upon the rocks, the rudder broke, a part of the keel and three or four planks were smashed, and some ribs stove in, which frightened us, for our barque filled immediately; and all that we could do was to wait until the sea fell, so that we might get ashore. For, otherwise, we were in danger of our lives, in consequence of the swell, which was very high and furious about us. The sea having fallen, we went on shore amid the storm, when the barque was speedily unloaded, and we saved a large portion of the provisions in her, with the help of the savage, Captain Secondon and his companions, who came to us with

[1] On the Granville side of Digby Strait. The French text reads east-north-west, an evident misprint. (Slafter.)

their canoes, to carry to our habitation what we had saved from our barque, which, all shattered as she was, went to pieces at the return of the tide.   But we, most happy at having saved our lives, returned to our settlement with our poor savages, who stayed there a large part of the winter; and we praised God for having rescued us from this shipwreck, from which we had not expected to escape so easily.

The loss of our barque caused us great regret, since we found ourselves, through want of a vessel, deprived of the prospect of being able to accomplish the voyage we had undertaken.   And we were unable to build another; for time was pressing, and although there was another barque on the stocks, yet it would have required too long to get it ready, and we could scarcely have made use of it before the return from France of the vessels we were daily expecting.

This was a great misfortune, and owing to the lack of foresight on the part of the master, who was obstinate, but little acquainted with seamanship, and trusting only his own head.   He was a good carpenter, skilful in building vessels, and careful in provisioning them with all necessaries, but in no wise adapted to sailing them.

Pont Gravé, having arrived at the settlement, received the evidence against Champdoré, who was accused of having run the barque on shore with evil intent.   Upon such information, he was imprisoned and handcuffed, with the intention of taking him to France and handing him over to Sieur de Monts, to be treated as justice might direct.

On the 15th of June, Pont Gravé, finding that the vessels did not return from France, had the handcuffs taken off from Champdoré, that he might finish the barque which was on the stocks, which service he discharged very well.

On the 16th of July, the time when we were to leave, in case the vessels had not returned, as was provided in the commission which Sieur de Monts had given to Pont Gravé, we set out from our settlement to go to Cape Breton or to Gaspé in search of means of returning to France, since we had received no intelligence from there.

Two of our men remained, of their own accord, to take care of the provisions which were left at the settlement, to each of whom Pont Gravé promised fifty crowns in money, and fifty more at which he agreed to estimate their pay when he should come to get them the following year.[1]

There was a captain of the savages named Mabretou,[2] who promised to take care of them, and that they should be treated as kindly as his own children. We found him a friendly savage all the time we were there, although he had the name of being the worst and most traitorous man of his tribe.

Chapter 12

Departure from Port Royal to return to France. Meeting Ralleau at Cape Sable, which caused us to turn back.

On the 17th of the month, in accordance with the resolution we had formed, we set out from the mouth of Port Royal with two barques, one of eighteen tons, the other of seven or eight, with the view of pursuing the voyage to Cape Breton or Canseau. We anchored in the strait of Long Island, where during the night our cable broke, and we came near being lost, owing to the violent tides which strike upon several rocky points in and about this place. But, through the diligent exertions of all, we were saved, and escaped once more.

On the 21st of the month there was a violent wind, which broke the irons of our rudder between Long Island and Cape Fourchu, and reduced us to such extremities that we were at a loss what to do. For the fury of the sea did not permit us to land, since the breakers ran mountain high along the coast, so that we resolved to perish in the sea rather than to land, hoping that the wind and tempest would abate, so that, with

---

[1] Lescarbot has preserved their names: La Taille and Miquelet.

[2] The spelling of Lescarbot and of Father Biard, Membertou, is adopted by Parkman. Membertou claimed to be more than one hundred years old, and to have been a married man at the time of the visit of Jacques Cartier. He was converted by the Jesuits, and made a most edifying end.

the wind astern, we might go ashore on some sandy beach. As each one thought by himself what might be done for our preservation, a sailor said that a quantity of cordage attached to the stern of our barque, and dragging in the water, might serve in some measure to steer our vessel. But this was of no avail; and we saw that, unless God should aid us by other means, this would not preserve us from shipwreck. As we were thinking what could be done for our safety, Champdoré, who had been again handcuffed, said to some of us that, if Pont Gravé desired it, he would find means to steer our barque. This we reported to Pont Gravé, who did not refuse this offer, and the rest of us still less. He accordingly had his handcuffs taken off the second time, and at once taking a rope, he cut it and fastened the rudder with it in such a skilful manner that it would steer the ship as well as ever. In this way, he made amends for the mistakes he had made leading to the loss of the previous barque, and was discharged from his accusation through our entreaties to Pont Gravé who, although somewhat reluctantly, acceded to it.

The same day we anchored near La Baye Courante,[1] two leagues from Cape Fourchu, and there our barque was repaired.

On the 23d of July, we proceeded near to Cape Sable.

On the 24th of the month, at two o'clock in the afternoon, we perceived a shallop, near Cormorant Island, coming from Cape Sable. Some thought it was savages going away from Cape Breton or the Island of Canseau. Others said it might be shallops sent from Canseau to get news of us. Finally, as we approached nearer, we saw that they were Frenchmen, which delighted us greatly. When it had almost reached us, we recognized Ralleau, the secretary of Sieur de Monts, which redoubled our joy. He informed us that Sieur de Monts had despatched a vessel of a hundred and twenty tons, commanded by Sieur de Poutrincourt, who had come with fifty men to act as Lieutenant-General, and live in the coun-

---

[1] The bay at the mouth of Argyll River, sometimes called Lobster Bay. (Slafter.)

try; that he had landed at Canseau, whence the above-
mentioned vessel had gone out to sea, in order, if possible, to
find us, while he, meanwhile, was proceeding along the coast
in a shallop, in order to meet us in case we should have set
out, supposing we had departed from Port Royal, as was in
fact the case: in so doing, they acted very wisely. All this
intelligence caused us to turn back; and we arrived at Port
Royal on the 25th of the month, where we found the above-
mentioned vessel and Sieur de Poutrincourt, and were greatly
delighted to see realized what we had given up in despair.[1]
He told us that his delay had been caused by an accident
which happened to the ship in leaving the boom at Rochelle,
where he had taken his departure, and that he had been hindered by bad weather on his voyage.

The next day, Sieur de Poutrincourt proceeded to set forth
his views as to what should be done; and, in accordance with
the opinion of all, he resolved to stay at Port Royal this
year, inasmuch as no discovery had been made since the departure of Sieur de Monts, and the period of four months
before winter was not long enough to search out a site and
construct another settlement, especially in a large vessel,
unlike a barque which draws little water, searches everywhere,
and finds places to one's mind for effecting settlements.
But he decided that, during this period, nothing more should
be done than to try to find some place better adapted for our
abode.

Thus deciding, Sieur de Poutrincourt despatched at once
some laborers to work on the land in a spot[2] which he deemed
suitable, up the river, a league and a half from the settlement
of Port Royal, and where we had thought of making our
abode. Here he ordered wheat, rye, hemp, and several other
kinds of seeds, to be sown, in order to ascertain how they
would flourish.

[1] Lescarbot, who was on board this vessel, the *Jonas*, has given a long
account of their voyage, and of their reception. He fixes the date of Poutrincourt's arrival on July 27, and that of Pontgravé and Champlain on the 31st,
which is probably correct. See Lescarbot, book IV., chs. IX.–XIII.

[2] Where the village of Annapolis now stands.

On the 22d of August, a small barque was seen approaching our settlement. It was that of Des Antons, of St. Malo, who had come from Canseau, where his vessel was engaged in fishing, to inform us that there were some vessels[1] about Cape Breton engaged in the fur-trade; and that, if we would send our ship, we might capture them on the point of returning to France. It was determined to do so as soon as some supplies, which were in the ship, could be unloaded.

This being done, Pont Gravé embarked, together with his companions, who had wintered with him at Port Royal, excepting Champdoré and Foulgeré de Vitré. I also stayed with De Poutrincourt, in order, with God's help, to complete the map of the coasts and countries which I had commenced. Every thing being put in order in the settlement, Sieur de Poutrincourt ordered provisions to be taken on board for our voyage along the coast of Florida.

On the 29th of August, we set out from Port Royal, as did also Pont Gravé and Des Antons, who were bound for Cape Breton and Canseau, to seize the vessels which were engaging in the fur-trade, as I have before stated. After getting out to sea, we were obliged to put back on account of bad weather. But the large vessel kept on her course, and we soon lost sight of her.

Chapter 13

Sieur de Poutrincourt sets out from Port Royal to make discoveries. All that was seen, and what took place as far as Mallebarre.

On the 5th of September, we set out again from Port Royal.[2] On the 7th, we reached the mouth of the river St. Croix, where we found a large number of savages, among others

---

[1] See Lescarbot, book IV., ch. XIII. This was an old offender, named Boyer, who succeeded on this occasion in making his escape.

[2] Lescarbot, who remained in charge at Port Royal, busied himself with gardening, and with digging drains.

Secondon and Messamouët. We came near being lost there
on a rocky islet, on account of Champdoré's usual obstinacy.[1]

The next day we proceeded in a shallop to the Island of
St. Croix, where Sieur de Monts had wintered, to see if we
could find any spikes of wheat and other seeds which we had
planted there. We found some wheat which had fallen on the
ground, and come up as finely as one could wish; also a large
number of garden vegetables, which also had come up fair
and large. It gave us great satisfaction to see that the soil
there was good and fertile.

After visiting the island, we returned to our barque, which
was one of eighteen tons, on the way catching a large number of mackerel, which are abundant there at this season. It
was decided to continue the voyage along the coast, which
was not a very well-considered conclusion, since we lost much
time in passing over again the discoveries made by Sieur de
Monts as far as the harbor of Mallebarre. It would have been
much better, in my opinion, to cross from where we were directly to Mallebarre, the route being already known, and then
use our time in exploring as far as the fortieth degree, or still
farther south, revisiting, upon our homeward voyage, the
entire coast at pleasure.

After this decision, we took with us Secondon and Messamouët, who went as far as Choüacoet in a shallop, where they
wished to make an alliance with the people of the country,
by offering them some presents.

On the 12th of September, we set out from the river St.
Croix.

On the 21st, we arrived at Choüacoet, where we saw Onemechin, chief of the river, and Marchin, who had harvested
their corn. We saw at the Island of Bacchus [2] some grapes
which were ripe and very good, and some others not yet ripe,
as fine as those in France; and I am sure that, if they were
cultivated, they would produce good wine.

---

[1] Lescarbot, book IV., ch XIV., gives numerous piquant details as to
this voyage.

[2] Richmond Island.

In this place, Sieur de Poutrincourt secured a prisoner that Onemechin had, to whom Messamouët made presents of kettles, hatchets, knives, and other things. Onemechin reciprocated the same with Indian corn, squashes, and Brazilian beans; which was not very satisfactory to Messamouët, who went away very ill-disposed towards them for not properly recognizing his presents, and with the intention of making war upon them in a short time. For these nations give only in exchange for something in return, except to those who have done them a special service, as by assisting them in their wars.

Continuing our course, we proceeded to the Island Cape,[1] where we encountered rather bad weather and fogs, and saw little prospect of being able to spend the night under shelter, since the locality was not favorable for this. While we were thus in perplexity, it occurred to me that, while coasting along with Sieur de Monts, I had noted on my map, at a distance of a league from here, a place which seemed suitable for vessels, but which we did not enter, because, when we passed it, the wind was favorable for continuing on our course. This place we had already passed, which led me to suggest to Sieur de Poutrincourt that we should stand in for a point in sight, where the place in question was, which seemed to me favorable for passing the night. We proceeded to anchor at the mouth, and went in the next day.[2]

Sieur de Poutrincourt landed with eight or ten of our company. We saw some very fine grapes just ripe, Brazilian peas, pumpkins, squashes, and very good roots,[3] which the savages cultivate, having a taste similar to that of chards. They made us presents of some of these, in exchange for little trifles which we gave them. They had already finished their harvest. We saw two hundred savages in this very pleasant place; and there are here a large number of very fine walnut-trees,[4] cypresses, sassafras, oaks, ashes, and beeches. The

---

[1] Cape Ann.   [2] Gloucester Harbor.
[3] The Jerusalem artichoke, indigenous to North America.
[4] Probably the hickory and the butter-nut. Champlain often gives to these indigenous trees the names of their nearest European relatives.

chief of this place is named Quiouhamenec, who came to see us with a neighbor of his, named Cohoüepech, whom we entertained sumptuously.   Onemechin, chief of Choüacoet, came also to see us, to whom we gave a coat, which he, however, did not keep a long time, but made a present of it to another, since he was uneasy in it, and could not adapt himself to it.   We saw also a savage here, who had so wounded himself in the foot, and lost so much blood, that he fell down in a swoon.   Many others surrounded him, and sang some time before touching him.   Afterwards, they made some motions with their feet and hands, shook his head and breathed upon him, when he came to himself.   Our surgeon dressed his wounds, when he went off in good spirits.[1]

The next day, as we were calking our shallop, Sieur de Poutrincourt in the woods noticed a number of savages who were going, with the intention of doing us some mischief, to a little stream, where a neck connects with the main land, at which our party were doing their washing.   As I was walking along this neck, these savages noticed me; and, in order to put a good face upon it, since they saw that I had discovered them thus seasonably, they began to shout and dance, and then came towards me with their bows, arrows, quivers, and other arms.   And, inasmuch as there was a meadow between them and myself, I made a sign to them to dance again.   This they did in a circle, putting all their arms in the middle.   But they had hardly commenced, when they observed Sieur de Poutrincourt in the wood with eight musketeers, which frightened them.   Yet they did not stop until they had finished their dance, when they withdrew in all directions, fearing lest some unpleasant turn might be served them.   We said nothing to them, however, and showed them only demonstrations of gladness.   Then we returned to launch our shallop, and take our departure.   They entreated us to wait a day, saying that more than two thousand of them

---

[1] Lescarbot adds that an hour or two later they found that he had tied around his head the rag with which the wound had been dressed, and was dancing with delight at his new adornment.

would come to see us. But, unable to lose any time, we were unwilling to stay here longer. I am of opinion that their object was to surprise us. Some of the land was already cleared up, and they were constantly making clearings. Their mode of doing it is as follows: after cutting down the trees at the distance of three feet from the ground, they burn the branches upon the trunk, and then plant their corn between these stumps, in course of time tearing up also the roots. There are likewise fine meadows here, capable of supporting a large number of cattle. This harbor is very fine, containing water enough for vessels, and affording a shelter from the weather behind the islands. It is in latitude 43°, and we gave it the name of Le Beauport.[1]

The last day of September we set out from Beauport, and, passing Cap St. Louis, stood on our course all night for Cap Blanc. In the morning, an hour before daylight, we found ourselves to the leeward of Cap Blanc, in Baye Blanche, with eight feet of water, and at a distance of a league from the shore. Here we anchored, in order not to approach too near before daylight, and to see how the tide was. Meanwhile, we sent our shallop to make soundings. Only eight feet of water were found, so that it was necessary to determine before daylight what we would do. The water sank as low as five feet, and our barque sometimes touched on the sand, yet without any injury, for the water was calm, and we had not less than three feet of water under us. Then the tide began to rise, which gave us encouragement.

When it was day, we saw a very low, sandy shore, off which we were, and more to the leeward. A shallop was sent to make soundings in the direction of land somewhat high, where we thought there would be deep water; and, in fact, we found seven fathoms. Here we anchored, and at once got ready the shallop, with nine or ten men to land and examine a place where we thought there was a good harbor to shelter ourselves in, if the wind should increase. An examination having been made, we entered in two, three, and four fathoms of water.

[1] Gloucester Harbor.

When we were inside, we found five and six. There were
many very good oysters here, which we had not seen before,
and we named the place Port aux Huistres.[1] It is in latitude 42°. Three canoes of savages came out to us. On
this day, the wind coming round in our favor, we weighed
anchor to go to Cap Blanc, distant from here five leagues
north a quarter north-east, and we doubled the cape.

On the next day, the 2d of October, we arrived off Mallebarre, where we stayed some time on account of the bad
weather. During this time, Sieur de Poutrincourt, with the
shallop, accompanied by twelve or fifteen men, visited the
harbor, where some hundred and fifty savages, singing and
dancing according to their custom, appeared before him.
After seeing this place, we returned to our vessel, and, the
wind coming favorable, sailed along the coast towards the
south.

Chapter 14

*Continuation of the above discoveries, and what was observed
of particular importance.*

When we were some six leagues from Mallebarre, we anchored near the coast, the wind not being fair, along which we
observed columns of smoke made by the savages, which led us
to determine to go to them, for which purpose the shallop
was made ready. But when near the coast, which is sandy,
we could not land, for the swell was too great. Seeing this,
the savages launched a canoe, and came out to us, eight or
nine of them, singing and making signs of their joy at seeing
us, and they indicated to us that lower down there was a
harbor where we could put our barque in a place of security.
Unable to land, the shallop came back to the barque; and the
savages, whom we had treated civilly, returned to the shore.

On the next day, the wind being favorable, we continued

---

[1] Oyster Harbor, now Barnstable Harbor.

our course to the north [1] five leagues, and hardly had we
gone this distance, when we found three and four fathoms of
water at a distance of a league and a half from the shore.
On going a little farther, the depth suddenly diminished to a
fathom and a half and two fathoms, which alarmed us, since
we saw the sea breaking all around, but no passage by which
we could retrace our course, for the wind was directly contrary.

Accordingly being shut in among the breakers and sand-
banks, we had to go at hap-hazard where there seemed to be
the most water for our barque, which was at most only four
feet: we continued among these breakers until we found as
much as four feet and a half. Finally, we succeeded, by the
grace of God, in going over a sandy point running out nearly
three leagues seaward to the south-south-east, and a very dangerous place. Doubling this cape, which we named Cap
Batturier, [2] which is twelve or thirteen leagues from Mallebarre, we anchored in two and a half fathoms of water, since
we saw ourselves surrounded on all sides by breakers and
shoals, except in some places where the sea was breaking but
little. The shallop was sent to find a channel, in order to go
to a place, which we concluded to be that which the savages
had indicated. We also thought there was a river there,
where we could lie in security.

When our shallop arrived there, our party landed and
examined the place, and, returning with a savage whom they
brought off, they told us that we could enter at full tide,
which was resolved upon. We immediately weighed anchor,
and, under the guidance of the savage who piloted us, proceeded to anchor at a roadstead before the harbor, in six
fathoms of water and a good bottom; for we could not enter,
as the night overtook us.

On the next day, men were sent to set stakes at the end of
a sand-bank at the mouth of the harbor, when, the tide rising,

---

[1] Obviously a mistake. The whole context shows that they were sailing
south.

[2] *I.e.*, Shoal Cape. Apparently the island of Monomoy, though the
aspect of the coast has greatly changed.

we entered in two fathoms of water. When we had arrived, we praised God for being in a place of safety. Our rudder had broken, which we had mended with ropes; but we were afraid that, amid these shallows and strong tides, it would break anew, and we should be lost. Within this harbor [1] there is only a fathom of water, and two at full tide. On the east, there is a bay extending back on the north some three leagues,[2] in which there is an island and two other little bays which adorn the landscape, where there is a considerable quantity of land cleared up, and many little hills, where they cultivate corn and the various grains on which they live. There are, also, very fine vines, many walnut-trees, oaks, cypresses, but only a few pines. All the inhabitants of this place are very fond of agriculture, and provide themselves with Indian corn [3] for the winter, which they store in the following manner:

They make trenches in the sand on the slope of the hills, some five to six feet deep, more or less. Putting their corn and other grains into large grass sacks, they throw them into these trenches, and cover them with sand three or four feet above the surface of the earth, taking it out as their needs require. In this way, it is preserved as well as it would be possible to do in our granaries.

We saw in this place some five to six hundred savages, all naked except their sexual parts, which they cover with a small piece of doe or seal-skin. The women are also naked, and, like the men, cover theirs with skins or leaves. They wear their hair carefully combed and twisted in various ways, both men and women, after the manner of the savages of Chouacoet. Their bodies are well-proportioned, and their skin olive-colored. They adorn themselves with feathers, beads of shell, and other gewgaws, which they arrange very neatly in embroidery work. As weapons, they have bows,

---

[1] They were now in Stage Harbor, in Chatham, Massachusetts.

[2] The narrow bay stretching from Morris Island to the north.

[3] Indian corn, indigenous to America, was seen by Columbus in the West Indies; Champlain is the first who has left a record of its cultivation in New England.

arrows, and clubs. They are not so much great hunters as good fishermen and tillers of the land.

In regard to their police, government, and belief, we have been unable to form a judgment; but I suppose that they are not different in this respect from our savages, the Souriquois and Canadians, who worship neither the moon nor the sun, nor any thing else, and pray no more than the beasts.[1] There are, however, among them some persons who, as they say, are in concert with the devil, in whom they have great faith. They tell them all that is to happen to them, but in so doing lie for the most part. Sometimes they succeed in hitting the mark very well, and tell them things similar to those which actually happen to them. For this reason, they have faith in them, as if they were prophets; while they are only impostors who delude them, as the Egyptians and Bohemians do the simple villagers. They have chiefs, whom they obey in matters of war, but not otherwise, and who engage in labor and hold no higher rank than their companions. Each one has only so much land as he needs for his support.

Their dwellings are separate from each other, according to the land which each one occupies. They are large, of a circular shape, and covered with thatch made of grasses or the husks of Indian corn. They are furnished only with a bed or two, raised a foot from the ground, made of a number of little pieces of wood pressed against each other, on which they arrange a reed mat, after the Spanish style, which is a kind of matting two or three fingers thick: on these they sleep. They have a great many fleas in summer, even in the fields. One day as we went out walking, we were beset by so many of them that we were obliged to change our clothes.

---

[1] This conclusion harmonizes, as Dr. Slafter points out, with the opinion of Thomas Morton, who says that the natives of New England are "*sine fide, sine lege, et sine rege*," and that they "have no worship nor religion at all." *New English Canaan*, 1637, Prince Society ed., pp. 140, 141.

Parkman, *Jesuits in North America* (Boston, 1897), pp. 60–70, discusses the religion of the Algonquins in a more scientific spirit, but comes to much the same conclusion so far as worship is concerned.

All the harbors, bays, and coasts from Choüacoet are filled
with every variety of fish, like those which we have before
our habitation, and in such abundance that I can confidently
assert that there was not a day or night when we did not see
and hear pass by our barque more than a thousand porpoises,
which were chasing the smaller fry. There are also many
shell-fish of various sorts, principally oysters. Game birds are
very plenty.

It would be an excellent place to erect buildings and lay
the foundations of a state, if the harbor were somewhat deeper
and the entrance safer. Before leaving the harbor, the rudder
was repaired; and we had some bread made from flour, which
we had brought for our subsistence, in case our biscuit should
give out. Meanwhile, we sent the shallop with five or six men
and a savage to see whether a passage might be found more
favorable for our departure than that by which we had entered.

After they had gone five or six leagues and were near the
land, the savage made his escape, since he was afraid of being
taken to other savages farther south, the enemies of his tribe,
as he gave those to understand who were in the shallop.
The latter, upon their return, reported that, as far as they
had advanced, there were at least three fathoms of water, and
that farther on there were neither shallows nor reefs.

We accordingly made haste to repair our barque, and make
a supply of bread for fifteen days. Meanwhile, Sieur de
Poutrincourt, accompanied by ten or twelve arquebusiers,
visited all the neighboring country, which is very fine, as I
have said before, and where we saw here and there a large
number of little houses.

Some eight or nine days after, while Sieur de Poutrincourt
was walking out, as he had previously done, we observed the
savages taking down their cabins and sending their women,
children, provisions, and other necessaries of life into the
woods. This made us suspect some evil intention, and that
they purposed to attack those of our company who were working on shore, where they stayed at night in order to guard

κ

that which could not be embarked at evening except with much trouble. This proved to be true; for they determined among themselves, after all their effects had been put in a place of security, to come and surprise those on land, taking advantage of them as much as possible, and to carry off all they had. But, if by chance they should find them on their guard, they resolved to come with signs of friendship, as they were wont to do, leaving behind their bows and arrows.

Now, in view of what Sieur de Poutrincourt had seen, and the order which it had been told him they observed when they wished to play some bad trick, when we passed by some cabins, where there was a large number of women, we gave them some bracelets and rings to keep them quiet and free from fear, and to most of the old and distinguished men hatchets, knives, and other things which they desired. This pleased them greatly, and they repaid it all in dances, gambols, and harangues, which we did not understand at all. We went wherever we chose without their having the assurance to say anything to us. It pleased us greatly to see them show themselves so simple in appearance.

We returned very quietly to our barque, accompanied by some of the savages. On the way, we met several small troops of them, who gradually gathered together with their arms, and were greatly astonished to see us so far in the interior, and did not suppose that we had just made a circuit of nearly four or five leagues about their territory. Passing near us, they trembled with fear, lest harm should be done them, as it was in our power to do. But we did them none, although we knew their evil intentions. Having arrived where our men were working, Sieur de Poutrincourt inquired if everything was in readiness to resist the designs of this rabble.

He ordered everything on shore to be embarked. This was done, except that he who was making the bread stayed to finish a baking, and two others with him. They were told that the savages had some evil intent, and that they should make haste to embark the coming evening, since they carried their plans into execution only at night, or at daybreak, which in their plots is generally the hour for making a surprise.

Evening having come, Sieur de Poutrincourt gave orders that the shallop should be sent ashore to get the men who remained. This was done as soon as the tide would permit, and those on shore were told that they must embark for the reason assigned. This they refused in spite of the remonstrances that were made setting forth the risks they ran and the disobedience to their chief. They paid no attention to it, with the exception of a servant of Sieur de Poutrincourt, who embarked. Two others disembarked from the shallop and went to the three on shore, who had stayed to eat some cakes made at the same time with the bread.

But, as they were unwilling to do as they were told, the shallop returned to the vessel. It was not mentioned to Sieur de Poutrincourt, who had retired, thinking that all were on board.

The next day, in the morning, the 15th of October, the savages did not fail to come and see in what condition our men were, whom they found asleep, except one, who was near the fire. When they saw them in this condition, they came, to the number of four hundred, softly over a little hill, and sent them such a volley of arrows that to rise up was death. Fleeing the best they could towards our barque, shouting, "Help! they are killing us!" a part fell dead in the water; the others were all pierced with arrows, and one died in consequence a short time after. The savages made a desperate noise with roarings, which it was terrible to hear.[1]

Upon the occurrence of this noise and that of our men, the sentinel, on our vessel, exclaimed, "To arms! They are killing our men!" Consequently, each one immediately seized

[1] In the original Champlain has drawn a wonderful picture of this affray. Lescarbot, book IV., ch. XVI., gives a much fuller account. Of the five culprits four were killed or died of their wounds (see p. 110); the fifth, who was wounded, but recovered, was Du Val (see p. 132), who was afterwards executed at Quebec for conspiracy against Champlain. Lescarbot mentions a report that two of the five had previously angered the Indians by firing upon them.

his arms; and we embarked in the shallop, some fifteen or sixteen of us, in order to go ashore. But, being unable to get there on account of a sand-bank between us and the land, we threw ourselves into the water, and waded from this bank to the shore, the distance of a musket-shot. As soon as we were there, the savages, seeing us within arrow range, fled into the interior. To pursue them was fruitless, for they are marvellously swift. All that we could do was to carry away the dead bodies and bury them near a cross, which had been set up the day before, and then to go here and there to see if we could get sight of any of them. But it was time wasted, therefore we came back. Three hours afterwards, they returned to us on the sea-shore. We discharged at them several shots from our little brass cannon; and, when they heard the noise, they crouched down on the ground to avoid the fire. In mockery of us, they beat down the cross and disinterred the dead, which displeased us greatly, and caused us to go for them a second time; but they fled, as they had done before. We set up again the cross, and reinterred the dead, whom they had thrown here and there amid the heath, where they kindled a fire to burn them. We returned without any result, as we had done before, well aware that there was scarcely hope of avenging ourselves this time, and that we should have to renew the undertaking when it should please God.

On the 16th of the month, we set out from Port Fortuné, to which we had given this name on account of the misfortune which happened to us there. This place is in latitude 41° 20', and some twelve or thirteen leagues from Mallebarre.

Chapter 15

The inclemency of the weather not permitting us at that time to continue our discoveries, we resolved to return to our settlement. What happened to us until we reached it.

After having gone some six or seven leagues, we sighted an island, which we named La Soupçonneuse,[1] because in the

---

[1] *I.e.*, the Doubtful; now Martha's Vineyard.

distance we had several times thought it was not an island.
Then the wind became contrary, which caused us to put back
to the place whence we had set out, where we stayed two or
three days, no savage during this time presenting himself to us.

On the 20th, we set out anew and coasted along to the
south-west nearly twelve leagues,[1] where we passed near a
river which is small and difficult of access in consequence of
the shoals and rocks at its mouth, and which I called after
my own name.[2]   This coast is, so far as we saw, low and
sandy.   The wind again grew contrary and very strong, which
caused us to put out to sea, as we were unable to advance on
one tack or the other; it, however, finally abated a little and
grew favorable.   But all we could do was to return again to
Port Fortuné, where the coast, though low, is fine and good,
yet difficult of access, there being no harbors, many reefs,
and shallow water for the distance of nearly two leagues
from land.   The most that we found was seven or eight
fathoms in some channels, which, however, continued only
a cable's length, when there were suddenly only two or three
fathoms; but one should not trust the water who has not
well examined the depth with the lead in hand.

Some hours after we had returned to port, a son of Pont
Gravé, named Robert, lost a hand in firing a musket, which
burst in several pieces, but without injuring any one near
him.

Seeing now the wind continuing contrary, and being unable to put to sea, we resolved meanwhile to get possession of
some savages of this place, and, taking them to our settlement,
put them to grinding corn at the hand-mill, as punishment
for the deadly assault which they had committed on five or
six of our company.   But it was very difficult to do this when

[1] Nearly twelve leagues in a southwesterly direction from their anchorage at Stage Harbor in Chatham would bring them to the entrance of Vineyard Sound. This was the limit of Champlain's explorations towards the
south.

[2] This river appears on Champlain's map, but cannot with security
be identified. Very likely it is the tidal passage between Wood's Hole and
Nonamesset.

we were armed, since, if we went to them prepared to fight,
they would turn and flee into the woods, where they were not
to be caught.   It was necessary, accordingly, to have recourse
to artifice, and this is what we planned: when they should
come to seek friendship with us, to coax them by showing
them beads and other gewgaws,[1] and assure them repeatedly
of our good faith; then to take the shallop well armed, and
conduct on shore the most robust and strong men we had,
each one having a chain of beads and a fathom of match on
his arm; and there, while pretending to smoke with them
(each one having an end of his match lighted so as not to
excite suspicion, it being customary to have fire at the end
of a cord in order to light the tobacco), coax them with pleasing words so as to draw them into the shallop; and, if they
should be unwilling to enter, each one approaching should
choose his man, and, putting the beads about his neck, should
at the same time put the rope on him to draw him by force.
But, if they should be too boisterous, and it should not be
possible to succeed, they should be stabbed, the rope being
firmly held; and, if by chance any of them should get away,
there should be men on land to charge upon them with swords.
Meanwhile, the little cannon on our barque were to be kept
ready to fire upon their companions in case they should come to
assist them, under cover of which firearms the shallop could
withdraw in security.   The plan above-mentioned was well
carried out as it had been arranged.

Some days after these events had occurred, there came
savages by threes and fours to the shore, making signs to us
to go to them.   But we saw their main body in ambuscade
under a hillock behind some bushes, and I suppose that they
were only desirous of beguiling us into the shallop in order to
discharge a shower of arrows upon us, and then take to flight.
Nevertheless, Sieur de Poutrincourt did not hesitate to go to
them with ten of us, well equipped and determined to fight
them, if occasion offered.   We landed at a place beyond
their ambuscade, as we thought, and where they could not

[1] *Patinostres.*

surprise us. There three or four of us went ashore together
with Sieur de Poutrincourt: the others did not leave the
shallop, in order to protect it and be ready for an emergency.
We ascended a knoll and went about the woods to see if we could
not discover more plainly the ambuscade. When they saw us
going so unconcernedly to them, they left and went to other
places, which we could not see, and of the four savages we saw
only two, who went away very slowly. As they withdrew,
they made signs to us to take our shallop to another place,
thinking that it was not favorable for the carrying out of their
plan. And, when we also saw that they had no desire to come
to us, we re-embarked and went to the place they indicated,
which was the second ambuscade they had made, in their endeavor to draw us unarmed to themselves by signs of friendship.
But this we were not permitted to do at that time, yet we approached very near them without seeing this ambuscade, which
we supposed was not far off. As our shallop approached the
shore, they took to flight, as also those in ambush, after whom
we fired some musket-shots, since we saw that their intention
was only to deceive us by flattery, in which they were disappointed; for we recognized clearly what their purpose was,
which had only mischief in view. We retired to our barque
after having done all we could.[1]

On the same day, Sieur de Poutrincourt resolved to return
to our settlement on account of four or five sick and wounded
men, whose wounds were growing worse through lack of
salves, of which our surgeon, by a great mistake on his part,
had brought but a small provision, to the detriment of the
sick and our own discomfort, as the stench from their wounds
was so great, in a little vessel like our own, that one could

[1] See p. 105. This same tribe of Nausets "sent a shower of arrows upon
the Pilgrims in 1620, at a place called by them the 'First Encounter,' and not
more than three miles from the spot where the same tribe, in 1605, had attacked the French, and slain one of de Monts's men." (Slafter.) See Brad-
ford's *History of Plimoth Plantation* ch. x. For an account of the massacre
of the Indians, which Champlain here passes over, though he refers to it on
p. 106, see Lescarbot, book iv., ch. xvi. It is a blot on Champlain's record,
but the provocation had been great, and the chief responsibility rests with the
leader of the expedition, the hot-tempered Poutrincourt.

scarcely endure it. Moreover, we were afraid that they would
generate disease. Also we had provisions only for going
eight or ten days farther, however much economy might be
practised; and we knew not whether the return would last as
long as the advance, which was nearly two months.

At any rate, our resolution being formed, we withdrew, but
with the satisfaction that God had not left unpunished the
misdeeds of these barbarians. We advanced no farther than
to latitude 41° 30′, which was only half a degree farther than
Sieur de Monts had gone on his voyage of discovery. We
set out accordingly from this harbor.

On the next day we anchored near Mallebarre, where we
remained until the 28th of the month, when we set sail. On
that day the air was very cold, and there was a little snow.
We took a direct course for Norumbegue or Isle Haute. Heading east-north-east, we were two days at sea without seeing
land, being kept back by bad weather. On the following
night, we sighted the islands, which are between Quinibequy
and Norumbegue. The wind was so strong that we were
obliged to put to sea until daybreak; but we went so far from
land, although we used very little sail, that we could not see
it again until the next day, when we saw Isle Haute, of which
we were abreast.

On the last day of October, between the Island of Monts
Déserts and Cap Corneille, our rudder broke in several pieces,
without our knowing the reason. Each one expressed his
opinion about it. On the following night, with a fresh breeze,
we came among a large number of islands and rocks, whither
the wind drove us; and we resolved to take refuge, if possible,
on the first land we should find.

We were for some time at the mercy of the wind and sea,
with only the foresail set. But the worst of it was that the
night was dark, and we did not know where we were going;
for our barque could not be steered at all, although we did
all that was possible, holding in our hands the sheets of the
foresail, which sometimes enabled us to steer it a little. We
kept continually sounding, to see if it were possible to find

a bottom for anchoring, and to prepare ourselves for what might happen. But we found none. Finally, as we were going faster than we wished, it was recommended to put an oar astern together with some men, so as to steer to an island which we saw, in order to shelter ourselves from the wind. Two other oars also were put over the sides in the after part of the barque, to assist those who were steering, in order to make the vessel bear up on one tack and the other. This device served us so well, that we headed where we wished, and ran in behind the point of the island we had seen, anchoring in twenty-one fathoms of water until daybreak, when we proposed to reconnoitre our position and seek for a place to make another rudder. The wind abated. At daybreak, we found ourselves near the Isles Rangées, entirely surrounded by breakers, and we praised God for having preserved us so wonderfully amid so many perils.

On the 1st of November, we went to a place which we deemed favorable for beaching our vessel and repairing our helm. On this day, I landed, and saw some ice two inches thick, it having frozen perhaps eight or ten days before. I observed also that the temperature of the place differed very much from that of Mallebarre and Port Fortuné, for the leaves of the trees were not yet dead and had not begun to fall when we set out, while here they had all fallen, and it was much colder than at Port Fortuné.

On the next day, as we were beaching our barque, a canoe came containing Etechemin savages, who told the savage Secondon in our barque that Iouaniscou, with his companions, had killed some other savages, and carried off some women as prisoners, whom they had executed near the Island of Monts Déserts.

On the 9th of the month, we set out from near Cap Corneille, and anchored the same day in the little passage of Sainte Croix River.[1]

On the morning of the next day, we landed our savage with some supplies which we gave him. He was well pleased and

[1] The southern strait leading into Eastport Harbor. (Slafter.)

satisfied at having made this voyage with us, and took away with him some heads of the savages that had been killed at Port Fortuné. The same day we anchored in a very pretty cove on the south of the Island of Manan.

On the 12th of the month, we made sail; and, when under way, the shallop, which we were towing astern, struck against our barque so violently and roughly that it made an opening and stove in her upper works, and again in the recoil broke the iron fastenings of our rudder. At first, we thought that the first blow had stove in some planks in the lower part, which would have sunk us; for the wind was so high that all we could do was to carry our foresail. But finding that the damage was slight, and that there was no danger, we managed with ropes to repair the rudder as well as we could, so as to serve us to the end of our voyage. This was not until the 14th of November, when, at the entrance to Port Royal, we came near being lost on a point; but God delivered us from this danger as well as from many others to which we had been exposed.

Chapter 16

Return from the foregoing discoveries, and what transpired during the winter.

Upon our arrival,[1] Lescarbot, who had remained at the settlement, assisted by the others who had stayed there, welcomed us with a humorous entertainment.

[1] This is Champlain's first reference to Lescarbot, who had come out with his friend Poutrincourt in 1606. Marc Lescarbot was a Paris lawyer, born at Vervins about 1580. In 1609, after his return to France, he published a *Histoire de la Nouvelle France*, part of which refers to his own experiences, and has been already referred to in these notes. New and revised editions were issued in 1612 and 1618. The edition of 1612 was republished in 1866 by Tross of Paris, and the edition of 1618 is now (1907) being republished by the Champlain Society of Toronto. The lively and somewhat heterodox lawyer, who was afterwards imprisoned for publishing a satire against the Jesuits, did not get on well with the sober-sided Champlain, and some references in this volume are bitterly commented on by Lescarbot

Having landed and had time to take breath, each one began to make little gardens, I among the rest attending to mine, in order in the spring to sow several kinds of seeds which had been brought from France, and which grew very well in all the gardens.

Sieur de Poutrincourt, moreover, had a water-mill built nearly a league and a half from our settlement, near the point where grain had been planted. This mill was built at a fall, on a little river [1] which is not navigable on account of the large number of rocks in it, and which falls into a small lake. In this place, there is such an abundance of herring in their season that shallops could be loaded with them if one were to take the trouble to bring the requisite apparatus. The savages also of this region come here sometimes to fish. A quantity of charcoal was made by us for our forge. During the winter, in order not to remain idle, I undertook the building of a road along the wood to a little river or brook, which we named La Truitière, [2] there being many trout there. I asked Sieur de Poutrincourt for two or three men, which he gave me to assist in making this passageway. I got along so well that in a little while I had the road through. It extends through to the trout-brook, and measures nearly two thousand paces. It served us as a walk under the shelter of the trees, which I had left on both sides. This led Sieur de Poutrincourt to determine to make another through the woods, in order that we might go straight to the mouth of Port Royal, it being a distance of nearly three leagues and a half by land from our settlement. He had this commenced and continued for about half a league from La Truitière; but he did not finish it, as the undertaking was too laborious, and he was occupied by other things at the time more necessary. Some time after our arrival, we saw a shallop containing savages, who told us that a sav-

in his edition of 1618. He was also a poet, and published *Les Muses de la Nouvelle France* (1611, 1618). In this are given the words of the play entitled *Le Théatre de Neptune,* which he had composed for this occasion. On Lescarbot see Mr. H. P. Biggar's article, "The French Hakluyt; Marc Lescarbot of Vervins," in the *American Historical Review,* VI. 671–692.

[1] Now Allen River.   [2] *I.e.,* Trout Brook.

age,[1] who was one of our friends, had been killed by those belonging to the place whence they came, which was Norumbegue, in revenge for the killing of the men of Norumbegue and Quinibequy by Iouaniscou, also a savage, and his followers, as I have before related; and that some Etechemins had informed the savage Secondon, who was with us at that time.

The commander of the shallop was the savage named Ouagimou, who was on terms of friendship with Bessabez, chief of the river Norumbegue, of whom he asked the body of Panounias, who had been killed. The latter granted it to him, begging him to tell his friends that he was very sorry for his death, and assuring him that it was without his knowledge that he had been killed, and that, inasmuch as it was not his fault, he begged him to tell them that he desired they might continue to live as friends. This Ouagimou promised to do upon his return. He said to us that he was very uneasy until he got away from them, whatever friendship they might show him, since they were liable to change; and he feared that they would treat him in the same manner as they had the one who had been killed. Accordingly, he did not tarry long after being dismissed. He took the body in his shallop from Norumbegue to our settlement, a distance of fifty leagues.

As soon as the body was brought on shore, his relatives and friends began to shout by his side, having painted their entire face with black, which is their mode of mourning. After lamenting much, they took a quantity of tobacco and two or three dogs and other things belonging to the deceased, and burned them some thousand paces from our settlement on the sea-shore. Their cries continued until they returned to their cabin.

The next day they took the body of the deceased and wrapped it in a red covering, which Mabretou, chief of this place, urgently implored me to give him, since it was handsome and large. He gave it to the relatives of the deceased, who

[1] This Indian Panounias and his wife had accompanied de Monts on his expedition of 1605. See p. 56.

thanked me very much for it. After thus wrapping up the body, they decorated it with several kinds of *matachiats;* that is, strings of beads and bracelets of diverse colors. They painted the face, and put on the head many feathers and other things, the finest they had. Then they placed the body on its knees between two sticks, with another under the arms to sustain it. Around the body were the mother, wife, and others of the relatives and friends of the deceased, both women and girls, howling like dogs.

While the women and girls were shrieking, the savage named Mabretou made an address to his companions on the death of the deceased, urging all to take vengeance for the wickedness and treachery committed by the subjects of Bessabez, and to make war upon them as speedily as possible. All agreed to do so in the spring.

After the harangue was finished and the cries had ceased, they carried the body of the deceased to another cabin. After smoking tobacco together, they wrapped it in an elk-skin likewise; and, binding it very securely, they kept it until there should be a larger number of savages present, from each one of whom the brother of the deceased expected to receive presents, it being their custom to give them to those who have lost fathers, wives, brothers, or sisters.

On the night of the 26th of December, there was a southeast wind, which blew down several trees. On the last day of December, it began to snow, which continued until the morning of the next day. On the 16th of January following, 1607, Sieur de Poutrincourt, desiring to ascend the river Équille, found it at a distance of some two leagues from our settlement sealed with ice, which caused him to return, not being able to advance any farther. On the 8th of February, some pieces of ice began to flow down from the upper part of the river into the harbor, which only freezes along the shore. On the 10th of May following, it snowed all night; and, towards the end of the month, there were heavy hoar-frosts, which lasted until the 10th or 12th of June, when all the trees were covered with leaves, except the oaks, which do not leaf

out until about the 15th.   The winter was not so severe as on
the preceding years, nor did the snow continue so long on the
ground.   It rained very often, so that the savages suffered
a severe famine, owing to the small quantity of snow.   Sieur
de Poutrincourt supported a part of them who were with us;
namely, Mabretou, his wife and children, and some others.

We spent this winter very pleasantly, and fared generously
by means of the ORDRE DE BON TEMPS,[1] which I introduced.
This all found useful for their health, and more advantageous
than all the medicines that could have been used.   By the
rules of the order, a chain was put, with some little ceremonies, on the neck of one of our company, commissioning him
for the day to go a hunting.   The next day it was conferred
upon another, and thus in succession.   All exerted themselves
to the utmost to see who would do the best and bring home
the finest game.   We found this a very good arrangement, as
did also the savages who were with us.

There were some cases of *mal de la terre* among us, which
was, however, not so violent as in the previous years.   Nevertheless, seven died from it, and another from an arrow
wound, which he had received from the savages at Port
Fortuné.

Our surgeon, named Master Éstienne, opened some of the
bodies, as we did the previous years, and found almost all the
interior parts affected.   Eight or ten of the sick got well by
spring.

At the beginning of March and of April, all began to prepare gardens, so as to plant seeds in May, which is the proper
time for it.   They grew as well as in France, but were somewhat later.   I think France is at least a month and a half
more forward.   As I have stated, the time to plant is in May,
although one can sometimes do so in April; yet the seeds
planted then do not come forward any faster than those
planted in May, when the cold can no longer damage the plants
except those which are very tender, since there are many which

---

[1] Lescarbot (book IV., ch. XVI.) gives a much more detailed and picturesque account of this order, and of their life through the winter.

cannot endure the hoar-frosts, unless great care and attention be exercised.

On the 24th of May, we perceived a small barque [1] of six or seven tons' burthen, which we sent men to reconnoitre; and it was found to be a young man from St. Malo, named Chevalier, who brought letters from Sieur de Monts to Sieur de Poutrincourt, by which he directed him to bring back his company to France.[2] He also announced to us the birth of Monseigneur, the Duke of Orleans,[3] to our delight, in honor of which event we made bonfires and chanted the *Te Deum*.

Between the beginning and the 20th of June, some thirty or forty [4] savages assembled in this place in order to make war upon the Almouchiquois, and revenge the death of Panounias, who was interred by the savages according to their custom, who gave afterwards a quantity of peltry to a brother of his. The presents being made, all of them set out from this

---

[1] The *barque*, in Champlain's use, was commonly rigged with two masts, and was of from about six to eighteen tons burden.

[2] Lescarbot (book IV., ch. XVII.) adds his usual abundance of picturesque detail. The first to sight the *barque* was the centenarian Membertou (Mabretou). Chevalier had come out in the *Jonas*, the same ship which had brought out Lescarbot and Poutrincourt in the year before. It had now stopped at Canso to fish for cod. It brought letters telling that the company of de Monts had been broken up; that the Dutch, led by a French traitor named La Jeunesse, had looted the fur-trading establishments on the St. Lawrence, and that de Monts' monopoly had been rescinded by the king's council. On this aspect of the story, see Biggar, *Early Trading Companies of New France*, p. 63. The fur-trade remained open till 1613.

What touched Lescarbot even more deeply was that Chevalier, on the plea that they were supposed to have perished during the winter, had eaten all the sweetmeats and other dainties sent out by their friends. To this loss he frequently recurs.

The sturdy though passionate de Poutrincourt, "after he had a long while mused thereon, said that, although he should have none to come with him but his own family, he would not forsake the enterprize." (Lescarbot, IV., XVII.)

[3] The second son of Henry IV. and Marie de Médicis, born April 16, 1607, died November 17, 1611, without having been given a Christian name. He must not be confused with his more celebrated brother Gaston (1608–1660), who did not become Duke of Orleans till his marriage in 1626.

[4] Lescarbot (IV., XVII.) says about 400, which is more likely.

place on the 29th of June for Choüacoet, which is the country of the Almouchiquois, to engage in the war.

Some days after the arrival of the above Chevalier, Sieur de Poutrincourt sent him to the rivers St. John and St. Croix to trade for furs. But he did not permit him to go without men to bring back the barque, since some had reported that he desired to return to France with the vessel in which he had come, and leave us in our settlement. Lescarbot was one of those who accompanied him, who up to this time had not left Port Royal. This is the farthest he went, only fourteen or fifteen leagues beyond Port Royal.[1]

While awaiting the return of Chevalier, Sieur de Poutrincourt went to the head of Baye Françoise in a shallop with seven or eight men. Leaving the harbor and heading northeast a quarter east for some twenty-five leagues along the coast, we arrived at a cape where Sieur de Poutrincourt desired to ascend a cliff more than thirty fathoms high, in doing which he came near losing his life. For, having reached the top of the rock, which is very narrow, and which he had ascended with much difficulty, the summit trembled beneath him. The reason was that, in course of time, moss had gathered there four or five feet in thickness, and, not being solid, trembled when one was on top of it, and very often when one stepped on a stone three or four others fell down. Accordingly, having gone up with difficulty, he experienced still greater in coming down, although some sailors, men very dexterous in climbing, carried him a hawser, a rope of medium size, by means of which he descended. This place was named Cap de Poutrincourt,[2] and is in latitude 45° 40'.

We went as far as the head of this bay, but saw nothing but certain white stones suitable for making lime, yet they are found only in small quantities. We saw also on some islands a great number of gulls. We captured as many of them as we wished. We made the tour of the bay, in order to go to the

---

[1] Lescarbot complains of this statement, in his edition of 1618. Champlain is a little unfair both to Cartier (see p. 22, note 3) and to Lescarbot.

[2] Now Cape Split.

Port aux Mines, where I had previously been, and whither I conducted Sieur de Poutrincourt, who collected some little pieces of copper with great difficulty. All this bay has a circuit of perhaps twenty leagues, with a little river[1] at its head, which is very sluggish and contains but little water. There are many other little brooks, and some places where there are good harbors at high tide, which rises here five fathoms. In one of these harbors three or four leagues north of Cap de Poutrincourt, we found a very old cross all covered with moss and almost all rotten, a plain indication that before this there had been Christians there. All of this country is covered with dense forests, and with some exceptions is not very attractive.

From the Port aux Mines we returned to our settlement. In this bay there are strong tidal currents running in a southwesterly direction.

On the 12th of July, Ralleau, secretary of Sieur de Monts, arrived with three others in a shallop from a place called Niganis,[2] distant from Port Royal some hundred and sixty or hundred and seventy leagues, confirming the report which Chevalier had brought to Sieur de Poutrincourt.

On the 3d[3] of July, three barques were fitted out to send the men and supplies, which were at our settlement, to Canseau, distant one hundred and fifteen leagues from our settlement, and in latitude 45° 20′, where the vessel[4] was engaged in fishing, which was to carry us back to France.

Sieur de Poutrincourt sent back all his companions, but remained with eight others at the settlement, so as to carry to France some grain not yet quite ripe.

On the 10th of August, Mabretou arrived from the war, who told us that he had been at Choüacoet, and had killed twenty savages and wounded ten or twelve; also that Onemechin, chief of that place, Marchin, and one other, had been

---

[1] The Shubenacadie.

[2] Niganish, in the island of Cape Breton.

[3] Probably a misprint for 30th, the date given by Lescarbot.

[4] The *Jonas*. Nearly three months before Port Royal was abandoned, Jamestown had been founded.

killed by Sasinou, chief of the river of Quinibequy, who was afterwards killed by the companions of Onemechin and Marchin. All this war was simply on account of the savage Panounias, one of our friends who, as I have said above, had been killed at Norumbegue by the followers of Onemechin and Marchin. At present, the chiefs in place of Onemechin, Marchin, and Sasinou are their sons: namely, for Sasinou, Pememen; Abriou for his father, Marchin; and for Onemechin, Queconsicq. The two latter were wounded by the followers of Mabretou, who seized them under pretence of friendship, as is their fashion, something which both sides have to guard against.[1]

Chapter 17

The settlement abandoned. Return to France of Sieur de Poutrincourt and all his company.

On the 11th of August, we set out from our settlement in a shallop, and coasted along as far as Cape Fourchu, where I had previously been.

Continuing our course along the coast as far as Cap de la Hève, where we first landed with Sieur de Monts, on the 8th of May, 1604, we examined the coast from this place as far as Canseau, a distance of nearly sixty leagues. This I had not yet done, and I observed it very carefully, making a map of it as of the other coasts.

Departing from Cap de la Hève, we went as far as Sesambre,[2] an island so called by some people from St. Malo, and distant fifteen leagues from La Hève. Along the route are a large number of islands, which we named Les Martyres, since some Frenchmen were once killed there by the savages. These islands lie in several inlets and bays. In one of them is

---

[1] Lescarbot tells us that Champdoré, sent by Poutrincourt, subsequently reconciled the belligerents.
[2] Now Sambro.

a river named St. Marguerite,[1] distant seven leagues from
Sesambre, which is in latitude 44° 25′. The islands and coasts
are thickly covered with pines, firs, birches, and other trees
of inferior quality. Fish and also fowl are abundant.

After leaving Sesambre, we passed a bay which is unobstructed, of seven or eight leagues in extent, with no islands
except at the extremity, where is the mouth of a small river,
containing but little water.[2] Then, heading north-east a
quarter east, we arrived at a harbor distant eight leagues from
Sesambre, which is very suitable for vessels of a hundred or
a hundred and twenty tons. At its entrance is an island
from which one can walk to the main land at low tide. We
named this place Port Saincte Helaine,[3] which is in latitude
44° 40′ more or less.

From this place we proceeded to a bay called La Baye
de Toutes Isles,[4] of some fourteen or fifteen leagues in extent,
a dangerous place on account of the presence of banks, shoals,
and reefs. The country presents a very unfavorable appearance, being filled with the same kind of trees which I have
mentioned before. Here we encountered bad weather.

Hence we passed on near a river, six leagues distant, called
Rivière de l'Isle Verte,[5] there being a green island at its entrance. This short distance which we traversed is filled with
numerous rocks extending nearly a league out to sea, where the
breakers are high, the latitude being 45° 15′.

Thence we went to a place where there is an inlet, with
two or three islands, and a very good harbor,[6] distant three
leagues from l'Isle Verte. We passed also by several islands
near and in a line with each other, which we named Isles
Rangées, and which are distant six or seven leagues from

---

[1] The bay is still called St. Margaret.
[2] Halifax Harbor, formerly Chebucto Bay. On his map Champlain calls
it Baye Saine.
[3] Perpisawick Inlet. (Slafter.) Jeddore. (Laverdière.)
[4] Really an archipelago, extending along the coast.
[5] *I.e.*, Green Island River, now River St. Mary, so called by Nicolas
Denys, in his *Description de l'Amérique Septentrionale* (1672). The island
is now called Wedge Island.
[6] Now Country Harbor.

l'Isle Verte. Afterwards we passed by another bay,[1] containing several islands, and proceeded to a place where we found a vessel engaged in fishing between some islands, which are a short distance from the main land, and distant four leagues from the Rangées. This place we named Port de Savalette,[2] the name of the master of the vessel engaged in fishing, a Basque, who entertained us bountifully, and was very glad to see us, since there were savages there who purposed some harm to him, which we prevented.

Leaving this place, we arrived on the 27th of the month at Canseau, distant six leagues from Port de Savalette, having passed on our way a large number of islands. At Canseau, we found that the three barques had arrived at port in safety. Champdoré and Lescarbot came out to receive us. We also found the vessel ready to sail, having finished its fishing and awaiting only fair weather to return. Meanwhile, we had much enjoyment among these islands, where we found the greatest possible quantity of raspberries.

All the coast which we passed along from Cape Sable to this place is moderately high and rocky, in most places bordered by numerous islands and breakers, which extend out to sea nearly two leagues in places, and are very unfavorable for the approach of vessels. Yet there cannot but be good harbors and roadsteads along the coasts and islands, if they were explored. As to the country, it is worse and less promising than in other places which we had seen, except on some rivers or brooks, where it is very pleasant; but there is no doubt that the winter in these regions is cold, lasting from six to seven months.

The harbor of Canseau is a place surrounded by islands, to which the approach is very difficult, except in fair weather, on account of the rocks and breakers about it. Fishing, both green and dry, is carried on here.

---

[1] Tor Bay.

[2] White Haven. The name was really given by Lescarbot, who has left a most interesting account of the old Basque fisherman, who had made forty-two voyages to these waters. (Lescarbot, IV., XIX.)

From this place to the Island of Cape Breton, which is in latitude 45° 45′ and 14° 50′ of the deflection of the magnetic needle, it is eight leagues, and to Cape Breton twenty-five. Between the two there is a large bay,[1] extending some nine or ten leagues into the interior and making a passage between the Island of Cape Breton and the main land through to the great Bay of St. Lawrence, by which they go to Gaspé and Isle Percée, where fishing is carried on. This passage along the Island of Cape Breton is very narrow. Although there is water enough, large vessels do not pass there at all on account of the strong currents and the impetuosity of the tides which prevail. This we named Le Passage Courant and it is in latitude 45° 45′.

The Island of Cape Breton is of a triangular shape, with a circuit of about eighty leagues. Most of the country is mountainous, yet in some parts very pleasant. In the centre of it there is a kind of lake, where the sea enters by the north a quarter north-west, and also by the south a quarter south-east.[2] Here are many islands filled with plenty of game, and shellfish of various kinds, including oysters, which, however, are not of very good flavor. In this place there are two harbors where fishing is carried on; namely, Le Port aux Anglois,[3] distant from Cape Breton [4] some two or three leagues, and Niganis, eighteen or twenty leagues north a quarter north-west. The Portuguese once made an attempt to settle this island, and spent a winter here;[5] but the inclemency of the season and the cold caused them to abandon their settlement.

On the 3d of September, we set out from Canseau. On the 4th, we were off Sable Island. On the 6th, we reached

---

[1] Chedabucto Bay, and the Strait (or Gut) of Canso.

[2] There are really two passages on the north-east (not west), known as the Great and the Little Bras d'Or, and none on the south, though a ship canal has now been cut, joining the Bras d'Or lakes with St. Peter's Bay. Champlain's map is more correct than his description.

[3] *I.e.*, English Harbor, now Louisburg.

[4] Distinguish Cape Breton (headland) from Cape Breton (island).

[5] Mr. Bourne conjectures that this may have been at the time of the exploration of Fagundes, 1521. See Harrisse, *Discovery of North America*, pp. 182 *et seqq.*

the Grand Bank, where the catching of green fish is carried
on, in latitude 45° 30'.   On the 26th, we entered the sound
near the shores of Brittany and England, in sixty-five fathoms of water and in latitude 49° 30'.   On the 28th, we put
in at Roscou,[1] in lower Brittany, where we were detained by
bad weather until the last day of September, when, the wind
coming round favorable, we put to sea in order to pursue our
route to St. Malo, which formed the termination of these
voyages, in which God had guided us without shipwreck or
danger.[2]

[1] Now Roscoff.
[2] Poutrincourt and Lescarbot went on to Honfleur.   Thence Poutrincourt proceeded to Paris, and by judicious presents of the products of the
country persuaded Henry IV. to renew de Monts' monopoly for a year.
(Lescarbot, IV., XVII.)

THE VOYAGES TO THE GREAT RIVER
ST. LAWRENCE FROM THE YEAR 1608
TO THAT OF 1612

BOOK II

THE VOYAGES TO THE GREAT RIVER ST. LAWRENCE FROM THE YEAR 1608 TO THAT OF 1612[1]

Chapter 1

Determination of Sieur de Monts to make explorations in the interior; his commission, and its infringement by the Basques, who disarmed the vessel of Pont Gravé; and the agreement between them which they subsequently made.

HAVING returned to France after a stay of three years in New France, I proceeded to Sieur de Monts, and related to him the principal events of which I had been a witness since his departure, and gave him the map and plan of the most remarkable coasts and harbors there.

Some time afterward, Sieur de Monts determined to continue his undertaking, and complete the exploration of the interior along the great river St. Lawrence, where I had been by order of the late King Henry the Great[2] in the year 1603, for a distance of some hundred and eighty leagues, commencing in latitude 48° 40', that is, at Gaspé, at the entrance of the river, as far as the great fall, which is in latitude 45° and some minutes, where our exploration ended and where boats could not pass as we then thought, since we

---

[1] Book II. runs to 1612 if one includes in it not only these ensuing eleven chapters, but also the so-called "Second Voyage."

[2] Henry IV. died on May 14, 1610.

had not made a careful examination of it as we have since done.

Now after Sieur de Monts had conferred with me several times in regard to his purposes concerning the exploration, he resolved to continue so noble and meritorious an undertaking, notwithstanding the hardships and labors of the past. He honored me with his lieutenancy for the voyage; and, in order to carry out his purpose, he had two vessels equipped, one commanded by Pont Gravé, who was commissioned to trade with the savages of the country and bring back the vessels, while I was to winter in the country.

Sieur de Monts, for the purpose of defraying the expenses of the expedition, obtained letters from his Majesty for one year, by which all persons were forbidden to traffic in peltry with the savages, on penalties stated in the following commission: —

HENRY BY THE GRACE OF GOD KING OF FRANCE AND NAVARRE, to our beloved and faithful councillors, the officers of our Admiralty in Normandy, Brittany, and Guienne, bailiffs, marshals, prevosts, judges, or their lieutenants, and to each one of them, according to his authority, throughout the extent of their powers, jurisdictions, and precincts, greeting:

Acting upon the information which has been given us by those who have returned from New France, respecting the good quality and fertility of the lands of that country, and the disposition of the people to accept the knowledge of God, We have resolved to continue the settlement previously undertaken there, in order that our subjects may go there to trade without hinderance. And in view of the proposition to us of Sieur de Monts, Gentleman in Ordinary of our chamber, and our Lieutenant-General in that country, to make a settlement, on condition of our giving him means and supplies for sustaining the expense of it, it has pleased us to promise and assure him that none of our subjects but himself shall be permitted to trade in peltry and other merchandise, for the period of one year only, in the lands, regions, harbors, rivers, and highways throughout the extent of his jurisdiction: this We desire to have fulfilled. For these causes and other considerations impelling us thereto, We command and decree that each one of you, throughout

the extent of your powers, jurisdictions, and precincts, shall act
in our stead and carry out our will in distinctly prohibiting and forbidding all merchants, masters, and captains of vessels, also sailors
and others of our subjects, of whatever rank and profession, to fit
out any vessels, in which to go themselves or send others in order
to engage in trade or barter in peltry and other things with the
savages of New France, to visit, trade, or communicate with them
during the space of one year, within the jurisdiction of Sieur de
Monts, on penalty of disobedience, and the entire confiscation of
their vessels, supplies, arms, and merchandise for the benefit of
Sieur de Monts; and, in order that the punishment of their disobedience may be assured, you will allow, as We have and do allow,
the aforesaid Sieur de Monts or his lieutenants to seize, apprehend,
and arrest all violators of our present prohibition and order, also
their vessels, merchandise, arms, supplies, and victuals, in order to
take and deliver them up to the hands of justice, so that action
may be taken not only against the persons, but also the property of
the offenders, as the case shall require. This is our will, and We
bid you to have it at once read and published in all localities and
public places within your authority and jurisdiction, as you may
deem necessary, by the first one of our officers or sergeants in accordance with this requisition, by virtue of these presents, or a copy
of the same, properly attested once only by one of our well-beloved
and faithful councillors, notaries, and secretaries, to which it is
Our will that credence should be given as to the present original,
in order that none of our subjects may claim ground for ignorance,
but that all may obey and act in accordance with Our will in this
matter. We order, moreover, all captains of vessels, mates, and
second mates, and sailors of the same, and others on board of vessels or ships in the ports and harbors of the aforesaid country, to
permit, as We have done, Sieur de Monts, and others possessing
power and authority from him, to search the aforesaid vessels which
shall have engaged in the fur-trade after the present prohibition
shall have been made known to them. It is Our will that, upon the
requisition of the aforesaid Sieur de Monts, his lieutenants, and
others having authority, you should proceed against the disobedient
and offenders, as the case may require: to this end, We give you
power, authority, commission, and special mandate, notwithstanding the act of our Council of the 17th day of July last, any
hue and cry, Norman charter, accusation, objection, or appeals of

whatsoever kind; on account of which, and for fear of disregarding which, it is Our will that there should be no delay, and, if any of these occur, We have withheld and reserved cognizance of the same to Ourselves and our Council, apart from all other judges, and have forbidden and prohibited the same to all our courts and judges : for this is Our pleasure.

Given at Paris the seventh day of January, in the year of grace, sixteen hundred and eight, and the nineteenth of Our reign,

                    Signed,   HENRY.

And lower down, By the King, Delomenie. And sealed with the single label of the great seal of yellow wax.[1]

Collated with the original by me, Councillor, Notary, and Secretary of the King.

I proceeded to Honfleur for embarkation, where I found the vessel of Pont Gravé in readiness. He left port on the 5th of April. I did so on the 13th, arriving at the Grand Bank on the 15th of May, in latitude 45° 15′. On the 26th, we sighted Cape St. Mary, in latitude 46° 45′, on the Island of Newfoundland. On the 27th of the month, we sighted Cape St. Lawrence,[2] on Cape Breton, and also the Island of St. Paul, distant eighty-three leagues from Cape St. Mary. On the 30th, we sighted Isle Percée and Gaspé, in latitude 48° 40′, distant from Cape St. Lawrence from seventy to seventy-five leagues.

On the 3d of June, we arrived before Tadoussac, distant from Gaspé from eighty to ninety leagues; and we anchored in the roadstead of Tadoussac, a league distant from the harbor, which latter is a kind of cove at the mouth of the river Saguenay, where the tide is very remarkable on account of its rapidity, and where there are sometimes violent

---

[1] More exactly, " sealed on a single strip [of the parchment itself on which the document was engrossed] with the great seal in yellow wax." Letters patent in this time bore the king's signature, the countersignature of his secretary after the words, *Par le roy*, and the great seal. Letters patent of a permanent nature bore the impression of the seal in green wax; those of a temporary nature generally in yellow wax. Giry, *Manuel de Diplomatique*, pp. 628, 759, 771–774.

[2] Cape North, the northernmost point of Cape Breton.

winds, bringing severe cold. It is maintained that from the harbor of Tadoussac it is some forty-five or fifty leagues to the first fall on this river, which comes from the north-north-west. The harbor is small, and can accommodate only about twenty vessels. It has water enough, and is under shelter of the river Saguenay and a little rocky island, which is almost cut by the river; elsewhere there are very high mountains with little soil and only rocks and sand, thickly covered with such wood as fir and birch. There is a small pond near the harbor, shut in by mountains covered with wood. There are two points at the mouth: one on the south-west side, extending out nearly a league into the sea, called Point St. Matthew, or otherwise Point aux Allouettes;[1] and another on the north-west side, extending out one-eighth of a league, and called Point of all Devils,[2] from the dangerous nature of the place. The winds from the south-south-east strike the harbor, which are not to be feared; but those, however, from the Saguenay are. The two points above mentioned are dry at low tide; our vessel was unable to enter the harbor, as the wind and tide were unfavorable. I at once had the boat lowered, in order to go to the port and ascertain whether Pont Gravé had arrived. While on the way, I met a shallop with the pilot of Pont Gravé and a Basque, who came to inform me of what had happened to them because they attempted to hinder the Basque vessels from trading, according to the commission obtained by Sieur de Monts from his Majesty, that no vessels should trade without permission of Sieur de Monts, as was expressed in it; and that, notwithstanding the notifications which Pont Gravé made in behalf of his Majesty, they did not desist from forcibly carrying on their traffic; and that they had used their arms and maintained themselves so well in their vessel that, discharging all their cannon upon that of Pont Gravé, and letting off many musket-shots, he was severely wounded, together with three of his men, one of whom died, Pont Gravé meanwhile making no resistance;

[1] *I.e.*, Lark Point, still so called.
[2] Now known as Pointe aux Vaches.

for at the first shower of musketry he was struck down. The Basques came on board of the vessel and took away all the cannon and arms, declaring that they would trade, notwithstanding the prohibition of the King, and that when they were ready to set out for France they would restore to him his cannon and ammunition, and that they were keeping them in order to be in a state of security. Upon hearing all these particulars, I was greatly annoyed at such a beginning, which we might have easily avoided.

Now, after hearing from the pilot all these things I asked him why the Basque had come on board of our vessel. He told me that he came in behalf of their master, named Darache, and his companions, to obtain assurance from me that I would do them no harm, when our vessel entered the harbor.

I replied that I could not give any until I had seen Pont Gravé. The Basque said that, if I had need of anything in their power, they would assist me accordingly. What led them to use this language was simply their recognition of having done wrong, as they confessed, and the fear that they would not be permitted to engage in the whale-fishery. After talking at length, I went ashore to see Pont Gravé, in order to deliberate as to what was to be done. I found him very ill. He related to me in detail all that had happened. We concluded that we could only enter the harbor by force, and that the settlement must not be given up for this year, so that we considered it best, in order not to make a bad cause out of a just one, and thus work our ruin, to give them assurances on my part so long as I should remain there, and that Pont Gravé should undertake nothing against them, but that justice should be done in France, and their differences should be settled there.

Darache, master of the vessel, begged me to go on board, where he gave me a cordial reception. After a long conference, I secured an agreement between Pont Gravé and him, and required him to promise that he would undertake nothing against Pont Gravé, or what would be prejudicial to the King and Sieur de Monts; that, if he did the contrary, I should regard my promise as null and void. This was agreed to, and signed by each.

In this place were a number of savages who had come for traffic in furs, several of whom came to our vessel with their canoes, which are from eight to nine paces long, and about a pace or pace and a half broad in the middle, growing narrower towards the two ends. They are very apt to turn over, in case one does not understand managing them, and are made of birch bark, strengthened on the inside by little ribs of white cedar, very neatly arranged; they are so light that a man can easily carry one. Each can carry a weight equal to that of a pipe.[1] When they want to go overland to a river where they have business, they carry them with them. From Choüacoet along the coast as far as the harbor of Tadoussac, they are all alike.

Chapter 2

Of the River Saguenay, and the savages who visited us there. Of the Island of Orleans, and all that we observed there worthy of note.

After this agreement, I had some carpenters set to work to fit up a little barque of twelve or fourteen tons, for carrying all that was needed for our settlement, which, however, could not be got ready before the last of June.

Meanwhile, I managed to visit some parts of the river Saguenay, a fine river, which has the incredible depth of some one hundred and fifty to two hundred fathoms.[2] About fifty leagues [3] from the mouth of the harbor, there is, as is said, a great waterfall, descending from a very high elevation with great impetuosity. There are some islands in this river, very

---

[1] A liquid measure, containing from 400 to 700 quarts.

[2] Corrected in the edition of 1632 to read 80 to 100. The deepest modern soundings give 146.

[3] The Saguenay is navigable 71 miles from its mouth to Chicoutimi. From Lake St. John to its mouth the distance is 112 miles.

barren, being only rocks covered with small firs and heathers. It is half a league broad in places, and a quarter of a league at its mouth, where the current is so strong that at three-quarters flood-tide in the river it is still running out. All the land that I have seen consists only of mountains and rocky promontories, for the most part covered with fir and birch, a very unattractive country on both sides of the river. In a word, it is mere wastes, uninhabited by either animals or birds; for, going out hunting in places which seemed to me the most pleasant, I found only some very small birds, such as swallows and river birds, which go there in summer. At other times, there are none whatever, in consequence of the excessive cold. This river flows from the north-west.

The savages told me that, after passing the first fall, they meet with eight others, when they go a day's journey without finding any. Then they pass ten others, and enter a lake,[1] which they are three days in crossing, and they are easily able to make ten leagues a day up stream. At the end of the lake there dwells a migratory people. Of the three rivers [2] which flow into this lake, one comes from the north, very near the sea, where they consider it much colder than in their own country; and the other two from other directions in the interior, where are migratory savages, living only from hunting, and where our savages carry the merchandise we give them for their furs, such as beaver, marten, lynx, and otter, which are found there in large numbers, and which they then carry to our vessels. These people of the north report to our savages that they see the salt sea; and, if that is true, as I think it certainly is, it can be nothing but a gulf entering the interior on the north.[3] The savages say that the distance from the north sea to the port of Tadoussac is perhaps forty-five or fifty days' journey, in consequence of the difficulties presented by the

---

[1] Lake St. John, twenty-six miles by twenty, first seen by Europeans in 1647.

[2] The Peribonka, Mistassini, and Ashuapmuchuan.

[3] Hudson's Bay, discovered by Henry Hudson in 1610. Champlain had heard of his discoveries, and borrows from his maps.

roads, rivers, and country, which is very mountainous, and where there is snow for the most part of the year. This is what I have definitely ascertained in regard to this river. I have often wished to explore it, but could not do so without the savages, who were unwilling that I or any of our party should accompany them. Nevertheless, they have promised that I shall do so. This exploration would be desirable, in order to remove the doubts of many persons in regard to the existence of this sea on the north, where it is maintained that the English have gone in these latter years to find a way to China.

I set out from Tadoussac the last day of the month to go to Quebec. We passed near an island called Hare Island,[1] distant six leagues from the above-named port: it is two leagues from the northern, and nearly four leagues from the southern shore. From Hare Island we proceeded to a little river, dry at low tide, up which some seven hundred or eight hundred paces there are two falls. We named it Salmon River,[2] since we caught some of these fish in it. Coasting along the north shore, we came to a point extending into the river, which we called Cap Dauphin,[3] distant three leagues from Salmon River. Thence we proceeded to another, which we named Eagle Cape,[4] distant eight leagues from Cap Dauphin. Between the two there is a large bay, at the extremity of which is a little river dry at low tide. From Eagle Cape we proceeded to Isle aux Coudres,[5] a good league distant, which is about a league and a half long. It is nearly level, and grows narrower towards the two ends. On the western end there are meadows, and rocky points extending some distance out into the river. On the south-west side it

---

[1] Still so called. The name was given by Jacques Cartier.

[2] Probably Black River, two leagues from Cape Salmon.

[3] Now Cape Salmon.

[4] Now Cap aux Oies, or Goose Cape. The present Eagle Cape (Cap à l'Aigle) is only about two leagues from Cape Salmon. Most of these places still retain their French names, owing to the predominatingly French population of the province of Quebec.

[5] Still so called.

K

is very reefy, yet very pleasant in consequence of the woods surrounding it. It is distant about half a league from the northern shore, where is a little river extending some distance into the interior. We named it Rivière du Gouffre,[1] since abreast of it the tide runs with extraordinary rapidity; and, although it has a calm appearance, it is always much agitated, the depth there being great: but the river itself is shallow, and there are many rocks at and about its mouth. Coasting along from Isle aux Coudres, we reached a cape which we named Cap de Tourmente,[2] five leagues distant; and we gave it this name because, however little wind there may be, the water rises there as if it were full tide. At this point, the water begins to be fresh. Thence we proceeded to the Island of Orleans, a distance of two leagues, on the south side of which are numerous islands, low, covered with trees and very pleasant, with large meadows, having plenty of game, some being, so far as I could judge, two leagues in length, others a trifle more or less. About these islands are many rocks, also very dangerous shallows, some two leagues distant from the main land on the south. All this shore, both north and south, from Tadoussac to the Island of Orleans, is mountainous, and the soil very poor. The wood is pine, fir, and birch only, with very ugly rocks, so that in most places one could not make his way.

Now we passed along south of the Island of Orleans,[3] which is a league and a half distant from the main land and half a league on the north side, being six leagues in length, and one in breadth, or in some places a league and a half. On the north side, it is very pleasant, on account of the great extent of woods and meadows there; but it is very dangerous sailing, in consequence of the numerous points and rocks between the main land and island, on which are numerous fine oaks and in some places nut-trees, and on the borders of the woods,

---

[1] *I.e.*, Whirlpool River, still so called.   [2] Still so called.
[3] Still so called. Discovered by Cartier in 1535, and named the Island of Bacchus, because of the quantity of grapes seen growing. See *Early English and French Voyages*, pp. 45–48.

vines and other trees such as we have in France. This place is the commencement of the fine and fertile country of the great river, and is distant one hundred and twenty leagues from its mouth. Off the end of the island is a torrrent of water on the north shore, proceeding from a lake ten leagues in the interior: it comes down from a height of nearly twenty-five fathoms,[1] above which the land is level and pleasant, although farther inland are seen high mountains appearing to be from fifteen to twenty leagues distant.

Chapter 3

Arrival at Quebec, where we constructed our place of abode; its situation. Conspiracy against the service of the King and my life by some of our men. Punishment of them, and all that transpired in the affair.

From the Island of Orleans to Quebec [2] the distance is a league. I arrived there on the 3d of July, when I searched for a place suitable for our settlement, but I could find none more convenient or better situated than the point of Quebec, so called by the savages, which was covered with nut-trees. I at once employed a portion of our workmen in cutting them down, that we might construct our habitation there: one I set to sawing boards, another to making a cellar and digging ditches, another I sent to Tadoussac with the barque to get supplies. The first thing we made was the storehouse for

[1] The Montmorency Falls, flowing from Snow Lake, some fifty miles in the interior. Named by Champlain after the Admiral, Charles de Montmorency, to whom he dedicated his voyage of 1603. The height of the falls is really two hundred and sixty-five feet.

[2] Quebec, an Algonquin word meaning "the narrowing of the waters." In Cartier's time, it was called by the Indians Stadaconé. This point, where the first settlement was made, was "close to the place where the Champlain Market now stands in the lower town of the present city, and partly on the site now occupied by the Church of Notre Dame des Victoires." S. E. Dawson, *The St. Lawrence*, p. 254.

keeping under cover our supplies, which was promptly accomplished through the zeal of all, and my attention to the work.

Some days after my arrival at Quebec, a locksmith [1] conspired against the service of the king. His plan was to put me to death, and, getting possession of our fort, to put it into the hands of the Basques or Spaniards, then at Tadoussac, beyond which vessels cannot go, from not having a knowledge of the route, nor of the banks and rocks on the way.

In order to execute his wretched plan, by which he hoped to make his fortune, he suborned four of the worst characters, as he supposed, telling them a thousand falsehoods, and presenting to them prospects of acquiring riches.

These four men, having been won over, all promised to act in such a manner as to gain the rest over to their side; so that, for the time being, I had no one with me in whom I could put confidence, which gave them still more hope of making their plan succeed: for four or five of my companions, in whom they knew that I put confidence, were on board of the barques, for the purpose of protecting the provisions and supplies necessary for our settlement.

In a word, they were so skilful in carrying out their intrigues with those who remained, that they were on the point of gaining all over to their cause, even my lackey, promising them many things which they could not have fulfilled.

Being now all agreed, they made daily different plans as to how they should put me to death, so as not to be accused of it, which they found to be a difficult thing. But the devil blindfolding them all and taking away their reason and every possible difficulty, they determined to take me while unarmed and strangle me; or to give a false alarm at night, and shoot me as I went out, in which manner they judged that they would accomplish their work sooner than otherwise. They made a mutual promise not to betray each other, on penalty that the first one who opened his mouth should be poniarded. They were to execute their plan in four days, before the

[1] He was the one survivor of the five who had been attacked by the Indians on the coast of Massachusetts. See p. 99, and Lescarbot (IV., XVI.).

arrival of our barques, otherwise they would have been unable to carry out their scheme.

On this very day, one of our barques arrived, with our pilot, Captain Testu, a very discreet man. After the barque was unloaded, and ready to return to Tadoussac, there came to him a locksmith, named Natel, an associate of Jean du Val, the head of the conspiracy, who told him that he had promised the rest to do just as they did; but that he did not in fact desire the execution of the plot, yet did not dare to make a disclosure in regard to it, from fear of being poniarded.

Antoine Natel made the pilot promise that he would make no disclosure in regard to what he should say, since, if his companions should discover it, they would put him to death. The pilot gave him his assurance in all particulars, and asked him to state the character of the plot which they wished to carry out. This Natel did at length, when the pilot said to him: "My friend, you have done well to disclose such a malicious design, and you show that you are an upright man, and under the guidance of the Holy Spirit. But these things cannot be passed by without bringing them to the knowledge of Sieur de Champlain, that he may make provision against them; and I promise you that I will prevail upon him to pardon you and the rest. And I will at once," said the pilot, "go to him without exciting any suspicion; and do you go about your business, listening to all they may say, and not troubling yourself about the rest."

The pilot came at once to me, in a garden which I was having prepared, and said that he wished to speak to me in a private place, where we could be alone. I readily assented, and we went into the wood, where he related to me the whole affair. I asked who had told it to him. He begged me to pardon him who had made the disclosure, which I consented to do, although he ought to have addressed himself to me. He was afraid, he replied, that you would become angry, and harm him. I told him that I was able to govern myself better than that, in such a matter; and desired him to have the man come to me, that I might hear his statement. He went, and brought him all trembling with fear lest I should do him some harm. I reassured him, telling him not to be afraid; that he was in a place of safety, and that I should pardon him for all that he had done, together with the others, provided he would tell me in full the truth in regard to the whole matter, and the motive which had impelled them to it. "Nothing," he said, "had impelled them, except that they had imagined that, by giving up the place into the hands of the Basques or Spaniards, they might all become rich, and that they did not want to go back to France." He also related to me the remaining particulars in regard to their conspiracy.

After having heard and questioned him, I directed him to go about his work. Meanwhile, I ordered the pilot to bring up his shallop, which he did. Then I gave two bottles of wine to a young man, directing him to say to these four worthies, the leaders of the conspiracy, that it was a present of wine, which his friends at Tadoussac had given him, and that he wished to share it with them. This they did not decline, and at evening were on board the barque where he was to give them the entertainment. I lost no time in going there shortly after; and caused them to be seized, and held until the next day.

Then were my worthies astonished indeed. I at once had all get up, for it was about ten o'clock in the evening, and pardoned them all, on condition that they would disclose to me the truth in regard to all that had occurred; which they did, when I had them retire.

The next day I took the depositions of all, one after the other, in the presence of the pilot and sailors of the vessel, which I had put down in writing; and they were well pleased, as they said, since they had lived only in fear of each other, especially of the four knaves who had ensnared them. But now they lived in peace, satisfied, as they declared, with the treatment which they had received.

The same day I had six pairs of handcuffs made for the authors of the conspiracy: one for our surgeon, named Bon-

nerme, one for another, named La Taille, whom the four
conspirators had accused, which, however, proved false, and
consequently they were given their liberty.

This being done, I took my worthies to Tadoussac, begging
Pont Gravé to do me the favor of guarding them, since I
had as yet no secure place for keeping them, and as we were
occupied in constructing our places of abode. Another object was to consult with him, and others on the ship, as to
what should be done in the premises. We suggested that,
after he had finished his work at Tadoussac, he should come to
Quebec with the prisoners, where we should have them con-
fronted with their witnesses, and, after giving them a hearing,
order justice to be done according to the offence which they had
committed.

I went back the next day to Quebec, to hasten the com-
pletion of our storehouse, so as to secure our provisions,
which had been misused by all those scoundrels, who spared
nothing, without reflecting how they could find more when
these failed; for I could not obviate the difficulty until the
storehouse should be completed and shut up.

Pont Gravé arrived some time after me, with the prisoners,
which caused uneasiness to the workmen who remained, since
they feared that I should pardon them, and that they would
avenge themselves upon them for revealing their wicked
design.

We had them brought face to face, and they affirmed
before them all which they had stated in their depositions, the
prisoners not denying it, but admitting that they had acted
in a wicked manner, and should be punished, unless mercy
might be exercised towards them; accusing, above all, Jean
du Val, who had been trying to lead them into such a conspiracy from the time of their departure from France. Du
Val knew not what to say, except that he deserved death,
that all stated in the depositions was true, and that he begged
for mercy upon himself and the others, who had given in
their adherence to his pernicious purposes.

After Pont Gravé and I, the captain of the vessel, surgeon,

mate, second mate, and other sailors, had heard their depositions and face to face statements, we adjudged that it would
be enough to put to death Du Val, as the instigator of the conspiracy; and that he might serve as an example to those who
remained, leading them to deport themselves correctly in
future, in the discharge of their duty; and that the Spaniards
and Basques, of whom there were large numbers in the country, might not glory in the event. We adjudged that the
three others be condemned to be hung, but that they should
be taken to France and put into the hands of Sieur de Monts,
that such ample justice might be done them as he should recommend; that they should be sent with all the evidence and
their sentence, as well as that of Jean du Val, who was strangled
and hung at Quebec, and his head was put on the end of a pike,
to be set up in the most conspicuous place on our fort.

Chapter 4

*Return of Pont Gravé to France. Description of our quarters
and the place where Jacques Cartier stayed in 1535.*

After all these occurrences, Pont Gravé set out from Quebec,
on the 18th of September, to return to France with the three
prisoners. After he had gone, all who remained conducted
themselves correctly in the discharge of their duty.

I had the work on our quarters continued, which was
composed of three buildings of two stories. Each one was
three fathoms long, and two and a half wide. The storehouse was six fathoms long and three wide, with a fine cellar
six feet deep. I had a gallery made all around our buildings,
on the outside, at the second story, which proved very convenient. There were also ditches, fifteen feet wide and six
deep. On the outer side of the ditches, I constructed several
spurs, which enclosed a part of the dwelling, at the points
where we placed our cannon. Before the habitation there is
a place four fathoms wide and six or seven long, looking out

upon the river-bank. Surrounding the habitation are very good gardens, and a place on the north side some hundred or hundred and twenty paces long and fifty or sixty wide. Moreover, near Quebec, there is a little river, coming from a lake in the interior, distant six or seven leagues from our settlement. I am of opinion that this river,[1] which is north a quarter north-west from our settlement, is the place where Jacques Cartier wintered, since there are still, a league up the river, remains of what seems to have been a chimney, the foundation of which has been found, and indications of there having been ditches surrounding their dwelling, which was small. We found, also, large pieces of hewn, worm-eaten timber, and some three or four cannon-balls. All these things show clearly that there was a settlement there founded by Christians; and what leads me to say and believe that it was that of Jacques Cartier is the fact that there is no evidence whatever that any one wintered and built a house in these places except Jacques Cartier, at the time of his discoveries. This place, as I think, must have been called St. Croix, as he named it; which name has since been transferred to another place fifteen leagues west of our settlement. But there is no evidence of his having wintered in the place now called St. Croix, nor in any other there, since in this direction there is no river or other place large enough for vessels except the main river or that of which I spoke above; here there is half a fathom of water at low tide, many rocks, and a bank at the mouth; for vessels, if kept in the main river, where there are strong currents and tides, and ice in the winter, drifting along, would run the risk of being lost; especially as there is a sandy point extending out into the river, and filled with rocks, between which we have found, within the last three years, a passage not before discovered; but one must go through cautiously, in consequence of the dangerous points there. This place is exposed to the northwest winds; and the river runs as if it were a fall, the tide ebbing two and a half fathoms. There are no signs of buildings

[1] Now the St. Charles, called by Jacques Cartier the St. Croix. *Early English and French Voyages*, pp. 70, 75.

here, nor any indications that a man of judgment would settle in this place, there being many other better ones, in case one were obliged to make a permanent stay. I have been desirous of speaking at length on this point, since many believe that the abode of Jacques Cartier was here, which I do not believe, for the reasons here given; for Cartier would have left to posterity a narrative of the matter, as he did in the case of all he saw and discovered; and I maintain that my opinion is the true one, as can be shown by the history which he has left in writing.[1]

As still farther proof that this place now called St. Croix is not the place where Jacques Cartier wintered, as most persons think, this is what he says about it in his discoveries, taken from his history; namely, that he arrived at the Isle aux Coudres on the 5th of December,[2] 1535, which he called by this name, as hazel-nuts were found there. There is a strong tidal current in this place; and he says that it is three leagues long, but it is quite enough to reckon a league and a half. On the 7th of the month, Notre Dame Day,[3] he set out from this island to go up the river, in which he saw fourteen islands, distant seven or eight leagues from Isle aux Coudres on the south. He errs somewhat in this estimation, for it is not more than three leagues.[4] He also says that the place where the islands are is the commencement of the land or province of Canada, and that he reached an island ten leagues long and five wide, where extensive fisheries are carried on, fish being here, in fact, very abundant, especially the sturgeon. But its length is not more than six leagues, and its breadth two; a fact well recognized now. He says also that he anchored

[1] Champlain is obviously correct, though a century later the Jesuit Charlevoix, in his *Histoire Générale de la Nouvelle France*, sustains the contrary opinion.

[2] This should read September 6. See *Early English and French Voyages*, p. 45.

[3] September 7 is not the day of Our Lady, but the even or vigil before it.

[4] Cartier is really the more correct of the two, for though the islands are only three leagues higher up the river than Isle aux Coudres, they lie so far in to the north shore that the distance is practically as stated by Cartier.

between this island and the main land on the north, the smallest
passage, and a dangerous one, where he landed two savages
whom he had taken to France, and that, after stopping in this
place some time with the people of the country, he sent for his
barques and went farther up the river, with the tide, seeking
a harbor and place of security for his ships.   He says, farther,
that they went on up the river, coasting along this island, the
length of which he estimates at ten leagues; and after it was
passed they found a very fine and pleasant bay, containing a
little river and bar harbor, which they found very favorable
for sheltering their vessels.   This they named St. Croix, since
he arrived there on this day;[1] and at the time of the voyage
of Cartier the place was called Stadaca,[2] but we now call
it Quebec.   He says, also, that after he had examined this
place he returned to get his vessels for passing the winter
there.

Now we may conclude, accordingly, that the distance is
only five leagues[3] from the Isle aux Coudres to the Isle of
Orleans, at the western extremity of which the river is very
broad; and at which bay, as Cartier calls it, there is no other
river than that which he called St. Croix, a good league distant from the Isle of Orleans, in which, at low tide, there
is only half a fathom of water.   It is very dangerous for
vessels at its mouth, there being a large number of spurs;
that is, rocks scattered here and there.   It is accordingly
necessary to place buoys in order to enter, there being, as I
have stated, three fathoms of water at ordinary tides, and
four fathoms, or four and a half generally, at the great tides
at full flood.   It is only fifteen hundred paces from our habitation, which is higher up the river; and, as I have stated,
there is no other river up to the place now called St. Croix,
where vessels can lie, there being only little brooks.   The
shores are flat and dangerous, which Cartier does not mention
until the time that he sets out from St. Croix, now called

---

[1] *I.e.*, September 14, the day on which the exaltation of the Holy Cross
is celebrated.

[2] Stadaconé.   [3] It is at least twenty-six nautical miles.

Quebec, where he left his vessels, and built his place of abode, as is seen from what follows.

On the 19th of September, he set out from St. Croix where his vessels were, setting sail with the tide up the river, which they found very pleasant, as well on account of the woods, vines, and dwellings, which were there in his time, as for other reasons. They cast anchor twenty-five leagues from the entrance to the land of Canada;[1] that is, at the western extremity of the Isle of Orleans, so called by Cartier. What is now called St. Croix was then called Achelacy, at a narrow pass where the river is very swift and dangerous on account of the rocks and other things, and which can only be passed at flood-tide. Its distance from Quebec and the river where Cartier wintered is fifteen leagues.

Now, throughout the entire extent of this river, from Quebec to the great fall, there are no narrows except at the place now called St. Croix, the name of which has been transferred from one place to another one, which is very dangerous, as my description shows. And it is very apparent, from his narrative, that this was not the site of his habitation, as is claimed; but that the latter was near Quebec, and that no one had entered into a special investigation of this matter before my doing so in my voyages. For the first time I was told that he dwelt in this place, I was greatly astonished, finding no trace of a river for vessels, as he states there was. This led me to make a careful examination, in order to remove the suspicion and doubt of many persons in regard to the matter.

While the carpenters, sawers of boards, and other workmen were employed on our quarters, I set all the others to work clearing up around our place of abode, in preparation for gardens in which to plant grain and seeds, that we

---

[1] Cartier distinguishes clearly the three realms of Canada (about Quebec), Hochelaga (about Montreal), and Saguenay. He represents Canada as beginning at the Isle aux Coudres. Under the French, Canada assumed a wider though indeterminate meaning, its limits being the cause of frequent quarrels with the English colonies to the south.

might see how they would flourish, as the soil seemed to be
very good.

Meanwhile, a large number of savages were encamped in
cabins near us, engaged in fishing for eels, which begin to
come about the 15th of September, and go away on the 15th
of October.   During this time, all the savages subsist on this
food, and dry enough of it for the winter to last until the month
of February, when there are about two and a half, or at most
three, feet of snow; and, when their eels and other things
which they dry have been prepared, they go to hunt the
beaver until the beginning of January.   At their departure
for this purpose, they intrusted to us all their eels and other
things, until their return, which was on the 15th of December.
But they did not have great success in the beaver-hunt, as
the amount of water was too great, the rivers having overrun
their banks, as they told us.   I returned to them all their
supplies, which lasted them only until the 20th of January.
When their supply of eels gave out, they hunted the elk and
such other wild beasts as they could find until spring, when I
was able to supply them with various things.   I paid especial
attention to their customs.[1]

These people suffer so much from lack of food that they
are sometimes obliged to live on certain shell-fish, and eat
their dogs and the skins with which they clothe themselves
against the cold.   I am of opinion that, if one were to show
them how to live, and teach them the cultivation of the soil
and other things, they would learn very aptly.   For many of
them possess good sense, and answer properly questions put to
them.   They have a bad habit of taking vengeance, and are
great liars, and you must not put much reliance on them, except judiciously, and with force at hand.   They make promises readily, but keep their word poorly.   The most of them
observe no law at all, so far as I have been able to see, and
are, besides, full of superstitions.   I asked them with what
ceremonies they were accustomed to pray to their God, when

---

[1] The account which follows is largely taken from ch. III. of the voyage
of 1603.

they replied that they had none, but that each prayed to him in his heart, as he wished. That is why there is no law among them, and they do not know what it is to worship and pray to God, living as they do like brute beasts. But I think that they would soon become good Christians, if people would come and inhabit their country, which they are for the most part desirous of. There are some savages among them, called by them Pilotois, whom they believe to have intercourse with the devil face to face, who tells them what they must do in regard to war and other things; and, if he should order them to execute any undertaking, they would obey at once. So, also, they believe that all their dreams are true; and, in fact, there are many who say that they have had visions and dreams about matters which actually come to pass or will do so. But, to tell the truth, these are diabolical visions, through which they are deceived and misled. This is all I have been able to learn about their brutish faith. All these people are well proportioned in body, without deformity, and are agile. The women, also, are well-formed, plump, and of a swarthy color, in consequence of certain pigments with which they rub themselves, and which give them a permanent olive color. They are dressed in skins: a part only of the body is covered. But in winter they are covered throughout, in good furs of elk, otter, beaver, bear, seals, deer, and roe, of which they have large quantities. In winter, when the snow is deep, they make a sort of snow-shoe of large size, two or three times as large as that used in France, which they attach to their feet, thus going over the snow without sinking in; otherwise, they could not hunt or walk in many places. They have a sort of marriage, which is as follows: When a girl is fourteen or fifteen years old, and has several suitors, she may keep company with all she likes. At the end of five or six years, she takes the one that pleases her for her husband, and they live together to the end of their lives. But if, after living some time together, they have no children, the man can disunite himself and take another woman, alleging that his own is good for nothing. Hence, the girls have greater freedom than the married women.

After marriage, the women are chaste, and their husbands generally jealous. They give presents to the fathers or relatives of the girls they have wedded. These are the ceremonies and forms observed in their marriages. In regard to their burials: When a man or a woman dies, they dig a pit, in which they put all their property, as kettles, furs, axes, bows, arrows, robes, and other things. Then they place the body in the pit and cover it with earth, putting on top many large pieces of wood, and another piece upright, painted red on the upper part. They believe in the immortality of the soul, and say that they shall be happy in other lands with their relatives and friends who are dead. In the case of captains or others of some distinction, they celebrate a banquet three times a year after their death, singing and dancing about the grave.

All the time they were with us, which was the most secure place for them, they did not cease to fear their enemies [1] to such an extent that they often at night became alarmed while dreaming, and sent their wives and children to our fort, the gates of which I had opened to them, allowing the men to remain about the fort, but not permitting them to enter, for their persons were thus as much in security as if they had been inside. I also had five or six of our men go out to reassure them, and to go and ascertain whether they could see anything in the woods, in order to quiet them. They are very timid and in great dread of their enemies, scarcely ever sleeping in repose in whatever place they may be, although I constantly reassured them, so far as I could, urging them to do as we did; namely, that they should have a portion watch while the others slept, that each one should have his arms in readiness like him who was keeping watch, and that they should not regard dreams as the actual truth to be relied upon, since they are mostly only false, to which I also added other words on the same subject. But these remonstrances were of little avail with them, and they said that we knew

---

[1] *I.e.*, the Iroquois.

better than they how to keep guard against all things; and that they, in course of time, if we continued to stay with them, would be able to learn it.

Chapter 5

Seeds and vines planted at Quebec. Commencement of the winter and ice. Extreme destitution of certain Indians.

On the 1st of October, I had some wheat sown, and on the 15th some rye. On the 3d, there was a white frost in some places, and the leaves of the trees began to fall on the 15th. On the 24th, I had some native vines set out, which flourished very well. But, after leaving the settlement to go to France, they were all spoiled from lack of attention, at which I was much troubled on my return. On the 18th of November, there was a great fall of snow, which remained only two days on the ground, during which time there was a violent gale of wind. There died during this month a sailor and our locksmith[1] of dysentery, so also many Indians from eating eels badly cooked, as I think. On the 5th of February, it snowed violently, and the wind was high for two days. On the 20th, some Indians appeared on the other side of the river, calling to us to go to their assistance, which was beyond our power, on account of the large amount of ice drifting in the river. Hunger pressed upon these poor wretches so severely that, not knowing what to do, they resolved, men, women, and children, to cross the river or die, hoping that I should assist them in their extreme want. Having accordingly made this resolve, the men and women took the children and embarked in their canoes, thinking that they could reach our shore by an opening in the ice made by the wind; but they were scarcely in the middle of the stream when their canoes were caught by the ice and broken into a thousand pieces. But they were skilful

---

[1] Probably the informer Natel. See p. 133.

enough to throw themselves with the children, which the
women carried on their backs, on a large piece of ice. As they
were on it, we heard them crying out so that it excited intense
pity, as before them there seemed nothing but death. But
fortune was so favorable to these poor wretches that a large
piece of ice struck against the side of that on which they were,
so violently as to drive them ashore. On seeing this favorable
turn, they reached the shore with as much delight as they ever
experienced, notwithstanding the great hunger from which
they were suffering. They proceeded to our abode, so thin
and haggard that they seemed like mere skeletons, most of them
not being able to hold themselves up. I was astonished to see
them, and observe the manner in which they had crossed, in
view of their being so feeble and weak. I ordered some bread
and beans to be given them. So great was their impatience
to eat them, that they could not wait to have them cooked.
I lent them also some bark, which other savages had given me,
to cover their cabins. As they were making their cabin, they
discovered a piece of carrion, which I had had thrown out
nearly two months before to attract the foxes, of which we
caught black and red ones, like those in France, but with
heavier fur. This carrion consisted of a sow and a dog, which
had sustained all the rigors of the weather, hot and cold.
When the weather was mild, it stank so badly that one could
not go near it. Yet they seized it and carried it off to their
cabin, where they forthwith devoured it half cooked. No
meat ever seemed to them to taste better. I sent two or three
men to warn them not to eat it, unless they wanted to die :
as they approached their cabin, they smelt such a stench from
this carrion half warmed up, each one of the Indians holding
a piece in his hand, that they thought they should disgorge,
and accordingly scarcely stopped at all. These poor wretches
finished their repast. I did not fail, however, to supply them
according to my resources ; but this was little, in view of the
large number of them. In the space of a month, they would
have eaten up all our provisions, if they had had them in
their power, they are so gluttonous : for, when they have

ᴌ

ədibles, they lay nothing aside, but keep consuming them day and night without respite, afterwards dying of hunger. They did also another thing as disgusting as that just mentioned. I had caused a bitch to be placed on the top of a tree, which allured the martens[1] and birds of prey, from which I derived pleasure, since generally this carrion was attacked by them. These savages went to the tree, and, being too weak to climb it, cut it down and forthwith took away the dog, which was only skin and bones, the tainted head emitting a stench, but which was at once devoured.

This is the kind of enjoyment they experience for the most part in winter; for in summer they are able to support themselves, and to obtain provisions so as not to be assailed by such extreme hunger, the rivers abounding in fish, while birds and wild animals fill the country about. The soil is very good and well adapted for tillage, if they would but take pains to plant Indian corn, as all their neighbors do, the Algonquins, Ochastaiguins,[2] and Iroquois, who are not attacked by such extremes of hunger, which they provide against by their carefulness and foresight, so that they live happily in comparison with the Montagnais, Canadians, and Souriquois along the seacoast. This is in the main their wretched manner of life. The snow and ice last three months there, from January to the 8th of April, when it is nearly all melted: at the latest, it is only seldom that any is seen at the end of the latter month at our settlement. It is remarkable that so much snow and ice as there is on the river, and which is from two to three fathoms thick, is all melted in less than twelve days. From Tadoussac to Gaspé, Cape

---

[1] *I.e.*, weasels.

[2] *I.e.*, the Hurons, about Lake Huron and Georgian Bay. The Algonquins had their headquarters near the Ottawa, the Iroquois or Five Nations in Northern New York. The Montagnais wandered on both sides of the Saguenay; the Canadians to the east of the Montagnais, the Souriquois in Nova Scotia and New Brunswick. Sagard (*Le Grand Voyage aux Pays des Hurons*, 1632) distinguishes Hurons, Algonquins, and Montagnais as "the nobles, the burghers, and the peasantry and paupers of the forest." See Parkman, *Pioneers of France in the New World*, 359.

Breton, Newfoundland, and the Great Bay,[1] the snow and ice
continue in most places until the end of May, at which time
the entire entrance of the great river is sealed with ice; although at Quebec there is none at all, showing a strange difference for one hundred and twenty leagues in longitude, for
the entrance to the river is in latitude 49° 50′ to 51°, and our
settlement in 46° 40′.

Chapter 6

The scurvy at Quebec. How the winter passed. Description of
the place. Arrival at Quebec of Sieur des Marais, son-
in-law of Pont Gravé.

The scurvy began very late; namely, in February, and
continued until the middle of April. Eighteen were attacked,
and ten died; five others dying of the dysentery. I had some
opened, to see whether they were tainted, like those I had seen
in our other settlements. They were found the same. Some
time after, our surgeon died.[2] All this troubled us very much,
on account of the difficulty we had in attending to the sick.
The nature of this disease I have described before.

It is my opinion that this disease proceeds only from eating
excessively of salt food and vegetables, which heat the blood
and corrupt the internal parts. The winter is also, in part,
its cause; since it checks the natural warmth, causing a
still greater corruption of the blood. There rise also from
the earth, when first cleared up, certain vapors which infect
the air: this has been observed in the case of those who have
lived at other settlements; after the first year when the sun
had been let in upon what was not before cleared up, as
well in our abode as in other places, the air was much better,
and the diseases not so violent as before. But the country
is fine and pleasant, and brings to maturity all kinds of grains

---

[1] *I.e.*, the wide expanse between Newfoundland and the mainland, after
passing westward through the Straits of Belle Isle.

[2] His name was Bonnerme. See p. 134.

and seeds, there being found all the various kinds of trees which we have here in our forests, and many fruits, although they are naturally wild; as, nut-trees, cherry-trees, plum-trees, vines, raspberries, strawberries, currants, both green and red, and several other small fruits, which are very good. There are also several kinds of excellent plants and roots. Fishing is abundant in the rivers; and game without limit on the numerous meadows bordering them. From the month of April to the 15th of December, the air is so pure and healthy that one does not experience the slightest indisposition. But January, February, and March are dangerous, on account of the sicknesses prevailing at this time, rather than in summer, for the reasons before given; for, as to treatment, all of my company were well clothed, provided with good beds, and well warmed and fed, that is, with the salt meats we had, which in my opinion injured them greatly, as I have already stated. As far as I have been able to see, the sickness attacks one who is delicate in his living and takes particular care of himself as readily as one whose condition is as wretched as possible. We supposed at first that the workmen only would be attacked with this disease; but this we found was not the case. Those sailing to the East Indies and various other regions, as Germany and England, are attacked with it as well as in New France. Some time ago, the Flemish, being attacked with this malady in their voyages to the Indies, found a very strange remedy, which might be of service to us; but we have never ascertained the character of it. Yet I am confident that, with good bread and fresh meat, a person would not be liable to it.

On the 8th of April, the snow had all melted; and yet the air was still very cold until April,[1] when the trees begin to leaf out.

Some of those sick with the scurvy were cured when spring came, which is the season for recovery. I had a savage of the country wintering with me, who was attacked with this disease from having changed his diet to salt meat; and he died

[1] In the edition of 1632, he corrects this to May.

from its effects, which clearly shows that salt food is not nourishing, but quite the contrary in this disease.

On the 5th of June, a shallop arrived at our settlement with Sieur des Marais,[1] a son-in-law of Pont Gravé, bringing us the tidings that his father-in-law had arrived at Tadoussac on the 28th of May. This intelligence gave me much satisfaction, as we entertained hopes of assistance from him. Only eight out of the twenty-eight at first forming our company were remaining, and half of these were ailing.

On the 7th of June, I set out from Quebec for Tadoussac on some matters of business, and asked Sieur des Marais to stay in my place until my return, which he did.

Immediately upon my arrival, Pont Gravé and I had a conference in regard to some explorations which I was to make in the interior, where the savages had promised to guide us. We determined that I should go in a shallop with twenty men, and that Pont Gravé should stay at Tadoussac to arrange the affairs of our settlement ; and this determination was carried out, he spending the winter there. This arrangement was especially desirable, since I was to return to France, according to the orders sent out by Sieur de Monts, in order to inform him of what I had done and the explorations I had made in the country.

After this decision, I set out at once from Tadoussac, and returned to Quebec, where I had a shallop fitted out with all that was necessary for making explorations in the country of the Iroquois, where I was to go with our allies, the Montagnais.

Chapter 7

Departure from Quebec and voyage to the Isle St. Éloi. Meeting there with the Algonquins and Ochataiguins.

With this purpose, I set out on the 18th of the month. Here the river begins to widen, in some places to the breadth

---

[1] Claude Godet, Sieur des Marets. He married Jeanne, the only daughter of Pont Gravé. His younger brother Jean was the Sieur du Parc, afterwards mentioned.

of a league or a league and a half. The country becomes more
and more beautiful. There are hills along the river in part,
and in part it is a level country, with but few rocks. The river
itself is dangerous in many places, in consequence of its banks
and rocks; and it is not safe sailing without keeping the lead
in hand. The river is very abundant in many kinds of fish,
not only such as we have here, but others which we have not.
The country is thickly covered with massive and lofty forests,
of the same kind of trees as we have about our habitation.
There are also many vines and nut-trees on the bank of the
river, and many small brooks and streams which are only
navigable with canoes. We passed near Point St. Croix,
which many maintain, as I have said elsewhere, is the place
where Jacques Cartier spent the winter. This point is sandy,
extending some distance out into the river, and exposed to the
north-west wind, which beats upon it. There are some meadows, covered however every full tide, which falls nearly two
fathoms and a half. This passage is very dangerous on account
of the large number of rocks stretching across the river, although there is a good but very winding channel, where the
river runs like a race, rendering it necessary to take the proper
time for passing. This place has deceived many, who thought
they could only pass at high tide from there being no channel:
but we have now found the contrary to be true, for one can go
down at low tide; but it would be difficult to ascend, in consequence of the strong current, unless there were a good wind.
It is consequently necessary to wait until the tide is a third
flood, in order to pass, when the current in the channel is six,
eight, ten, twelve, and fifteen fathoms deep.

Continuing our course, we reached a very pleasant river,
nine leagues distant from St. Croix and twenty-four from
Quebec. This we named St. Mary's River.[1] The river all
the way from St. Croix is very pleasant.

Pursuing our route, I met some two or three hundred savages, who were encamped in huts near a little island called
St. Éloi, a league and a half distant from St. Mary. We

------

[1] Now the Sainte Anne.

made a reconnoissance, and found that they were tribes of savages, called Ochateguins and Algonquins, on their way to Quebec, to assist us in exploring the territory of the Iroquois, with whom they are in deadly hostility, sparing nothing belonging to their enemies.

After reconnoitring, I went on shore to see them, and inquired who their chief was. They told me there were two, one named Yroquet, and the other Ochasteguin, whom they pointed out to me. I went to their cabin, where they gave me a cordial reception, as is their custom.

I proceeded to inform them of the object of my voyage, with which they were greatly pleased. After some talk, I withdrew. Some time after, they came to my shallop, and presented me with some peltry, exhibiting many tokens of pleasure. Then they returned to the shore.

The next day, the two chiefs came to see me, when they remained some time without saying a word, meditating and smoking all the while. After due reflection, they began to harangue in a loud voice all their companions who were on the bank of the river, with their arms in their hands, and listening very attentively to what their chiefs said to them, which was as follows: that nearly ten moons ago, according to their mode of reckoning, the son of Yroquet had seen me, and that I had given him a good reception, and declared that Pont Gravé and I desired to assist them against their enemies, with whom they had for a long time been at warfare, on account of many cruel acts committed by them against their tribe, under color of friendship; that, having ever since longed for vengeance, they had solicited all the savages, whom I saw on the bank of the river, to come and make an alliance with us, and that their never having seen Christians also impelled them to come and visit us; that I should do with them and their companions as I wished; that they had no children with them, but men versed in war and full of courage, acquainted with the country and rivers in the land of the Iroquois; that now they entreated me to return to our settlement, that they might see our houses, and that, after three days, we should all

together come back to engage in the war; that, as a token of
firm friendship and joy, I should have muskets and arquebuses
fired, at which they would be greatly pleased. This I did,
when they uttered great cries of astonishment, especially those
who had never heard nor seen the like.

After hearing them, I replied that, if they desired, I should
be very glad to return to our settlement, to gratify them
still more; and that they might conclude that I had no other
purpose than to engage in the war, since we carried with us
nothing but arms, and not merchandise for barter, as they had
been given to understand; and that my only desire was to
fulfil what I had promised them; and that, if I had known
of any who had made evil reports to them, I should regard
them as enemies more than they did themselves. They told
me that they believed nothing of them, and that they never
had heard any one speak thus. But the contrary was the
case; for there were some savages who told it to ours. I contented myself with waiting for an opportunity to show them
in fact something more than they could have expected from
me.

Chapter 8

*Return to Quebec. Continuation afterwards with the savages to
the fall of the river of the Iroquois.*

The next day, we set out all together for our settlement,
where they enjoyed themselves some five or six days, which
were spent in dances and festivities, on account of their eagerness for us to engage in the war.

Pont Gravé came forthwith from Tadoussac with two little
barques full of men, in compliance with a letter, in which I
begged him to come as speedily as possible.

The savages seeing him arrive rejoiced more than ever, inasmuch as I told them that he had given some of his men to
assist them, and that perhaps we should go together.

On the 28th of the month,[1] we equipped some barques for assisting these savages. Pont Gravé embarked on one and I on the other, when we all set out together. The first of June,[2] we arrived at St. Croix, distant fifteen leagues from Quebec, where Pont Gravé and I concluded that, for certain reasons, I should go with the savages, and he to our settlement and to Tadoussac. This resolution being taken, I embarked in my shallop all that was necessary, together with Des Marais and La Routte, our pilot, and nine men.

I set out from St. Croix on the 3d of June[3] with all the savages. We passed the Trois Rivières,[4] a very beautiful country, covered with a growth of fine trees. From this place to St. Croix is a distance of fifteen leagues. At the mouth of the above-named river[5] there are six islands, three of which are very small, the others some fifteen to sixteen hundred paces long, very pleasant in appearance. Near Lake St. Peter,[6] some two leagues up the river, there is a little fall not very difficult to pass. This place is in latitude 46°, lacking some minutes. The savages of the country gave us to understand that some days' journey up this river there is a lake, through which the river flows. The length of the lake is ten days' journey, when some falls are passed, and afterwards three or four other lakes of five or six days' journey in length. Having reached the end of these, they go four or five leagues by land, and enter still another lake,[7] where the Sacqué has its principal source. From this lake, the savages go to Tadoussac. The Trois Rivières extends forty days' journey of the savages. They say that at the end of this river there is a people, who are great hunters, without a fixed abode, and who are less than six days' journey from the North Sea. What little of the country I have seen is sandy,

---

[1] June 28, 1609.   [2] July 1.   [3] July 3.
[4] Three Rivers, so called because the St. Maurice flows by three mouths into the St. Lawrence.
[5] *I.e.*, the St. Maurice.
[6] Cartier's Lake of Angoulême. *Early English and French Voyages,* p. 55.
[7] Lake St. John, the source of the Saguenay.

very high, with hills, covered with large quantities of pine and fir on the river border; but some quarter of a league inland the woods are very fine and open, and the country level.

Thence we continued our course to the entrance of Lake St. Peter, where the country is exceedingly pleasant and level, and crossed the lake, in two, three, and four fathoms of water, which is some eight leagues long and four wide. On the north side, we saw a very pleasant river, extending some twenty leagues into the interior, which I named St. Suzanne; on the south side, there are two, one called Rivière du Pont, the other, Rivière de Gennes, which are very pretty, and in a fine and fertile country.[1] The water is almost still in the lake, which is full of fish. On the north bank, there are seen some slight elevations at a distance of some twelve or fifteen leagues from the lake. After crossing the lake, we passed a large number of islands of various sizes, containing many nut-trees and vines, and fine meadows, with quantities of game and wild animals, which go over from the main land to these islands. Fish are here more abundant than in any other part of the river that we had seen. From these islands, we went to the mouth of the River of the Iroquois,[2] where we stayed two days, refreshing ourselves with good venison, birds, and fish, which the savages gave us. Here there sprang up among them some difference of opinion on the subject of the war, so that a portion only determined to go with me, while the others returned to their country with their wives and the merchandise which they had obtained by barter.

Setting out from the mouth of this river, which is some four hundred to five hundred paces broad, and very beautiful, running southward,[3] we arrived at a place in latitude 45°, and twenty-two or twenty-three leagues from the Trois Rivières. All this river from its mouth to the first fall, a distance

---

[1] Now Rivière du Loup, on the north side; on the south side are three, now called Nicolet, St. Francis, and Yamaska.

[2] Richelieu.

[3] Champlain went southward, but up-stream. The Richelieu flows northward.

of fifteen leagues, is very smooth, and bordered with woods,
like all the other places before named, and of the same sorts.
There are nine or ten fine islands before reaching the fall
of the Iroquois, which are a league or a league and a half
long, and covered with numerous oaks and nut-trees. The
river is nearly half a league wide in places, and very abundant in fish. We found in no place less than four feet of
water. The approach to the fall is a kind of lake,[1] where
the water descends, and which is some three leagues in circuit. There are here some meadows, but not inhabited by
savages on account of the wars. There is very little water at
the fall, which runs with great rapidity. There are also many
rocks and stones, so that the savages cannot go up by water,
although they go down very easily. All this region is very
level, covered with forests, vines, and nut-trees. No Christians
had been in this place before us; and we had considerable
difficulty in ascending the river with oars.

As soon as we had reached the fall, Des Marais, La Routte,
and I, with five men, went on shore to see whether we could
pass this place; but we went some league and a half without
seeing any prospect of being able to do so, finding only water
running with great swiftness, and in all directions many stones,
very dangerous, and with but little water about them. The
fall is perhaps six hundred paces broad. Finding that it was
impossible to cut a way through the woods with the small
number of men that I had, I determined, after consultation
with the rest, to change my original resolution, formed on the
assurance of the savages that the roads were easy, but which
we did not find to be the case, as I have stated. We accordingly returned to our shallop, where I had left some men as
guards, and to indicate to the savages upon their arrival that
we had gone to make explorations along the fall.

After making what observations I wished in this place, we
met, on returning, some savages, who had come to reconnoitre,
as we had done. They told us that all their companions had

---

[1] Chambly Basin, leading to Chambly rapids.

arrived at our shallop, where we found them greatly pleased, and delighted that we had gone in this manner without a guide, aided only by the reports they had several times made to us.

Having returned, and seeing the slight prospect there was of passing the fall with our shallop, I was much troubled. And it gave me especial dissatisfaction to go back without seeing a very large lake, filled with handsome islands, and with large tracts of fine land bordering on the lake, where their enemies live according to their representations. After duly thinking over the matter, I determined to go and fulfil my promise, and carry out my desire. Accordingly, I embarked with the savages in their canoes, taking with me two men, who went cheerfully. After making known my plan to Des Marais and others in the shallop, I requested the former to return to our settlement with the rest of our company, giving them the assurance that, in a short time, by God's grace, I would return to them.

I proceeded forthwith to have a conference with the captains of the savages, and gave them to understand that they had told me the opposite of what my observations found to be the case at the fall; namely, that it was impossible to pass it with the shallop, but that this would not prevent me from assisting them as I had promised. This communication troubled them greatly; and they desired to change their determination, but I urged them not to do so, telling them that they ought to carry out their first plan, and that I, with two others, would go to the war with them in their canoes, in order to show them that, as for me, I would not break my word given to them, although alone; but that I was unwilling then to oblige any one of my companions to embark, and would only take with me those who had the inclination to go, of whom I had found two.

They were greatly pleased at what I said to them, and at the determination which I had taken, promising, as before, to show me fine things.

Chapter 9

*Departure from the fall of the Iroquois River. Description of
a large lake. Encounter with the enemy at this lake;
their manner of attacking the Iroquois, and their behavior in battle.*

I set out accordingly from the fall of the Iroquois River
on the 2d of July.[1] All the savages set to carrying their
canoes, arms, and baggage overland, some half a league, in
order to pass by the violence and strength of the fall, which
was speedily accomplished. Then they put them all in the
water again, two men in each with the baggage; and they
caused one of the men of each canoe to go by land some three
leagues, the extent of the fall, which is not, however, so violent
here as at the mouth, except in some places, where rocks ob-
struct the river, which is not broader than three hundred or
four hundred paces. After we had passed the fall, which was
attended with difficulty, all the savages, who had gone by
land over a good path and level country, although there are
a great many trees, re-embarked in their canoes. My men
went also by land; but I went in a canoe. The savages
made a review of all their followers, finding that there were
twenty-four canoes, with sixty men. After the review was
completed, we continued our course to an island,[2] three leagues
long, filled with the finest pines I had ever seen. Here they
went hunting, and captured some wild animals. Proceeding
about three leagues farther on, we made a halt, in order to
rest the coming night.

They all at once set to work, some to cut wood, and others
to obtain the bark of trees for covering their cabins, for the
sake of sheltering themselves, others to fell large trees for
constructing a barricade on the river-bank around their cabins, which they do so quickly that in less than two hours so

---

[1] Read 12th of July.
[2] The Island of Ste. Thérèse (Laverdière); the Isle aux Noix (Slafter).

much is accomplished that five hundred of their enemies would find it very difficult to dislodge them without killing large numbers. They make no barricade on the river-bank, where their canoes are drawn up, in order that they may be able to embark, if occasion requires. After they were established in their cabins, they despatched three canoes, with nine good men, according to their custom in all their encampments, to reconnoitre for a distance of two or three leagues, to see if they can perceive anything, after which they return. They rest the entire night, depending upon the observation of these scouts, which is a very bad custom among them; for they are sometimes while sleeping surprised by their enemies, who slaughter them before they have time to get up and prepare for defence. Noticing this, I remonstrated with them on the mistake they made, and told them that they ought to keep watch, as they had seen us do every night, and have men on the lookout, in order to listen and see whether they perceived anything, and that they should not live in such a manner like beasts. They replied that they could not keep watch, and that they worked enough in the day-time in the chase, since, when engaged in war, they divide their troops into three parts: namely, a part for hunting scattered in several places; another to constitute the main body of their army, which is always under arms; and the third to act as *avant-coureurs*, to look out along the rivers, and observe whether they can see any mark or signal showing where their enemies or friends have passed. This they ascertain by certain marks which the chiefs of different tribes make known to each other; but, these not continuing always the same, they inform themselves from time to time of changes, by which means they ascertain whether they are enemies or friends who have passed. The hunters never hunt in advance of the main body, or *avant-coureurs*, so as not to excite alarm or produce disorder, but in the rear and in the direction from which they do not anticipate their enemy. Thus they advance until they are within two or three days' march of their enemies, when they proceed by night stealthily and all in a body, except the *van-couriers*.

By day, they withdraw into the interior of the woods, where they rest, without straying off, neither making any noise nor any fire, even for the sake of cooking, so as not to be noticed in case their enemies should by accident pass by. They make no fire, except in smoking, which amounts to almost nothing. They eat baked Indian meal, which they soak in water, when it becomes a kind of porridge. They provide themselves with such meal to meet their wants, when they are near their enemies, or when retreating after a charge, in which case they are not inclined to hunt, retreating immediately.

In all their encampments, they have their Pilotois, or Ostemoy, a class of persons who play the part of soothsayers, in whom these people have faith. One of these builds a cabin, surrounds it with small pieces of wood, and covers it with his robe: after it is built, he places himself inside, so as not to be seen at all, when he seizes and shakes one of the posts of his cabin, muttering some words between his teeth, by which he says he invokes the devil, who appears to him in the form of a stone, and tells him whether they will meet their enemies and kill many of them. This Pilotois lies prostrate on the ground, motionless, only speaking with the devil: on a sudden, he rises to his feet, talking, and tormenting himself in such a manner that, although naked, he is all of a perspiration. All the people surround the cabin, seated on their buttocks, like apes. They frequently told me that the shaking of the cabin, which I saw, proceeded from the devil, who made it move, and not the man inside, although I could see the contrary; for, as I have stated above, it was the Pilotois who took one of the supports of the cabin, and made it move in this manner. They told me also that I should see fire come out from the top, which I did not see at all. These rogues counterfeit also their voice, so that it is heavy and clear, and speak in a language unknown to the other savages. And, when they represent it as broken, the savages think that the devil is speaking, and telling them what is to happen in their war, and what they must do.

But all these scapegraces, who play the soothsayer, out of a hundred words do not speak two that are true, and impose upon these poor people. There are enough like them in the world, who take food from the mouths of the people by their impostures, as these worthies do. I often remonstrated with the people, telling them that all they did was sheer nonsense, and that they ought not to put confidence in them.

Now, after ascertaining from their soothsayers what is to be their fortune, the chiefs take sticks a foot long, and as many as there are soldiers. They take others, somewhat larger, to indicate the chiefs. Then they go into the wood, and seek out a level place, five or six feet square, where the chief, as sergeant-major, puts all the sticks in such order as seems to him best. Then he calls all his companions, who come all armed; and he indicates to them the rank and order they are to observe in battle with their enemies. All the savages watch carefully this proceeding, observing attentively the outline which their chief has made with the sticks. Then they go away, and set to placing themselves in such order as the sticks were in, when they mingle with each other, and return again to their proper order, which manœuvre they repeat two or three times, and at all their encampments, without needing a sergeant to keep them in the proper order, which they are able to keep accurately without any confusion. This is their rule in war.

We set out on the next day, continuing our course in the river as far as the entrance of the lake. There are many pretty islands here, low, and containing very fine woods and meadows, with abundance of fowl and such animals of the chase as stags, fallow-deer, fawns, roe-bucks, bears, and others, which go from the main land to these islands. We captured a large number of these animals. There are also many beavers, not only in this river, but also in numerous other little ones that flow into it. These regions, although they are pleasant, are not inhabited by any savages, on account of their wars; but they withdraw as far as possible from the rivers into the interior, in order not to be suddenly surprised.

The next day we entered the lake,[1] which is of great extent, say eighty or a hundred leagues long, where I saw four fine islands, ten, twelve, and fifteen leagues long, which were formerly inhabited by the savages, like the River of the Iroquois; but they have been abandoned since the wars of the savages with one another prevail. There are also many rivers falling into the lake, bordered by many fine trees of the same kinds as those we have in France, with many vines finer than any I have seen in any other place; also many chestnut-trees on the border of this lake, which I had not seen before. There is also a great abundance of fish, of many varieties; among others, one called by the savages of the country *Chaousarou*,[2] which varies in length, the largest being, as the people told me, eight or ten feet long. I saw some five feet long, which were as large as my thigh; the head being as big as my two fists, with a snout two feet and a half long, and a double row of very sharp and dangerous teeth. Its body is, in shape, much like that of a pike; but it is armed with scales so strong that a poniard could not pierce them. Its color is silver-gray. The extremity of its snout is like that of swine. This fish makes war upon all others in the lakes and rivers. It also possesses remarkable dexterity, as these people informed me, which is exhibited in the following manner. When it wants to capture birds, it swims in among the rushes, or reeds, which are found on the banks of the lake in several places, where it puts its snout out of water and keeps perfectly still: so that, when the birds come and light on its snout, supposing it to be only the stump of a tree, it adroitly closes it, which it had kept ajar, and pulls the birds by the feet down under water. The savages gave me the head of one of them, of which they make great account, saying that, when they have the headache, they bleed themselves with the teeth of this fish on the spot where they suffer pain, when it suddenly passes away.

[1] Lake Champlain. The distances are at least threefold overstated. In 1632 he reduces the length to fifty or sixty leagues, though leaving the dimensions of the islands unchanged.   [2] The garpike.

M

Continuing our course over this lake on the western side, I noticed, while observing the country, some very high mountains on the eastern side, on the top of which there was snow.[1] I made inquiry of the savages whether these localities were inhabited, when they told me that the Iroquois dwelt there, and that there were beautiful valleys in these places, with plains productive in grain, such as I had eaten in this country, together with many kinds of fruit without limit. They said also that the lake extended near mountains, some twenty-five leagues distant from us, as I judge. I saw, on the south, other mountains, no less high than the first, but without any snow.[2] The savages told me that these mountains were thickly settled, and that it was there we were to find their enemies; but that it was necessary to pass a fall[3] in order to go there (which I afterwards saw), when we should enter another lake,[4] nine or ten leagues long. After reaching the end of the lake, we should have to go, they said, two leagues by land, and pass through a river[5] flowing into the sea on the Norumbegue coast, near that of Florida, whither it took them only two days to go by canoe, as I have since ascertained from some prisoners we captured, who gave me minute information in regard to all they had personal knowledge of, through some Algonquin interpreters, who understood the Iroquois language.

Now, as we began to approach within two or three days' journey of the abode of their enemies, we advanced only at night, resting during the day. But they did not fail to practise constantly their accustomed superstitions, in order to ascertain what was to be the result of their undertaking; and they often asked me if I had had a dream, and seen their enemies, to which I replied in the negative. Yet I did not cease to encourage them, and inspire in them hope. When

---

[1] The Green Mountains of Vermont. "Champlain was probably deceived as to the snow on their summits in July. What he saw was doubtless white limestone." (Slafter.)

[2] The Adirondacks.   [3] Ticonderoga.   [4] Lake George.

[5] The Hudson, separated only by a small portage from Lake George.

night came, we set out on the journey until the next day, when we withdrew into the interior of the forest, and spent the rest of the day there. About ten or eleven o'clock, after taking a little walk about our encampment, I retired. While sleeping, I dreamed that I saw our enemies, the Iroquois, drowning in the lake near a mountain, within sight. When I expressed a wish to help them, our allies, the savages, told me we must let them all die, and that they were of no importance. When I awoke, they did not fail to ask me, as usual, if I had had a dream. I told them that I had, in fact, had a dream. This, upon being related, gave them so much confidence that they did not doubt any longer that good was to happen to them.

When it was evening, we embarked in our canoes to continue our course; and, as we advanced very quietly and without making any noise, we met on the 29th of the month the Iroquois, about ten o'clock at evening, at the extremity of a cape[1] which extends into the lake on the western bank. They had come to fight. We both began to utter loud cries, all getting their arms in readiness. We withdrew out on the water, and the Iroquois went on shore, where they drew up all their canoes close to each other and began to fell trees with poor axes, which they acquire in war sometimes, using also others of stone. Thus they barricaded themselves very well.

Our forces also passed the entire night, their canoes being drawn up close to each other, and fastened to poles, so that they might not get separated, and that they might be all in readiness to fight, if occasion required. We were out upon the water, within arrow range of their barricades. When they were armed and in array, they despatched two canoes by themselves to the enemy to inquire if they wished to fight, to which the latter replied that they wanted nothing else: but they said that, at present, there was not much light, and that it would be necessary to wait for daylight, so as to be able to

[1] Crown Point (Laverdière). The ensuing battle took place at or near Ticonderoga.

recognize each other; and that, as soon as the sun rose, they would offer us battle. This was agreed to by our side. Meanwhile, the entire night was spent in dancing and singing, on both sides, with endless insults and other talk; as, how little courage we had, how feeble a resistance we should make against their arms, and that, when day came, we should realize it to our ruin. Ours also were not slow in retorting, telling them they would see such execution of arms as never before, together with an abundance of such talk as is not unusual in the siege of a town. After this singing, dancing, and bandying words on both sides to the fill, when day came, my companions and myself continued under cover, for fear that the enemy would see us. We arranged our arms in the best manner possible, being, however, separated, each in one of the canoes of the savage Montagnais. After arming ourselves with light armor, we each took an arquebuse, and went on shore. I saw the enemy go out of their barricade, nearly two hundred in number, stout and rugged[1] in appearance. They came at a slow pace towards us, with a dignity and assurance which greatly amused[2] me, having three chiefs at their head. Our men also advanced in the same order, telling me that those who had three large plumes were the chiefs, and that they had only these three, and that they could be distinguished by these plumes, which were much larger than those of their companions, and that I should do what I could to kill them. I promised to do all in my power, and said that I was very sorry they could not understand me, so that I might give order and shape to their mode of attacking their enemies, and then we should, without doubt, defeat them all; but that this

[1] "Robust" would be a better translation.

[2] "Pleased" or "delighted" would be more accurate. "A deliberation and gravity that gave him a soldier's content," says H. D. Sedgwick in his *Champlain* (Boston, 1902); "a steadiness which excited the admiration of Champlain" (Parkman). The Iroquois owed their strength not so much to their ferocity, for they were naturally less warlike than the Algonquins, but to their superior discipline.

This mode of fighting, in close array, shown also in a drawing which in the original accompanies this portion of the text, contrasts strongly with that which the Indians followed after they became acquainted with fire-arms.

could not now be obviated, and that I should be very glad to show them my courage and good-will when we should engage in the fight.

As soon as we had landed, they began to run for some two hundred paces towards their enemies, who stood firmly, not having as yet noticed my companions, who went into the woods with some savages. Our men began to call me with loud cries; and, in order to give me a passage-way, they opened in two parts, and put me at their head, where I marched some twenty paces in advance of the rest, until I was within about thirty paces of the enemy, who at once noticed me, and, halting, gazed at me, as I did also at them. When I saw them making a move to fire at us, I rested my musket against my cheek, and aimed directly at one of the three chiefs. With the same shot, two fell to the ground; and one of their men was so wounded that he died some time after. I had loaded my musket with four balls. When our side saw this shot so favorable for them, they began to raise such loud cries that one could not have heard it thunder. Meanwhile, the arrows flew on both sides. The Iroquois were greatly astonished that two men had been so quickly killed, although they were equipped with armor woven from cotton thread, and with wood which was proof against their arrows. This caused great alarm among them. As I was loading again, one of my companions fired a shot from the woods, which astonished them anew to such a degree that, seeing their chiefs dead, they lost courage, and took to flight, abandoning their camp and fort, and fleeing into the woods, whither I pursued them, killing still more of them. Our savages also killed several of them, and took ten or twelve prisoners. The remainder escaped with the wounded. Fifteen or sixteen were wounded on our side with arrow-shots; but they were soon healed.[1]

[1] Champlain has been greatly blamed for thus rousing the fury of the Iroquois. But while he probably underestimated their power, he could hardly avoid taking part with the Hurons and Algonquins against them, if either trade or colonization was to proceed with any security.

In his autograph letter of 1635 to Richelieu he urges a vigorous Indian

After gaining the victory, our men amused themselves by taking a great quantity of Indian corn and some meal from their enemies, also their armor, which they had left behind that they might run better. After feasting sumptuously, dancing and singing, we returned three hours after, with the prisoners. The spot where this attack took place is in latitude 43° and some minutes, and the lake was called Lake Champlain.

Chapter 10

Return from the battle, and what took place on the way.

After going some eight leagues, towards evening they took one of the prisoners, to whom they made a harangue, enumerating the cruelties which he and his men had already practised towards them without any mercy, and that, in like manner, he ought to make up his mind to receive as much. They commanded him to sing, if he had courage, which he did; but it was a very sad song.

Meanwhile, our men kindled a fire; and, when it was well burning, they each took a brand, and burned this poor creature gradually, so as to make him suffer greater torment. Sometimes they stopped, and threw water on his back. Then they tore out his nails, and applied fire to the extremities of his fingers and private member. Afterwards, they flayed the top of his head,[1] and had a kind of gum poured all hot upon

policy, and promises utterly to crush the Iroquois with one hundred and twenty light-armed troops.

These vigorous measures were not taken, and the Iroquois, supplied with fire-arms by the Dutch and English settlers of New York, long harassed the French settlements. At the time of the battle, Henry Hudson's ship, the *Half Moon*, was at anchor in Penobscot Bay. The Dutch and English whom he represented won a friend unknown to themselves when Champlain routed the Iroquois.

[1] Scalping was the habit of the Canadian Indians, whereas it was in these early days the habit of the Indians of southern New England to behead. Friederici, *Skalpieren und ähnliche Gebräuche* (Braunschweig, 1906), pp. 14, 15.

it; then they pierced his arms near the wrists, and, drawing up the sinews with sticks, they tore them out by force; but, seeing that they could not get them, they cut them. This poor wretch uttered terrible cries, and it excited my pity to see him treated in this manner, and yet showing such firmness that one would have said, at times, that he suffered hardly any pain at all. I remonstrated with them, saying that we practised no such cruelties, but killed them at once; and that, if they wished me to fire a musket-shot at him, I should be willing to do so. They refused, saying that he would not in that case suffer any pain. I went away from them, pained to see such cruelties as they practised upon his body. When they saw that I was displeased, they called me, and told me to fire a musket-shot at him. This I did without his seeing it, and thus put an end, by a single shot, to all the torments he would have suffered, rather than see him tyrannized over. After his death, they were not yet satisfied, but opened him, and threw his entrails into the lake. Then they cut off his head, arms, and legs, which they scattered in different directions; keeping the scalp, which they had flayed off, as they had done in the case of all the rest whom they had killed in the contest. They were guilty also of another monstrosity in taking his heart, cutting it into several pieces, and giving it to a brother of his to eat, as also to others of his companions, who were prisoners: they took it into their mouths, but would not swallow it. Some Algonquin savages, who were guarding them, made some of them spit it out, when they threw it into the water. This is the manner in which these people behave towards those whom they capture in war, for whom it would be better to die fighting, or to kill themselves on the spur of the moment, as many do, rather than fall into the hands of their enemies. After this execution, we set out on our return with the rest of the prisoners, who kept singing as they went along, with no better hopes for the future than he had had who was so wretchedly treated.

Having arrived at the falls of the Iroquois, the Algonquins returned to their own country; so also the Ochateguins, with a part of the prisoners: well satisfied with the results of the war, and that I had accompanied them so readily. We separated accordingly with loud protestations of mutual friendship; and they asked me whether I would not like to go into their country, to assist them with continued fraternal relations; and I promised that I would do so.

I returned with the Montagnais. After informing myself from the prisoners in regard to their country, and of its probable extent, we packed up the baggage for the return, which was accomplished with such despatch that we went every day in their canoes twenty-five or thirty leagues, which was their usual rate of travelling. When we arrived at the mouth of the river Iroquois, some of the savages dreamed that their enemies were pursuing them. This dream led them to move their camp forthwith, although the night was very inclement on account of the wind and rain; and they went and passed the remainder of the night, from fear of their enemies, amid high reeds on Lake St. Peter. Two days after, we arrived at our settlement, where I gave them some bread and peas; also some beads, which they asked me for, in order to ornament the heads of their enemies, for the purpose of merry-making upon their return. The next day, I went with them in their canoes as far as Tadoussac, in order to witness their ceremonies. On approaching the shore, they each took a stick, to the end of which they hung the heads of their enemies, who had been killed, together with some beads, all of them singing. When they were through with this, the women undressed themselves, so as to be in a state of entire nudity, when they jumped into the water, and swam to the prows of the canoes to take the heads of their enemies, which were on the ends of long poles before their boats: then they hung them about their necks, as if it had been some costly chain, singing and dancing meanwhile. Some days after, they presented me with one of these heads, as if it were something very precious; and also with a pair of arms taken from their enemies, to keep and show to the king. This, for the sake of gratifying them, I promised to do.

After some days, I went to Quebec, whither some Algonquin savages came, expressing their regret at not being present at the defeat of their enemies, and presenting me with
some furs, in consideration of my having gone there and
assisted their friends.

Some days after they had set out for their country, distant
about a hundred and twenty leagues from our settlement, I
went to Tadoussac to see whether Pont Gravé had returned
from Gaspé, whither he had gone. He did not arrive until
the next day, when he told me that he had decided to return
to France. We concluded to leave an upright man, Captain
Pierre Chavin of Dieppe, to command at Quebec, until Sieur
de Monts should arrange matters there.

Chapter 11

*Return to France, and what occurred up to the time of
re-embarkation.*

After forming this resolution, we went to Quebec to establish him in authority, and leave him every thing requisite
and necessary for the settlement, together with fifteen men.
Every thing being arranged, we set out on the first day of
September for Tadoussac, in order to fit out our vessel for
returning to France.

We set out accordingly from the latter place on the 5th
of the month, and on the 8th anchored at Isle Percée. On
Thursday the 10th, we set out from there, and on the 18th,
the Tuesday following, we arrived at the Grand Bank. On
the 2d of October, we got soundings. On the 8th, we anchored at Conquet [1] in Lower Brittany. On Saturday the
10th, we set out from there, arriving at Honfleur on the 13th.

After disembarking, I did not wait long before taking post
to go to Sieur de Monts, who was then at Fontainebleau,

---

[1] In the department of Finisterre, thirteen miles west of Brest.

where His Majesty was. Here I reported to him in detail all that had transpired in regard to the winter quarters and our new explorations, and my hopes for the future in view of the promises of the savages called Ochateguins, who are good Iroquois.[1] The other Iroquois, their enemies, dwell more to the south. The language of the former does not differ much from that of the people recently discovered and hitherto unknown to us, which they understand when spoken.

I at once waited upon His Majesty, and gave him an account of my voyage, which afforded him pleasure and satisfaction. I had a girdle made of porcupine quills, very well worked, after the manner of the country where it was made, and which His Majesty thought very pretty. I had also two little birds, of the size of blackbirds and of a carnation color;[2] also, the head of a fish caught in the great lake of the Iroquois, having a very long snout and two or three rows of very sharp teeth. A representation of this fish may be found on the great lake, on my geographical map.

After I had concluded my interview with His Majesty Sieur de Monts determined to go to Rouen to meet his associates, the Sieurs Collier and Le Gendre, merchants of Rouen, to consider what should be done the coming year. They resolved to continue the settlement, and finish the explorations up the great river St. Lawrence, in accordance with the promises of the Ochateguins, made on condition that we should assist them in their wars, as I had given them to understand.

Pont Gravé was appointed to go to Tadoussac, not only for traffic, but to engage in anything else that might realize means for defraying the expenses.

Sieur Lucas Le Gendre, of Rouen, one of the partners, was ordered to see to the purchase of merchandise and supplies, the repair of the vessels, obtaining crews, and other things necessary for the voyage.

---

[1] The Ochateguins, called by the French Hurons, from their manner of doing their hair (*hure* = a wild boar's head), were a branch of the Iroquois nation, though at this time at deadly feud with them. Their real name was Yendots or Wyandots.

[2] The scarlet tanager.

After these matters were arranged, Sieur de Monts returned to Paris, I accompanying him, where I stayed until the end of February.   During this time, Sieur de Monts endeavored to obtain a new commission for trading in the newly discovered regions, and where no one had traded before.   This he was unable to accomplish, although his requests and proposals were just and reasonable.

But, finding that there was no hope of obtaining this commission, he did not cease to prosecute his plan, from his desire that every thing might turn out to the profit and honor of France.

During this time, Sieur de Monts did not express to me his pleasure in regard to me personally, until I told him it had been reported to me that he did not wish to have me winter in Canada, which, however, was not true, for he referred the whole matter to my pleasure.

I provided myself with whatever was desirable and necessary for spending the winter at our settlement in Quebec. For this purpose I set out from Paris the last day of February following, and proceeded to Honfleur, where the embarkation was to be made.   I went by way of Rouen, where I stayed two days.   Thence I went to Honfleur, where I found Pont Gravé and Le Gendre, who told me they had embarked what was necessary for the settlement.   I was very glad to find that we were ready to set sail, but uncertain whether the supplies were good and adequate for our sojourn and for spending the winter.

THE SECOND VOYAGE TO NEW FRANCE
IN THE YEAR 1610

THE SECOND[1] VOYAGE TO NEW FRANCE IN THE YEAR 1610

Chapter 1

Departure from France to return to New France, and occurrences until our arrival at the settlement.

THE weather having become favorable, I embarked at Honfleur with a number of artisans on the 7th of the month of March. But, encountering bad weather in the Channel, we were obliged to put in on the English coast at a place called Porlan,[2] in the roadstead of which we stayed some days, when we weighed anchor for the Isle d'Huy,[3] near the English coast, since we found the roadstead of Porlan very bad. When near this island, so dense a fog arose, that we were obliged to put in at the Hougue.[4]

Ever since the departure from Honfleur, I had been afflicted with a very severe illness, which took away my hopes of being able to make the voyage; so that I embarked in a boat to return to Havre in France, to be treated there, being very ill on board the vessel. My expectation was, on recovering my health, to embark again in another vessel, which had not yet left Honfleur, in which Des Marais, son-in-law of Pont Gravé, was to embark; but I had myself carried, still very ill, to Honfleur, where the vessel on which I had set out put in on the 15th of March, for some ballast, which it needed in order to be properly trimmed. Here it remained until the 8th of April. During this time, I recovered in a great degree; and, though still feeble and weak, I nevertheless embarked again.

[1] The second in which Champlain had had full responsibility.
[2] Portland.   [3] The Isle of Wight.
[4] A hamlet in the Isle of Wight.

We set out anew on the 18th[1] of April, arriving at the Grand Bank on the 19th, and sighting the Islands of St. Pierre on the 22d. When off Menthane, we met a vessel from St. Malo, on which was a young man, who, while drinking to the health of Pont Gravé, lost control of himself and was thrown into the sea by the motion of the vessel and drowned, it being impossible to render him assistance on account of the violence of the wind.

On the 26th of the month, we arrived at Tadoussac, where there were vessels which had arrived on the 18th, a thing which had not been seen for more than sixty years,[2] as the old mariners said who sail regularly to this country. This was owing to the mild winter and the small amount of ice, which did not prevent the entrance of these vessels. We learned from a young nobleman, named Sieur du Parc,[3] who had spent the winter at our settlement, that all his companions were in good health, only a few having been ill, and they but slightly. He also informed us that there had been scarcely any winter, and that they had usually had fresh meat the entire season, and that their hardest task had been to keep up good cheer.

This winter shows how those undertaking in future such enterprises ought to proceed, it being very difficult to make a new settlement without labor; and without encountering adverse fortune the first year, as has been the case in all our first settlements. But, in fact, by avoiding salt food and using fresh meat, the health is as good here as in France.

The savages had been waiting from day to day for us to go to the war with them. When they learned that Pont Gravé and I had arrived together, they rejoiced greatly, and came to speak with us.

[1] Read 8th. Laverdière ingeniously suggests that the manuscript read *le dit huit*, changed by the printer to *le dix-huit*.

[2] The Abbé Ferland, *Cours d'Histoire du Canada*, p. 157, points out that this implies that for more than sixty years the Basque, Breton, and Norman adventurers had pushed their journeys in quest of fish and fur as far as Tadoussac.

[3] Brother of Des Marais, or Des Marets, previously mentioned.

I went on shore to assure them that we would go with them, in conformity with the promises they had made me, namely, that upon our return from the war they would show me the Trois Rivières, and take me to a sea so large that the end of it cannot be seen, whence we should return by way of the Saguenay to Tadoussac. I asked them if they still had this intention, to which they replied that they had, but that it could not be carried out before the next year, which pleased [1] me. But I had promised the Algonquins and Ochateguins that I would assist them also in their wars, they having promised to show me their country, the great lake, some copper mines, and other things, which they had indicated to me. I accordingly had two strings to my bow, so that, in case one should break, the other might hold.

On the 28th of the month, I set out from Tadoussac for Quebec, where I found Captain Pierre,[2] who commanded there, and all his companions in good health. There was also a savage captain with them, named Batiscan,[3] with some of his companions, who were awaiting us, and who were greatly pleased at my arrival, singing and dancing the entire evening. I provided a banquet for them, which gratified them very much. They had a good meal, for which they were very thankful, and invited me with seven others to an entertainment of theirs, not a small mark of respect with them. We each one carried a porringer, according to custom, and brought it home full of meat, which we gave to whomsoever we pleased.

Some days after I had set out from Tadoussac, the Montagnais arrived at Quebec, to the number of sixty able-bodied men, *en route* for the war. They tarried here some days, enjoying themselves, and not omitting to ply me frequently with questions, to assure themselves that I would not fail in

---

[1] Read "displeased." Between "du plaisir" and "du déplaisir" confusion was easy.

[2] Pierre Chavin. See p. 169.

[3] The name is perpetuated in that of a river and a harbor between Quebec and Montreal.

N

my promises to them.   I assured them, and again made
promises to them, asking them if they had found me breaking
my word in the past.   They were greatly pleased when I
renewed my promises to them.

They said to me: "Here are numerous Basques and Misti-
goches" (this is the name they give to the Normans and
people of St. Malo), "who say they will go to the war with
us.   What do you think of it?   Do they speak the truth?"
I answered no, and that I knew very well what they really
meant; that they said this only to get possession of their com-
modities.   They replied to me : "You have spoken the truth.
They are women, and want to make war only upon our beavers."
They went on talking still farther in a facetious mood, and in
regard to the manner and order of going to the war.

They determined to set out, and await me at the Trois
Rivières, thirty leagues above Quebec, where I had promised
to join them, together with four barques loaded with merchandise, in order to traffic in peltries, among others with
the Ochateguins, who were to await me at the mouth of the
river of the Iroquois, as they had promised the year before,
and to bring there as many as four hundred men to go to
the war.

Chapter 2

*Departure from Quebec to assist our allied savages in their war
against the Iroquois, their enemies; and all that transpired until our return to the settlement.*

I set out from Quebec on the 14th of June, to meet the Montagnais, Algonquins, and Ochateguins, who were to be at the
mouth of the river of the Iroquois.   When I was eight leagues
from Quebec, I met a canoe, containing two savages, one an
Algonquin, and the other a Montagnais, who entreated me to
advance as rapidly as possible, saying that the Algonquins and
Ochateguins would in two days be at the rendezvous, to the
number of two hundred, with two hundred others to come a

little later, together with Yroquet, one of their chiefs. They asked me if I was satisfied with the coming of these savages. I told them I could not be displeased at it, since they had kept their word. They came on board my barque, where I gave them a good entertainment. Shortly after conferring with them about many matters concerning their wars, the Algonquin savage, one of their chiefs, drew from a sack a piece of copper a foot long, which he gave me. This was very handsome and quite pure. He gave me to understand that there were large quantities where he had taken this, which was on the bank of a river, near a great lake. He said that they gathered it in lumps, and, having melted it,[1] spread it in sheets, smoothing it with stones. I was very glad of this present, although of small value.

Arriving at Trois Rivières, I found all the Montagnais awaiting me, and the four barques as I stated above, which had gone to trade with them.

The savages were delighted to see me, and I went on shore to speak with them. They entreated me, together with my companions, to embark on their canoes and no others, when we went to the war, saying that they were our old friends. This I promised them, telling them that I desired to set out at once, since the wind was favorable; and that my barque was not so swift as their canoes, for which reason I desired to go on in advance. They earnestly entreated me to wait until the morning of the next day, when we would all go together, adding that they would not go faster than I should. Finally, to satisfy them, I promised to do this, at which they were greatly pleased.

On the following day, we all set out together, and continued our route until the morning of the next day, the 19th of the month, when we arrived at an island [2] off the river of the Iroquois, and waited for the Algonquins, who were

---

[1] This, with what Cartier says, *Early English and French Voyages*, p. 72, proves that the Indians had the arts of melting and beating copper, though of iron they were ignorant before the coming of the whites.

[2] Isle St. Ignace.

to be there the same day.   While the Montagnais were felling
trees to clear a place for dancing, and for arranging themselves
for the arrival of the Algonquins, an Algonquin canoe was
suddenly seen coming in haste, to bring word that the Algonquins had fallen in with a hundred Iroquois, who were strongly
barricaded, and that it would be difficult to conquer them,
unless they should come speedily, together with the Mati-
goches, as they call us.

The alarm at once sounded among them, and each one got
into his canoe with his arms.   They were quickly in readiness,
but with confusion; for they were so precipitate that, instead
of making haste, they hindered one another.   They came to
our barque and the others, begging me, together with my companions, to go with them in their canoes, and they were so
urgent that I embarked with four others.   I requested our
pilot, La Routte, to stay in the barque, and send me some four
or five more of my companions, if the other barques would
send some shallops with men to aid us; for none of the barques
were inclined to go with the savages, except Captain Thibaut,
who, having a barque there, went with me.   The savages cried
out to those who remained, saying that they were woman-hearted,
and that all they could do was to make war upon their peltry.

Meanwhile, after going some half a league, all the savages
crossing the river landed, and, leaving their canoes, took their
bucklers, bows, arrows, clubs, and swords, which they attach
to the end of large sticks, and proceeded to make their way in
the woods, so fast that we soon lost sight of them, they leaving
us, five in number, without guides.   This displeased us; but,
keeping their tracks constantly in sight, we followed them,
although we were often deceived.   We went through dense
woods, and over swamps and marshes, with the water always
up to our knees, greatly encumbered by a pike-man's corselet,
with which each one was armed.   We were also tormented in
a grievous and unheard-of manner by quantities of mosquitoes, which were so thick that they scarcely permitted us to
draw breath.   After going about half a league under these
circumstances, and no longer knowing where we were, we per-

ceived two savages passing through the woods, to whom we called and told them to stay with us, and guide us to the whereabouts of the Iroquois, otherwise we could not go there, and should get lost in the woods. They stayed to guide us. After proceeding a short distance, we saw a savage coming in haste to us, to induce us to advance as rapidly as possible, giving me to understand that the Algonquins and Montagnais had tried to force the barricade of the Iroquois but had been repulsed, that some of the best men of the Montagnais had been killed in the attempt, and several wounded, and that they had retired to wait for us, in whom was their only hope. We had not gone an eighth of a league with this savage, who was an Algonquin captain, before we heard the yells and cries on both sides, as they jeered at each other, and were skirmishing slightly while awaiting us. As soon as the savages perceived us, they began to shout, so that one could not have heard it thunder. I gave orders to my companions to follow me steadily, and not to leave me on any account. I approached the barricade of the enemy, in order to reconnoitre it. It was constructed of large trees placed one upon another, and of a circular shape, the usual form of their fortifications. All the Montagnais and Algonquins approached likewise the barricade. Then we commenced firing numerous musket-shots through the brush-wood, since we could not see them, as they could us. I was wounded while firing my first shot at the side of their barricade by an arrow, which pierced the end of my ear and entered my neck. I seized the arrow, and tore it from my neck. The end of it was armed with a very sharp stone. One of my companions also was wounded at the same time in the arm by an arrow, which I tore out for him. Yet my wound did not prevent me from doing my duty: our savages also, on their part, as well as the enemy, did their duty, so that you could see the arrows fly on all sides as thick as hail.[1] The Iroquois were astonished at

---

[1] If Champlain's drawing may be trusted, the Indians fired high in air, that their arrows might come down upon the heads of their enemies. The stockade was of course roofless.

the noise of our muskets, and especially that the balls penetrated better than their arrows.   They were so frightened at the effect produced that, seeing several of their companions fall wounded and dead, they threw themselves on the ground whenever they heard a discharge, supposing that the shots were sure.   We scarcely ever missed firing two or three balls at one shot, resting our muskets most of the time on the side of their barricade.   But, seeing that our ammunition began to fail, I said to all the savages that it was necessary to break down their barricades and capture them by storm; and that, in order to accomplish this, they must take their shields, cover themselves with them, and thus approach so near as to be able to fasten stout ropes to the posts that supported the barricades, and pull them down by main strength, in that way making an opening large enough to permit them to enter the fort.   I told them that we would meanwhile, by our musketry-fire, keep off the enemy, as they endeavored to prevent them from accomplishing this; also that a number of them should get behind some large trees, which were near the barricade, in order to throw them down upon the enemy, and that others should protect these with their shields, in order to keep the enemy from injuring them.   All this they did very promptly.   And, as they were about finishing the work, the barques, distant a league and a half, hearing the reports of our muskets, knew that we were engaged in conflict; and a young man from St. Malo, full of courage, Des Prairies by name, who like the rest had come with his barque to engage in peltry traffic, said to his companions that it was a great shame to let me fight in this way with the savages without coming to my assistance; that for his part he had too high a sense of honor to permit him to do so, and that he did not wish to expose himself to this reproach.   Accordingly, he determined to come to me in a shallop with some of his companions, together with some of mine whom he took with him. Immediately upon his arrival, he went towards the fort of the Iroquois, situated on the bank of the river.   Here he landed, and came to find me.   Upon seeing him, I ordered

our savages who were breaking down the fortress to stop, so
that the new-comers might have their share of the sport. I
requested Sieur des Prairies and his companions to fire some
salvos of musketry, before our savages should carry by storm
the enemy, as they had decided to do. This they did, each
one firing several shots, in which all did their duty well.
After they had fired enough, I addressed myself to our savages, urging them to finish the work. Straightway, they
approached the barricade, as they had previously done, while
we on the flank were to fire at those who should endeavor
to keep them from breaking it down. They behaved so well
and bravely that, with the help of our muskets, they made an
opening, which, however, was difficult to go through, as there
was still left a portion as high as a man, there being also
branches of trees there which had been beaten down, forming
a serious obstacle. But, when I saw that the entrance was
quite practicable, I gave orders not to fire any more, which they
obeyed. At the same instant, some twenty or thirty, both of
savages and of our own men, entered, sword in hand, without finding much resistance. Immediately, all who were
unharmed took to flight. But they did not proceed far; for
they were brought down by those around the barricade, and
those who escaped were drowned in the river. We captured
some fifteen prisoners, the rest being killed by musket-shots,
arrows, and the sword. When the fight was over, there came
another shallop, containing some of my companions. This,
although behind time, was yet in season for the booty, which,
however, was not of much account. There were only robes
of beaver-skin, and dead bodies covered with blood, which
the savages would not take the trouble to plunder, laughing
at those in the last shallop, who did so; for the others did not
engage in such low business. This, then, is the victory obtained by God's grace, for gaining which they gave us much
praise.

The savages scalped the dead, and took the heads as a
trophy of victory, according to their custom. They returned
with fifty wounded Montagnais and Algonquins and three dead,

singing and leading their prisoners with them.   They attached to sticks in the prows of their canoes the heads and a dead body cut into quarters, to eat in revenge, as they said.   In this way they went to our barques off the River of the Iroquois.

My companions and I embarked in a shallop, where I had my wound dressed by the surgeon, De Boyer, of Rouen, who likewise had come here for the purpose of traffic.   The savages spent all this day in dancing and singing.

The next day, Sieur de Pont Gravé arrived with another shallop, loaded with merchandise.   Moreover, there was also a barque containing Captain Pierre, which he had left behind, it being able to come only with difficulty, as it was rather heavy and a poor sailer.

The same day there was some trading in peltry, but the other barques carried off the better part of the booty.   It was doing them a great favor to search out a strange people for them, that they might afterwards carry off the profit without any risk or danger.

That day, I asked the savages for an Iroquois prisoner which they had, and they gave him to me.   What I did for him was not a little; for I saved him from many tortures which he must have suffered in company with his fellow-prisoners, whose nails they tore out, also cutting off their fingers, and burning them in several places.   They put to death on the same day two or three, and, in order to increase their torture, treated them in the following manner.

They took the prisoners to the border of the water, and fastened them perfectly upright to a stake.   Then each came with a torch of birch bark, and burned them, now in this place, now in that.   The poor wretches, feeling the fire, raised so loud a cry that it was something frightful to hear; and frightful indeed are the cruelties which these barbarians practise towards each other.   After making them suffer greatly in this manner and burning them with the above-mentioned bark, taking some water, they threw it on their bodies to increase their suffering.   Then they applied the fire anew, so that the skin fell from their bodies, they continuing to utter loud cries and exclamations, and dancing until the poor wretches fell dead on the spot.

As soon as a body fell to the ground dead, they struck it violent blows with sticks, when they cut off the arms, legs, and other parts; and he was not regarded by them as manly, who did not cut off a piece of the flesh, and give it to the dogs. Such are the courtesies prisoners receive. But still they endure all the tortures inflicted upon them with such constancy that the spectator is astonished.

As to the other prisoners, which remained in possession of the Algonquins and Montagnais, it was left to their wives and daughters to put them to death with their own hands; and, in such a matter, they do not show themselves less inhuman, than the men, but even surpass them by far in cruelty; for they devise by their cunning more cruel punishments, in which they take pleasure, putting an end to their lives by the most extreme pains.

The next day there arrived the Captain Yroquet, also another Ochateguin, with some eighty men, who regretted greatly not having been present at the defeat. Among all these tribes there were present nearly two hundred men, who had never before seen Christians, for whom they conceived a great admiration.

We were some three days together on an island off the river of the Iroquois, when each tribe returned to its own country.

I had a young lad,[1] who had already spent two winters at Quebec, and who was desirous of going with the Algonquins to learn their language. Pont Gravé and I concluded that, if he entertained this desire, it would be better to send him to this place than elsewhere, that he might ascertain the nature of their country, see the great lake, observe the rivers and tribes there, and also explore the mines and objects of special interest in the localities occupied by these tribes, in order that he might inform us, upon his return, of the facts

[1] Apparently Étienne Brulé, on whom see C. W. Butterfield, *History of Brulé's Discoveries and Explorations* (Cleveland, 1898).

of the case. We asked him if it was his desire to go, for I did not wish to force him. But he answered the question at once by consenting to the journey with great pleasure.

Going to Captain Yroquet, who was strongly attached to me, I asked him if he would like to take this young boy to his country to spend the winter with him, and bring him back in the spring. He promised to do so, and treat him as his own son, saying that he was greatly pleased with the idea. He communicated the plan to all the Algonquins, who were not greatly pleased with it, from fear that some accident might happen to the boy, which would cause us to make war upon them. This hesitation cooled the desire of Yroquet, who came and told me that all his companions failed to find the plan a good one. Meanwhile, all the barques had left, excepting that of Pont Gravé, who, having some pressing business on hand, as he told me, went away too. But I stayed with my barque to see how the matter of the journey of this boy, which I was desirous should take place, would result. I accordingly went on shore, and asked to speak with the captains, who came to me, and we sat down for a conference, together with many other savages of age and distinction in their troops. Then I asked them why Captain Yroquet, whom I regarded as my friend, had refused to take my boy with him. I said that it was not acting like a brother or friend to refuse me what he had promised, and what could result in nothing but good to them; taking the boy would be a means of increasing still more our friendship with them and forming one with their neighbors; that their scruples at doing so only gave me an unfavorable opinion of them; and that if they would not take the boy, as Captain Yroquet had promised, I would never have any friendship with them, for they were not children to break their promises in this manner. They then told me that they were satisfied with the arrangement, only they feared that, from change of diet to something worse than he had been accustomed to, some harm might happen to the boy, which would provoke my displeasure. This they said was the only cause of their refusal.

I replied that the boy would be able to adapt himself without difficulty to their manner of living and usual food, and that, if through sickness or the fortunes of war any harm should befall him, this would not interrupt my friendly feelings toward them, and that we were all exposed to accidents, which we must submit to with patience. But I said that if they treated him badly, and if any misfortune happened to him through their fault, I should in truth be displeased, which, however, I did not expect from them, but quite the contrary.

They said to me: "Since, then, this is your desire, we will take him, and treat him like ourselves. But you shall also take a young man in his place, to go to France. We shall be greatly pleased to hear him report the fine things he shall have seen." I accepted with pleasure the proposition, and took the young man. He belonged to the tribe of the Ochateguins, and was also glad to go with me. This presented an additional motive for treating my boy still better than they might otherwise have done. I fitted him out with what he needed, and we made a mutual promise to meet at the end of June.

We parted with many promises of friendship. Then they went away towards the great fall of the River of Canada, while I returned to Quebec. On my way, I met Pont Gravé on Lake St. Peter, who was waiting for me with a large patache, which he had fallen in with on this lake, and which had not been expeditious enough to reach the place where the savages were, on account of its poor sailing qualities.

We all returned together to Quebec, when Pont Gravé went to Tadoussac, to arrange some matters pertaining to our quarters there. But I stayed at Quebec to see to the reconstruction of some palisades about our abode, until Pont Gravé should return, when we could confer together as to what was to be done.

On the 4th of June,[1] Des Marais arrived at Quebec, greatly

---

[1] Read 4th of July.

to our joy; for we were afraid that some accident had happened to him at sea.

Some days after, an Iroquois prisoner, whom I had kept
guarded, got away in consequence of my giving him too much
liberty, and made his escape, urged to do so by fear, notwithstanding the assurances given him by a woman of his
tribe we had at our settlement.

A few days after, Pont Gravé wrote me that he was
thinking of passing the winter at the settlement, being moved
to do so by many considerations. I replied that, if he
expected to fare better than I had done in the past, he would
do well.

He accordingly hastened to provide himself with the supplies necessary for the settlement.

After I had finished the palisade about our habitation, and
put every thing in order, Captain Pierre returned in a barque
in which he had gone to Tadoussac to see his friends. I also
went there to ascertain what would result from the second
trading, and to attend to some other special business which I
had there. Upon my arrival, I found there Pont Gravé, who
stated to me in detail his plans, and the reasons inducing him
to spend the winter. I told him frankly what I thought of
the matter; namely, that I believed he would not derive much
profit from it, according to the appearances that were plainly
to be seen.

He determined accordingly to change his plan, and despatched a barque with orders for Captain Pierre to return
from Quebec on account of some business he had with him;
with the intelligence also that some vessels, which had arrived
from Brouage, brought the news that Monsieur de Saint Luc [1]
had come by post from Paris, expelled those of the religion [2]
from Brouage, re-enforced the garrison with soldiers, and
then returned to Court; that the king had been killed,[3] and

---

[1] Son of a former governor of Brouage, Champlain's birthplace.
[2] *I.e.*, the Huguenots.
[3] Henry IV. was assassinated on May 14, 1610.

two or three days after him the Duke of Sully,[1] together with two other lords, whose names they did not know.

All these tidings gave great sorrow to the true French in these quarters. As for myself, it was hard for me to believe it, on account of the different reports about the matter, and which had not much appearance of truth. Still, I was greatly troubled at hearing such mournful news.

Now, after having stayed three or four days longer at Tadoussac, I saw the loss which many merchants must suffer, who had taken on board a large quantity of merchandise, and fitted out a great number of vessels, in expectation of doing a good business in the fur-trade, which was so poor on account of the great number of vessels, that many will for a long time remember the loss which they suffered this year.

Sieur de Pont Gravé and I embarked, each of us in a barque, leaving Captain Pierre on the vessel. We took Du Parc to Quebec, where we finished what remained to be done at the settlement. After every thing was in good condition, we resolved that Du Parc, who had wintered there with Captain Pierre, should remain again, and that Captain Pierre should return to France with us, on account of some business that called him there.

We accordingly left Du Parc in command there, with sixteen men, all of whom we enjoined to live soberly, and in the fear of God, and in strict observance of the obedience due to the authority of Du Parc, who was left as their chief and commander, just as if one of us had remained. This they all promised to do, and to live in peace with each other.

As to the gardens, we left them all well supplied with kitchen vegetables of all sorts, together with fine Indian corn, wheat, rye, and barley, which had been already planted. There were also vines which I had set out when I spent the winter there, but these they made no attempt to preserve; for, upon my return, I found them all in ruins, and I was

---

[1] The report of Sully's death was unfounded; but his power was broken, and he lived in retirement till his death in 1641.

greatly displeased that they had given so little attention to the preservation of so fine and good a plot, from which I had anticipated a favorable result.

After seeing that every thing was in good order, we set out from Quebec on the 8th of August for Tadoussac, in order to prepare our vessel, which was speedily done.

Chapter 3

Return to France.   Meeting a whale; the mode of capturing them.

On the 13th of the month, we set out from Tadoussac, arriving at Île Percée the next day, where we found a large number of vessels engaged in the fishery, dry and green.

On the 18th of the month, we departed from Île Percée, passing in latitude 42°, without sighting the Grand Bank, where the green fishery is carried on, as it is too narrow at this altitude.

When we were about half way across, we encountered a whale, which was asleep.   The vessel, passing over him, awakening him betimes, made a great hole in him near the tail, without damaging our vessel; but he threw out an abundance of blood.

It has seemed to me not out of place to give here a brief description of the mode of catching whales, which many have not witnessed, and suppose that they are shot, owing to the false assertions about the matter made to them in their ignorance by impostors, and on account of which such ideas have often been obstinately maintained in my presence.

Those, then, most skilful in this fishery are the Basques, who, for the purpose of engaging in it, take their vessels to a place of security, and near where they think whales are plenty. Then they equip several shallops manned by competent men and provided with hawsers, small ropes made of the best hemp to be found, at least a hundred and fifty fathoms long.

They are also provided with many halberds of the length of
a short pike, whose iron is six inches broad; others are from
a foot and a half to two feet long, and very sharp. Each
shallop has a harpooner, the most agile and adroit man they
have, whose pay is next highest to that of the masters, his
position being the most dangerous one. This shallop being
outside of the port, the men look in all quarters for a whale,
tacking about in all directions. But, if they see nothing,
they return to the shore, and ascend the highest point they
can find, and from which they can get the most extensive
view. Here they station a man on the look-out. They are
aided in catching sight of a whale both by his size and the
water he spouts through his blow-holes, which is more than
a puncheon at a time, and two lances high. From the amount
of this water, they estimate how much oil he will yield. From
some they get as many as one hundred and twenty puncheons,
from others less. Having caught sight of this monstrous
fish, they hasten to embark in their shallops, and by rowing
or sailing they advance until they are upon him.

Seeing him under water, the harpooner goes at once to
the prow of the shallop with his harpoon, an iron two feet
long and half a foot wide at the lower part, and attached to
a stick as long as a small pike, in the middle of which is a
hole to which the hawser is made fast. The harpooner,
watching his time, throws his harpoon at the whale, which
enters him well forward. As soon as he finds himself wounded,
the whale goes down. And if by chance turning about, as he
does sometimes, his tail strikes the shallop, it breaks it like
glass. This is the only risk they run of being killed in har-
pooning. As soon as they have thrown the harpoon into him,
they let the hawser run until the whale reaches the bottom.
But sometimes he does not go straight to the bottom, when
he drags the shallop eight or nine leagues or more, going as
swiftly as a horse. Very often they are obliged to cut their
hawser, for fear that the whale will take them under water.
But, when he goes straight to the bottom, he rests there awhile,
and then returns quietly to the surface, the men taking aboard

again the hawser as he rises. When he comes to the top, two or three shallops are stationed around with halberds, with which they give him several blows. Finding himself struck, the whale goes down again, leaving a trail of blood, and grows weak to such an extent that he has no longer any strength nor energy, and returning to the surface is finally killed. When dead, he does not go down again: fastening stout ropes to him, they drag him ashore to their head-quarters, the place where they try out the fat of the whale, to obtain his oil. This is the way whales are taken, and not by cannon-shots, which many suppose, as I have stated above.

To resume the thread of my narrative: after wounding the whale, as mentioned, we captured a great many porpoises, which our mate harpooned to our pleasure and amusement. We also caught a great many fish having a large ear, with a hook and line, attaching to the hook a little fish resembling a herring, and letting it trail behind the vessel. The large ear,[1] thinking it in fact a living fish, comes up to swallow it, thus finding himself at once caught by the hook, which is concealed in the body of the little fish. This fish is very good, and has certains tufts which are very handsome, and resemble those worn on plumes.

On the 22d of September, we arrived on soundings. Here we saw twenty vessels some four leagues to the west of us, which, as they appeared from our vessel, we judged to be Flemish.

On the 25th of the month, we sighted the Isle de Grenezé,[2] after experiencing a strong blow, which lasted until noon.

On the 27th of the month, we arrived at Honfleur.

[1] Mackerel.   [2] Guernsey.

THIRD VOYAGE OF SIEUR DE CHAMPLAIN
IN THE YEAR 1611

THIRD VOYAGE OF SIEUR DE CHAMPLAIN
IN THE YEAR 1611

Chapter 1

Departure from France to return to New France. The dangers and other events which occurred up to the time of arrival at the settlement.

WE set out from Honfleur on the first day of March. The wind was favorable until the eighth, when we were opposed by a wind south-southwest and west-northwest, driving us as far as latitude 42°, without our being able to make a southing, so as to sail straight forward on our course. Accordingly after encountering several heavy winds, and being kept back by bad weather, we nevertheless, through great difficulty and hardship, and by sailing on different tacks, succeeded in arriving within eighty leagues of the Grand Bank, where the fresh[1] fishery is carried on. Here we encountered ice thirty or forty fathoms high, or more, which led us to consider what course we ought to take, fearing that we might fall in with more during the night, or that the wind changing would drive us on to it. We also concluded that this would not be the last, since we had set out from France too early in the season. We sailed accordingly during that day with short sail, as near the wind as we could. When night came, the fog arose so thick and obscure that we could scarcely see the ship's length. About eleven o'clock at night, more ice was seen, which alarmed

---

[1] Or rather, " green fishing." This was the fishing carried on on the banks by vessels remaining at sea for several months, and was distinguished from the "dry fishing" carried on from the shore in small boats, which returned toward nightfall, and exposed their catch to be dried by the sun and wind. See Lescarbot, ed. 1609, p. 823.

us. But through the energy of the sailors we avoided it. Supposing that we had passed all danger, we met with still more ice, which the sailors saw ahead of our vessel, but not until we were almost upon it. When all had committed themselves to God, having given up all hope of avoiding collision with this ice, which was already under our bowsprit, they cried to the helmsman to bear off; and this ice, which was very extensive, drove in such a manner that it passed by without striking our vessel, which stopped short, and remained as still as if it had never moved, to let it pass. Although the danger was over, our blood was not so quickly cooled, so great had been our fear, and we praised God for delivering us from so imminent a peril. This experience being over, we passed the same night two or three other masses of ice, not less dangerous than the former ones. There was at the same time a dripping fog, and it was so cold that we could scarcely get warm. The next day we met several other large and very high masses of ice, which, in the distance, looked like islands. We, however, avoided them all, and reached the Grand Bank, where we were detained by bad weather for the space of six days. The wind growing a little milder, and very favorable, we left the banks in latitude 44° 30′, which was the farthest south we could go. After sailing some sixty leagues west-northwest, we saw a vessel coming down to make us out, but which afterwards bore off to the east-northeast, to avoid a large bank of ice, which covered the entire extent of our line of vision. Concluding that there was a passage through the middle of this great floe, which was divided into two parts, we entered, in pursuance of our course, between the two, and sailed some ten leagues without seeing anything contrary to our conjecture of a fine passage through, until evening, when we found the floe closed up. This gave us much anxiety as to what was to be done, the night being at hand and there being no moon, which deprived us of all means of returning to the point whence we had come. Yet, after due deliberation, it was resolved to try to find again the entrance by which we had come, which we set about accomplishing. But the night coming on with fog, rain, snow, and a wind so violent that we could scarcely carry our mainsail, every trace of our way was lost. For, as we were expecting to avoid the ice so as to pass out, the wind had already closed up the passage, so that we were obliged to return to the other tack. We were unable to remain longer than a quarter of an hour on one tack before taking another, in order to avoid the numerous masses of ice drifting about on all sides. We thought more than twenty times that we should never escape with our lives. The entire night was spent amid difficulties and hardships. Never was the watch better kept, for nobody wished to rest, but to strive to escape from the ice and danger. The cold was so great, that all the ropes of the vessel were so frozen and covered with large icicles that the men could not work her nor stick to the deck. Thus we ran, on this tack and that, awaiting with hope the daylight. But when it came, attended by a fog, and we saw that our labor and hardship could not avail us anything, we determined to go to a mass of ice, where we should be sheltered from the violent wind which was blowing; to haul everything down, and allow ourselves to be driven along with the ice, so that when at some distance from the rest of the ice we could make sail again, and go back to the above-mentioned bank and manage as before, until the fog should pass away, when we might go out as quickly as possible. Thus we continued the entire day until the morning of the next day, when we set sail, now on this tack now on that, finding ourselves everywhere enclosed amid large floes of ice, as if in lakes on the mainland. At evening we sighted a vessel on the other side of one of these banks of ice, which, I am sure, was in no less anxiety than ourselves. Thus we remained four or five days, exposed to these risks and extreme hardships, until one morning on looking out in all directions, although we could see no opening, yet in one place it seemed as if the ice was not thick, and that we could easily pass through. We got under way, and passed by a large number of *bourguignons*; that is, pieces of ice separated from the large banks by the violence of the winds. Having reached this bank of ice, the sailors proceeded to provide them-

selves with large oars and pieces of wood, in order to keep off
the blocks of ice we met. In this way we passed this bank,
but not without touching some pieces of ice, which did no
good to our vessel, although they inflicted no essential damage.
Being outside, we praised God for our deliverance. Continuing
our course on the next day, we encountered other pieces, in
which we became so involved that we found ourselves surrounded on all sides, except where we had entered. It was
accordingly necessary to turn back, and endeavor to double
the southern point. This we did not succeed in doing until
the second day, passing by several small pieces of ice, which
had been separated from the main bank. This latter was in
latitude 44° 30′. We sailed until the morning of the next
day, towards the northwest, north-northwest, when we met
another large ice bank, extending as far as we could see east
and west. This, in the distance, seemed like land, for it was
so level that it might properly be said to have been made so
on purpose. It was more than eighteen feet high, extending
twice as far under water. We calculated that we were only
some fifteen leagues from Cape Breton, it being the 26th day
of the month. These numerous encounters with ice troubled
us greatly. We were also fearful that the passage [1] between
Capes Breton and Raye would be closed, and that we should
be obliged to keep out to sea a long time before being able
to enter. Unable to do anything else, we were obliged to
run out to sea again some four or five leagues, in order to
double another point of the above-mentioned grand ice bank,
which continued on our west-southwest. After turning on
the other tack to the northwest, in order to double this point,
we sailed some seven leagues, and then steered to the north-
northwest some three leagues, when we observed another
ice bank. The night approached, and the fog came on so
that we put to sea to pass the remainder of the night, purposing
at daybreak to return and reconnoitre the last mentioned ice.
On the twenty-seventh day of the month, we sighted land

---

[1] The Cabot Strait. Though not freezing over like the Strait of Belle-
Isle, it is sometimes blocked by drift ice in spring for a fortnight or more.

west-northwest of us, seeing no ice on the north-northeast. We approached nearer for the sake of a better observation, and found that it was Canseau. This led us to bear off to the north for Cape Breton Island; but we had scarcely sailed two leagues when we encountered an ice bank on the north-east. Night coming on, we were obliged to put out to sea until the next day, when we sailed northeast, and encountered more ice, bearing east, east-southeast from us, along which we coasted heading northeast and north for more than fifteen leagues. At last we were obliged to sail towards the west, greatly to our regret, inasmuch as we could find no passage, and should be obliged to withdraw and sail back on our track. Unfortunately for us we were overtaken by a calm, so that it seemed as if the swell of the sea would throw us upon the icebank just mentioned, and we got ready to launch our little boat, to use in case of necessity. If we had taken refuge on the above-mentioned ice it would only have been to languish and die in misery. While we were deliberating whether to launch our boat, a fresh breeze arose to our great delight, and thus we escaped from the ice. After we had sailed two leagues, night came on, with a very thick fog, causing us to haul down our sail, as we could not see, and as there were several large pieces of ice in our way, which we were afraid of striking. Thus we remained the entire night until the next day, which was the twenty-ninth, when the fog increased to such an extent that we could scarcely see the length of the vessel. There was also very little wind. Yet we did not fail to set sail, in order to avoid the ice. But, although expecting to extricate ourselves, we found ourselves so involved in it that we could not tell on which side to tack. We were accordingly again compelled to lower sail, and drift until the ice should allow us to make sail. We made a hundred tacks on one side and the other, several times fearing that we were lost. The most self-possessed would have lost all judgment in such a juncture; even the greatest navigator in the world. What alarmed us still more was the short distance we could see, and the fact that the night was coming on, and that we could not make a shift of a quarter of a league without finding a bank or some ice, and a great deal of floating ice, the smallest piece of which would have been sufficient to cause the loss of any vessel whatever. Now, while we were still sailing along amid the ice, there arose so strong a wind that in a short time the fog broke away, affording us a view, and suddenly giving us a clear air and fair sun. Looking around about us, we found that we were shut up in a little lake, not so much as a league and a half in circuit. On the north we perceived the island of Cape Breton, nearly four leagues distant, and it seemed to us that the passage-way to Cape Breton was still closed. We also saw a small ice bank astern of our vessel, and the ocean beyond that, which led us to resolve to go beyond the bank, which was divided. This we succeeded in accomplishing without striking our vessel, putting out to sea for the night, and passing to the southeast of the ice. Thinking now that we could double this ice bank, we sailed east-northeast some fifteen leagues, perceiving only a little piece of ice. At night we hauled down the sail until the next day, when we perceived another ice bank to the north of us, extending as far as we could see. We had drifted to within nearly half a league of it, when we hoisted sail, continuing to coast along this ice in order to find the end of it. While sailing along, we sighted on the first day of May a vessel amid the ice, which, as well as ourselves, had found it difficult to escape from it. We backed our sails in order to await the former, which came full upon us, since we were desirous of ascertaining whether it had seen other ice. On its approach we saw that it was the son[1] of Sieur de Poutrincourt, on his way to visit his father at the settlement of Port Royal. He had left France three months before, not without much reluctance, I think, and still they were nearly a hundred and forty leagues from Port Royal, and well out of their true course. We told them we had sighted the islands of Canseau, much to

---

[1] Charles de Biencourt, Sieur de Saint Just, was closely associated with his father, Sieur de Poutrincourt (see p. 32) in his work at Port Royal, and after his father's death endeavored unsuccessfully to carry it on. He died about 1623.

their satisfaction, I think, as they had not as yet sighted any land, and were steering straight between Cape St. Lawrence and Cape Raye, in which direction they would not have found Port Royal, except by going overland. After a brief conference with each other, we separated, each following his own course. The next day we sighted the islands of St. Pierre, finding no ice. Continuing our course we sighted on the following day, the third of the month, Cape Raye, also without finding ice. On the fourth we sighted the island of St. Paul, and Cape St. Lawrence,[1] being some eight leagues north of the latter. The next day we sighted Gaspé. On the seventh we were opposed by a northwest wind, which drove us out of our course nearly thirty-five leagues, when the wind lulled, and was in our favor as far as Tadoussac, which we reached on the 13th of May. Here we discharged a cannon to notify the savages, in order to obtain news from our settlement at Quebec. The country was still almost entirely covered with snow. There came out to us some canoes, informing us that one of our pataches had been in the harbor for a month, and that three vessels had arrived eight days before. We lowered our boat and visited these savages, who were in a very miserable condition, having only a few articles to barter to satisfy their immediate wants. Besides, they desired to wait until several vessels should meet, so that there might be a better market for their merchandise. Therefore they are mistaken who expect to gain an advantage by coming first, for these people are very sagacious and cunning.

On the 17th of the month I set out from Tadoussac for the great Fall,[2] to meet the Algonquin savages and other tribes, who had promised the year before to go there with my man, whom I had sent to them, that I might learn from him what he might see during the winter. Those at this harbor who suspected where I was going, in accordance with the promises which I had made to the savages, as stated above, began to build several small barques, that they might follow me as soon

[1] The northernmost point of Cape Breton.
[2] The Lachine Rapids, above Montreal.

as possible.   And several, as I learned before setting out from France, had some ships and pataches fitted out in view of our voyage, hoping to return rich, as from a voyage to the Indies.

Pont Gravé remained at Tadoussac, expecting, if he did nothing there, to take a patache and meet me at the fall. Between Tadoussac and Quebec our barque made much water, which obliged me to stop at Quebec and repair the leak. This was on the 21st of May.

Chapter 2

Landing at Quebec to repair the barque.   Departure from Quebec for the Fall, to meet the savages, and search out a place appropriate for a settlement.

On going ashore I found Sieur du Parc, who had spent the winter at the settlement. He and all his companions were very well, and had not suffered any sickness.   Game, both large and small, had been abundant during the entire winter, as they told me. I found there the Indian captain, named Batiscan, and some Algonquins, who said they were waiting for me, being unwilling to return to Tadoussac without seeing me.   I proposed to them to take one of our company to the Trois Rivières to explore the place, but being unable to obtain anything from them this year I put it off until the next.   Still I did not fail to inform myself particularly regarding the origin of the people living there, of which they told me with exactness. I asked them for one of their canoes, which they were unwilling to part with on any terms, because of their own need of it. For I had planned to send two or three men to explore the neighborhood of the Trois Rivières, and ascertain what there was there.   This, to my great regret, I was unable to accomplish, and postponed the project to the first opportunity that might present itself.

Meanwhile I urged on the repairs to our barque.   When it was ready, a young man from La Rochelle, named Tresart, asked me to permit him to accompany me to the above-men-

tioned fall. This I refused, replying that I had special plans
of my own, and that I did not wish to conduct any one to my
prejudice, adding that there were other companies than mine
there, and that I did not care to open up a way and serve as
a guide, and that he could make the voyage well enough alone
and without my help.

The same day I set out from Quebec, and arrived at the
great fall on the twenty-eighth of May. But I found none of
the savages who had promised me to be there on this day. I
entered at once a poor canoe, together with the savage I had
taken to France and one of my own men. After examining
the two shores, both in the woods and on the river bank, in
order to find a spot favorable for the location of a settlement,
and to get a place ready for building, I went some eight leagues
by land along the great fall and through the woods, which are
very open, as far as a lake,[1] whither our savage conducted
me. Here I observed the country very carefully. But in
all that I saw, I found no place more favorable than a little
spot to which barques and shallops can easily ascend, with
the help of a strong wind or by taking a winding course, in
consequence of the strong current. But above this place,
which we name La Place Royale, at the distance of a league
from Mont Royal, there are a great many little rocks and
shoals, which are very dangerous. Near Place Royale there
is a little river,[2] extending some distance into the interior, along
the entire length of which there are more than sixty acres of
land cleared up and like meadows, where grain can be sown
and gardens made. Formerly savages tilled these lands, but
they abandoned them on account of their wars, in which they
were constantly engaged.[3] There is also a large number of
other fine pastures, where any number of cattle can graze.
There are also the various kinds of trees found in France,

[1] The Lake of Two Mountains.

[2] The Rivière St. Pierre, now lost in the sewerage of the city of Montreal.

[3] In 1535 Jacques Cartier had found on the spot a flourishing Indian
village known as Hochelaga. The inhabitants were probably Iroquois.
See *Early English and French Voyages*, pp. 57–63, and Laverdière, III.,
p. 243, note 2.

together with many vines, nut and plum trees, cherries, strawberries, and other kinds of good fruit. Among the rest there
is a very excellent one, with a sweet taste like that of plan-
tains, a fruit of the Indies, as white as snow, with a leaf resembling that of nettles, and which creeps up the trees and
along the ground like ivy. Fish are very abundant, including
all the varieties we have in France, and many very good ones
which we do not have. Game is also plenty, the birds being
of various kinds. There are stags, hinds, does, caribous,
rabbits, lynxes, bears, beavers, also other small animals, and
all in such large numbers, that while we were at the fall we
were abundantly supplied with them.

After a careful examination, we found this place one of
the finest on this river. I accordingly forthwith gave orders
to cut down and clear up the woods in the Place Royale,[1]
so as to level it and prepare it for building. The water can
easily be made to flow around it, making of it a little island,
so that a habitation can be formed as one may wish.

There is a little island some twenty fathoms from Place
Royale, about a hundred paces long, where a good and strong
settlement might be made. There are also many meadows,
containing very good and rich potter's clay, as well adapted
for brick as for building purposes, and consequently a very
useful article. I had a portion of it worked up, from which
I made a wall four feet thick, three or four high, and ten
fathoms long, to see how it would stand during the winter,
when the freshets came down, although I thought the water
would not reach up to it, the ground there being twelve feet
above the river, which was very high. In the middle of the
river there was an island about three-quarters of a league
around, where a good and strong town could be built. This
we named Isle de Sainte Hélène.[2] This river at the fall is

---

[1] Now Pointe à Callières. "It is the centre of the present city of Montreal. The Custom House now stands upon the site he chose, and the Montreal ocean steamships discharge their cargoes there." Dawson, *The St.
Lawrence*, p. 262.
[2] After his wife, Hélène Boullé (see Introduction). It is still so called.

like a lake, containing two or three islands, and bordered by
fine meadows.

On the first day of June, Pont Gravé arrived at the fall,
having been unable to accomplish anything at Tadoussac.
A numerous company attended and followed after him to
share in the booty, without the hope of which they would have
been far in the rear.

Now, while awaiting the savages, I had two gardens made,
one in the meadows, the other in the woods, which I had cleared
up. On the 2d of June I sowed some seeds, all of which came
up finely, and in a short time, attesting the good quality of
the soil.

We resolved to send Savignon, our savage, together with
another, to meet his countrymen, so as to hasten their arrival. They hesitated about going in our canoe, of which
they were distrustful, it being a very poor one. They set out
on the 5th. The next day four or five barques arrived as
an escort for us, since they could do nothing at Tadoussac.

On the 7th I went to explore a little river,[1] along which
the savages sometimes go to war, and which flows into the
fall of the river of the Iroquois. It is very pleasant, with
meadow land more than three leagues in circuit, and much
arable land. It is distant a league from the great fall, and a
league and a half from Place Royale.

On the 9th our savage arrived. He had gone somewhat
beyond the lake, which is ten leagues long, and which I had
seen before. But he met no one, and they were unable to
go any farther, as their canoe gave out, which obliged them
to return. They reported that after passing the fall they saw
an island, where there was such a quantity of herons that the
air was completely filled with them. There was a young man
belonging to Sieur de Monts named Louis, who was very fond
of the chase. Hearing this, he wished to go and satisfy his
curiosity, earnestly entreating our savage to take him to the
place. To this the savage consented, taking also a captain

[1] The River St. Lambert, whence a short portage leads to Little River,
which flows into the basin of Chambly. (Laverdière.)

of the Montagnais, a very respectable person, whose name was Outetoucos. On the following morning Louis caused the two savages to be called, and went with them in a canoe to the island of the herons. This island is in the middle of the Fall. Here they captured as many herons and other birds as they wanted, and embarked again in their canoe. Outetoucos, contrary to the wish of the other savage, and against his remonstrances, desired to pass through a very dangerous place, where the water fell more than three feet, saying that he had formerly gone this way, which, however, was false. He had a long discussion in opposition to our savage, who wished to take him on the south side, along the mainland, where they usually go. This, however, Outetoucos did not wish, saying that there was no danger. Our savage finding him obstinate yielded to his desire. But he insisted that at least a part of the birds in the canoe should be taken out, as it was overloaded, otherwise he said it would inevitably fill and be lost. But to this he would not consent, saying that it would be time enough when they found themselves in the presence of danger. They accordingly permitted themselves to be carried along by the current. But when they reached the precipice, they wanted to throw overboard their load in order to escape. It was now, however, too late, for they were completely in the power of the rapid water, and were straightway swallowed up in the whirlpools of the fall, which turned them round a thousand times. For a long time they clung to the boat. Finally the swiftness of the water wearied them so that this poor Louis, who could not swim at all, entirely lost his presence of mind, and, the canoe going down, he was obliged to abandon it. As it returned to the surface, the two others, who kept holding on to it, saw Louis no more, and thus he died a sad death. The two others continued to hold on to the canoe. When, however, they were out of danger, this Outetoucos, being naked and having confidence in his swimming powers, abandoned it in the expectation of reaching the shore, although the water still ran there with great rapidity. But he was drowned, for he had been so weakened and overcome by his efforts that it was impossible for him to save himself after abandoning the canoe. Our savage Savignon, understanding himself better, held firmly to the canoe until it reached an eddy, whither the current had carried it. Here he managed so well that, notwithstanding his suffering and weariness, he approached the shore gradually, when, after throwing the water out of the canoe, he returned in great fear that they would take vengeance upon him, as the savages do among themselves, and related to us this sad story, which caused us great sorrow.

On the next day I went in another canoe to the Fall, together with the savage and another member of our company, to see the place where they had met with their accident, and find, if possible, the remains. But when he showed me the spot, I was horrified at beholding such a terrible place, and astonished that the deceased should have been so lacking in judgment as to pass through such a fearful place, when they could have gone another way. For it is impossible to go along there, as there are seven or eight descents of water one after the other, the lowest three feet high, the seething and boiling of the water being fearful. A part of the Fall was all white with foam, indicating the worst spot, the noise of which was like thunder, the air resounding with the echo of the cataracts. After viewing and carefully examining this place, and searching along the river bank for the dead bodies, another very light shallop having proceeded meanwhile on the other bank also, we returned without finding anything.

Chapter 3

Two hundred savages return the Frenchman who had been entrusted to them, and receive the savage who had come back from France. Various interviews on both sides.

On the thirteenth day of the month two hundred Charioquois [1] savages, together with the captains, Ochateguin, Iro-

---

[1] In the edition of 1632 Champlain has *Sauvages Hurons.*

quet, and Tregouaroti, brother of our savage, brought back
my servant.[1] We were greatly pleased to see them. I went
to meet them in a canoe with our savage. As they were
approaching slowly and in order, our men prepared to salute
them, with a discharge of arquebuses, muskets, and small
pieces. When they were near at hand, they all set to shouting
together, and one of the chiefs gave orders that they should
make their harangue, in which they greatly praised us, com-
mending us as truthful, inasmuch as I had kept the promise
to meet them at this Fall. After they had made three more
shouts, there was a discharge of musketry twice from thirteen
barques or pataches that were there. This alarmed them so,
that they begged me to assure them that there should be no
more firing, saying that the greater part of them had never
seen Christians, nor heard thunderings of that sort, and that
they were afraid of its harming them, but that they were
greatly pleased to see our savage in health, whom they supposed to be dead, as had been reported by some Algonquins,
who had heard so from the Montagnais. The savage commended the treatment I had shown him in France, and the
remarkable objects he had seen, at which all wondered, and
went away quietly to their cabins, expecting that on the
next day I would show them the place where I wished to
have them dwell. I saw also my servant, who was dressed
in the costume of the savages, who commended the treatment he had received from them. He informed me of all he
had seen and learned during the winter, from the savages.

The next day I showed them a spot for their cabins, in
regard to which the elders and principal ones consulted very
privately. After their long consultation they sent for me alone
and my servant, who had learned their language very well.
They told him they desired a close alliance with me, and were
sorry to see here all these shallops, and that our savage had
told them he did not know them at all nor their intentions,
and that it was clear that they were attracted only by their

---

[1] This was the young man previously mentioned, apparently Étienne
Brulé, who had passed the winter among them. See p. 185.

desire of gain and their avarice, and that when their assistance
was needed they would refuse it, and would not act as I did
in offering to go with my companions to their country and
assist them, of all of which I had given them proofs in the past.
They praised me for the treatment I had shown our savage,
which was that of a brother, and had put them under such
obligations of good will to me, that they said they would endeavor to comply with anything I might desire from them,
but that they feared that the other boats would do them
some harm. I assured them that they would not, and that we
were all under one king, whom our savage had seen, and belonged to the same nation, though matters of business were
confined to individuals, and that they had no occasion to fear,
but might feel as much security as if they were in their own
country. After considerable conversation, they made a
present of a hundred castors.[1] I gave them in exchange
other kinds of merchandise. They told me there were more
than four hundred savages of their country who had purposed
to come, but had been prevented by the following representations of an Iroquois prisoner, who had belonged to me, but had
escaped to his own country. He had reported, they said, that
I had given him his liberty and some merchandise, and that
I purposed to go to the Fall with six hundred Iroquois to meet
the Algonquins and kill them all, adding that the fear aroused
by this intelligence had alone prevented them from coming.
I replied that the prisoner in question had escaped without
my leave, that our savage knew very well how he went away,
and that there was no thought of abandoning their alliance,
as they had heard, since I had engaged in war with them, and
sent my servant to their country to foster their friendship,
which was still farther confirmed by my keeping my promise
to them in so faithful a manner.

They replied that, so far as they were concerned, they
had never thought of this; that they were well aware that
all this talk was far from the truth, and that if they had
believed the contrary they would not have come, but that

[1] *I.e.,* beaver-skins.

P

the others were afraid, never having seen a Frenchman except my servant. They told me also that three hundred Algonquins would come in five or six days, if we would wait for them, to unite with themselves in war against the Iroquois; that, however, they would return without doing so unless I went. I talked a great deal with them about the source of the great river and their country, and they gave me detailed information about their rivers, falls, lakes, and lands, as also about the tribes living there, and what is to be found in the region. Four of them assured me that they had seen a sea at a great distance from their country, but that it was difficult to go there, not only on account of the wars, but of the intervening wilderness. They told me also that, the winter before, some savages had come from the direction of Florida, beyond the country of the Iroquois, who lived near our ocean, and were in alliance with these savages. In a word they made me a very exact statement, indicating by drawings all the places where they had been, and taking pleasure in talking to me about them; and for my part I did not tire of listening to them, as they confirmed points in regard to which I had been before in doubt. After all this conversation was concluded, I told them that we would trade for the few articles they had, which was done the next day. Each one of the barques carried away its portion; we on our side had all the hardship and venture; the others, who had not troubled themselves about any explorations, had the booty, the only thing that urges them to activity, in which they employ no capital and venture nothing.

The next day, after bartering what little they had, they made a barricade about their dwelling, partly in the direction of the wood, and partly in that of our pataches; and this they said they did for their security, in order to avoid the surprises of their enemies, which we took for the truth. On the coming night, they called our savage, who was sleeping on my patache, and my servant, who went to them. After a great deal of conversation, about midnight they had me called also. Entering their cabins, I found them all seated in council. They

had me sit down near them, saying that when they met for
the purpose of considering a matter, it was their custom to
do so at night, that they might not be diverted by anything
from attention to the subject in hand; that at night one
thought only of listening, while during the day the thoughts
were distracted by other objects.

But in my opinion, confiding in me, they desired to tell me
privately their purpose. Besides, they were afraid of the
other pataches, as they subsequently gave me to understand.
For they told me that they were uneasy at seeing so many
Frenchmen, who were not especially united to one another,
and that they had desired to see me alone; that some of
them had been beaten; that they were as kindly disposed
towards me as towards their own children, confiding so much
in me that they would do whatever I told them to do, but
that they greatly mistrusted the others; that if I returned
I might take as many of their people as I wished, if it were
under the guidance of a chief; and that they sent for me to
assure me anew of their friendship, which would never be broken,
and to express the hope that I might never be ill disposed
towards them; and being aware that I had determined to
visit their country, they said they would show it to me at the
risk of their lives, giving me the assistance of a large number
of men, who could go everywhere; and that in future we should
expect such treatment from them as they had received from us.

Straightway they brought fifty castors and four strings of
beads, which they value as we do gold chains, saying that
I should share these with my brother, referring to Pont Gravé,
we being present together; that these presents were sent
by other captains, who had never seen me; that they desired to continue friends to me; that if any of the French
wished to go with them, they should be greatly pleased to have
them do so; and that they desired more than ever to establish a firm friendship. After much conversation with them
I proposed that inasmuch as they were desirous to have me
visit their country, I would petition His Majesty to assist us
to the extent of forty or fifty men, equipped with what was

necessary for the journey, and that I would embark with them on condition that they would furnish us the necessary provisions for the journey, and that I would take presents for the chiefs of the country through which we should pass, when we would return to our settlement to spend the winter; that moreover, if I found their country favorable and fertile, we would make many settlements there, by which means we should have frequent intercourse with each other, living happily in the future in the fear of God, whom we would make known to them.   They were well pleased with this proposition, and begged me to shake hands upon it, saying that they on their part would do all that was possible for its fulfilment; that, in regard to provisions, we should be as well supplied as they themselves, assuring me again that they would show me what I desired to see.   Thereupon, I took leave of them at daybreak, thanking them for their willingness to carry out my wishes, and entreating them to continue to entertain the same feelings.

On the next day, the 17th, they said that they were going castor-hunting, and that they would all return.   On the following morning they finished bartering what little they had, when they embarked in their canoes, asking us not to take any steps towards taking down their dwellings, which we promised them.   Then they separated from each other, pretending to go a hunting in different directions.   They left our savage with me that we might have less distrust in them.   But they had appointed themselves a rendezvous above the Fall, where they knew well enough that we could not go with our barques. Meanwhile, we awaited them in accordance with what they had told us.

The next day there came two savages, one Iroquet, the other the brother of our Savignon.   They came to get the latter, and ask me in behalf of all their companions to go alone with my servant to where they were encamped, as they had something of importance to tell me, which they were unwilling to communicate to any Frenchmen.   I promised them that I would go.

The following day I gave some trifles to Savignon, who
set out much pleased, giving me to understand that he was
about to live a very irksome life in comparison with that
which he had led in France. He expressed much regret at
separation, but I was very glad to be relieved of the care
of him. The two captains told me that on the morning of
the next day they would send for me, which they did. I
embarked, accompanied by my servant, with those who came.
Having arrived at the Fall, we went some eight leagues into
the woods, where they were encamped on the shore of a lake,
where I had been before. They were much pleased at seeing
me, and began to shout after their custom. Our Indian came
out to meet me, and ask me to go to the cabin of his brother,
where he at once had some meat and fish put on the fire for
my entertainment. While I was there, a banquet was held,
to which all the leading Indians were invited. I was not
forgotten, although I had already eaten sufficiently; but, in
order not to violate the custom of the country, I attended.
After banqueting, they went into the woods to hold their
council, and meanwhile I amused myself in looking at the
country round about, which is very pleasant.

Some time after they called me, in order to communicate to me what they had resolved upon. I proceeded to
them accordingly with my servant. After I had seated myself by their side, they said they were very glad to see me,
and to find that I had not failed to keep my word in what I
had promised them; saying that they felt it an additional proof
of my affection that I continued the alliance with them, and
that before setting out they desired to take leave of me, as
it would have been a very great disappointment to them to
go away without seeing me, thinking that I would in that
case have been ill disposed towards them. They said also
that what had led them to say they were going a-hunting,
and build the barricade, was not the fear of their enemies
nor the desire of hunting, but their fear of all the other pataches
accompanying me, inasmuch as they had heard it said that
on the night they sent for me they were all to be killed, and

that I should not be able to protect them from the others, who were much more numerous; so that in order to get away they made use of this ruse.   But they said if there had been only our two pataches they would have stayed some days longer, and they begged that, when I returned with my companions, I would not bring any others.   To this I replied that I did not bring these, but that they followed without my invitation; that in the future, however, I would come in another manner; at which explanation they were much pleased.

And now they began again to repeat what they had promised me in regard to the exploration of the country, while I promised, with the help of God, to fulfil what I had told them.   They besought me again to give them a man, and I replied that if there was any one among us who was willing to go, I should be well pleased.

They told me there was a merchant, named Bouyer, commander of a patache, who had asked them to take a young man, which request, however, they had been unwilling to grant before ascertaining whether this was agreeable to me, as they did not know whether we were friends, since he had come in my company to trade with them; also that they were in no wise under any obligations to him, but that he had offered to make them large presents.

I replied that we were in no wise enemies, and that they had often seen us conversing with each other; but that in regard to traffic each did what he could, and that the above-named Bouyer was perhaps desirous of sending this young man as I had sent mine, hoping for some return in the future, which I could also lay claim to from them; that, however, they must judge towards whom they had the greatest obligations, and from whom they were to expect the most.

They said there was no comparison between the obligations in the two cases, not only in view of the help I had rendered them in their wars against their enemies, but also of the offer of my personal assistance in the future, in all of which they had found me faithful to the truth, adding that all depended on my pleasure.   They said moreover that what made them speak of the matter was the presents he had offered them, and that, if this young man should go with them, it would not put them under such obligations to this Bouyer as they were under to me, and that it would have no influence upon the future, since they only took him on account of the presents from Bouyer.

I replied that it was indifferent to me whether they took him or not, and in fact that if they took him for a small consideration I should be displeased at it, but if in return for valuable presents, I should be satisfied, provided he stayed with Iroquet; which they promised me. Then there was made on both sides a final statement of our agreements. They had with them one who had three times been made prisoner by the Iroquois, but had been successful in escaping. This one resolved to go, with nine others, to war, for the sake of revenge for the cruelties his enemies had caused him to suffer. All the captains begged me to dissuade him if possible, since he was very valiant, and they were afraid that, advancing boldly towards the enemy, and supported by a small force only, he would never return. To satisfy them I endeavored to do so, and urged all the reasons I could, which, however, availed little; for he, showing me a portion of his fingers cut off, also great cuts and burns on his body, as evidences of the manner they had tortured him, said that it was impossible for him to live without killing some of his enemies and having vengeance, and that his heart told him he must set out as soon as possible, as he did, firmly resolved to behave well.

After concluding with them, I asked them to take me back in our patache. To accomplish this, they got ready eight canoes in order to pass the Fall, stripping themselves naked, and directing me to go in my shirt. For it often happens that some are lost in passing the Fall. Consequently, they keep close to each other, so as to render assistance at once, if any canoe should happen to turn over. They said to me, If yours should unfortunately overturn, not knowing how to swim, you must not think of abandoning it, and must cling to the little pieces in the middle of it, for we can easily rescue you. I am sure that even the most self-possessed persons in the world, who have not seen this place nor passed it in little boats such as they have, could not do so without the greatest apprehension. But these people are so skilful in passing falls, that it is an easy matter for them. I passed with them, which I had never before done, nor any other Christian, except my above-mentioned servant. Then we reached our barques, where I lodged a large number of them, and had some conversation with the before-mentioned Bouyer in view of the fear he entertained that I should prevent his servant from going with the savages. They returned the next day with the young man, who proved expensive to his master, who had expected, in my opinion, to recover the losses of his voyage, which were very considerable, like those of many others.

One of our young men also determined to go with these savages, who are Charioquois, living at a distance of some one hundred and fifty leagues from the Fall. He went with the brother of Savignon, one of the captains, who promised me to show him all that could be seen. Bouyer's man went with the above-mentioned Iroquet, an Algonquin, who lives some eighty leagues from the Fall. Both went off well pleased and contented.

After the departure of the savages, we awaited the three hundred others who, as had been told us, were to come, in accordance with the promise I had made them. Finding that they did not come, all the pataches determined to induce some Algonquin savages, who had come from Tadoussac, to go to meet them, in view of a reward that would be given them on their return, which was to be at the latest not over nine days from the time of their departure, so that we might know whether to expect them or not, and be able to return to Tadoussac. This they agreed to, and a canoe left with this purpose.

On the fifth of July a canoe arrived from the Algonquins, who were to come to the number of three hundred. From it we learned that the canoe which had set out from us had

arrived in their country, and that their companions, wearied
by their journey, were resting, and that they would soon arrive, in fulfilment of the promise they had made; that at most
they would not be more than eight days behindhand, but that
there would be only twenty-four canoes, as one of their captains
and many of their comrades had died of a fever that had broken
out among them. They also said that they had sent many
to the war, which had hindered their progress. We determined to wait for them.

But finding that this period had elapsed without their
arrival, Pont Gravé set out from the Fall on the eleventh of
the month, to arrange some matters at Tadoussac, while I
stayed to await the savages.

The same day a patache arrived, bringing provisions for
the numerous barques of which our party consisted. For
our bread, wine, meat, and cider had given out some days
before, obliging us to have recourse to fishing, the fine river
water, and some radishes which grow in great abundance in
the country; otherwise we should have been obliged to return.
The same day an Algonquin canoe arrived, assuring us that
on the next day the twenty-four canoes were to come, twelve
of them prepared for war.

On the twelfth the Algonquins arrived with some little
merchandise. Before trafficking they made a present to a
Montagnais Indian, the son of Anadabijou, who had lately
died, in order to mitigate his grief at the death of his father.
Shortly after they resolved to make some presents to all
the captains of the pataches. They gave to each of them
ten castors, saying they were very sorry they had no more, but
that the war, to which most of them were going, was the reason;
they begged, however, that what they offered might be accepted
in good part, saying that they were all friends to us, and to
me, who was seated near them, more than to all the others,
who were well-disposed towards them only on account of their
castors, and had not always assisted them like myself, whom
they had never found double-tongued like the rest.

I replied that all those whom they saw gathered together

were their friends; that, in case an opportunity should present itself, they would not fail to do their duty; that we were all friends; that they should continue to be well disposed towards us; that we would make them presents in return for those they gave us; and that they should trade in peace. This they did, and carried away what they could.

The next day they brought me privately forty castors, assuring me of their friendship, and that they were very glad of the conclusion which I had reached with the savages who had gone away, and that we should make a settlement at the fall, which I assured them we would do, making them a present in return.

After everything had been arranged, they determined to go and obtain the body of Outetoucos, who was drowned at the Fall, as we have before mentioned. They went to the spot where he had been buried, disinterred him and carried him to the island of St. Hélène, where they performed their usual ceremony, which is to sing and dance over the grave with festivities and banquets following. I asked them why they disinterred the body. They replied that if their enemies should find the grave they would do so, and divide the body into several pieces, which they would then hang to trees in order to offend them. For this reason they said that they transferred it to a place off from the road, and in the most secret manner possible.

On the 15th there arrived fourteen canoes, the chief over which was named Tecouehata. Upon their arrival all the other savages took up arms and performed some circular evolutions. After going around and dancing to their satisfaction, the others who were in their canoes also began to dance, making various movements of the body. After finishing their singing, they went on shore with a small quantity of furs, and made presents similar to those of the others. These were reciprocated by some of equal value. The next day they trafficked in what little they had, and presented me personally with thirty castors, for which I made them an acknowledgment. They begged me to continue my good will to them, which I promised to do. They spoke with me very especially respecting certain explorations towards the north, which might prove advantageous; and said, in reference to them, that if any one of my company would like to go with them, they would show him what would please me, and would treat him as one of their own children. I promised to give them a young man, at which they were much pleased. When he took leave of me to go with them, I gave him a detailed memorandum of what he was to observe while with them. After they had bartered what little they had, they separated into three parties; one for the war, another for the great Fall, another for a little river which flows into that of the great Fall. Thus they set out on the 18th day of the month, on which day we also departed.

The same day we made the thirty leagues from this Fall to the Trois Rivières. On the 19th we arrived at Quebec, which is also thirty leagues from the Trois Rivières. I induced the most of those in each boat to stay at the settlement, when I had some repairs made and some rose-bushes set out. I had also some oak wood put on board to make trial of in France, not only for marine wainscoting but also for windows. The next day, the 20th of July, I set out. On the 23d I arrived at Tadoussac, whence I resolved to return to France, in accordance with the advice of Pont Gravé. After arranging matters relating to our settlement, according to the directions which Sieur de Monts had given me, I embarked in the vessel of Captain Tibaut, of La Rochelle, on the 11th of August. During our passage we had an abundance of fish, such as *orades*, mackerel,[1] and *pilotes*, the latter similar to herrings, and found about certain planks covered with *pousse-pieds*, a kind of shell-fish attaching itself thereto, and growing there gradually. Sometimes the number of these little fish is so great that it is surprising to behold. We caught also some porpoises and other species of fish. The weather was favorable as far as Belle-Isle,[2] where we were overtaken by fogs,

---

[1] *Grande-oreille*, *i.e.*, large-ear. See p. 192.
[2] Belle-Isle-en-mer, off the west coast of France.

which continued three or four days. The weather then becoming fair, we sighted Alvert,[1] and arrived at La Rochelle on the 16th of September, 1611.

Chapter 4

Arrival at La Rochelle. Dissolution of the partnership between Sieur de Monts and his associates, the Sieurs Colier and le Gendre of Rouen. Jealousy of the French in regard to the new discoveries in New France.

Upon my arrival at La Rochelle I proceeded to visit Sieur de Monts, at Pons [2] in Saintonge, to inform him of all that had occurred during the expedition, and of the promise which the Ochateguins and Algonquins had made me, on condition that we would assist them in their wars, as I had agreed. Sieur de Monts, after listening to it all, determined to go to the Court to arrange the matter. I started before him to go there also. But on the way I was unfortunately detained by the falling of a horse upon me, which came near killing me. This fall detained me some time; but as soon as I had sufficiently recovered from its effects I set out again to complete my journey and meet Sieur de Monts at Fontainebleau, who, upon his return to Paris, had a conference with his associates. The latter were unwilling to continue in the association, as there was no commission forbidding any others from going to the new discoveries and trading with the inhabitants of the country. Sieur de Monts, seeing this, bargained with them for what remained at the settlement at Quebec, in consideration of a sum of money which he gave them for their share. He sent also some men to take care of the settlement, in the expectation of obtaining a commission from His Majesty.

---

[1] Pointe d'Arvert, a cape nine miles from Brouage, and twenty-seven miles south of La Rochelle.

[2] De Monts was governor of this town, which was about fifty miles southeast of La Rochelle.

But while he was engaged in the pursuit of this object some important matters demanded his attention, so that he was obliged to abandon it, and he left me the duty of taking the necessary steps for it. As I was about arranging the matter, the vessels arrived from New France with men from our settlement, those whom I had sent into the interior with the savages. They brought me very important information, saying that more than two hundred savages had come, expecting to find me at the great Fall of St. Louis, where I had appointed a rendezvous, with the intention of assisting them according to their request. But, finding that I had not kept my promise, they were greatly displeased. Our men, however, made some apologies, which were accepted, and assured them that they would not fail to come the following year or never. The savages agreed to this on their part. But several others left the old trading-station of Tadoussac, and came to the fall with many small barques to see if they could engage in traffic with these people, whom they assured that I was dead, although our men stoutly declared the contrary. This shows how jealousy against meritorious objects gets possession of bad natures; and all they want is that men should expose themselves to a thousand dangers, to discover peoples and territories, that they themselves may have the profit and others the hardship. It is not reasonable that one should capture the lamb and another go off with the fleece. If they had been willing to participate in our discoveries, use their means, and risk their persons, they would have given evidence of their honor and nobleness, but on the contrary they show clearly that they are impelled by pure malice that they may enjoy the fruit of our labors equally with ourselves.

On this subject, and to show how many persons strive to pervert praiseworthy enterprises, I will instance again the people of St. Malo and others, who say that the profit of these discoveries belongs to them, since Jacques Cartier, who first visited Canada and the islands of Newfoundland, was from their city; as if that city had contributed to the expenses of these discoveries of Jacques Cartier, who went there by the order and at the expense of King Francis I. in the years 1534 and 1535 to discover these territories now called New France. If then Cartier made any discovery at the expense of His Majesty, all his subjects have the same rights and liberties in them as the people of St. Malo, who cannot prevent others who make farther discoveries at their own expense, as is shown in the case of the discoveries above described, from profiting by them in peace. Hence they ought not to claim any rights if they themselves make no contributions, and their reasons for doing so are weak and foolish.

To prove more conclusively that they who maintain this position do so without any foundation, let us suppose that a Spaniard or other foreigner had discovered lands and wealth at the expense of the King of France. Could the Spaniards or other foreigners claim these discoveries and this wealth, on the ground that the discoverer was a Spaniard or foreigner? No! There would be no sense in doing so, and they would always belong to France. Hence the people of St. Malo cannot make these claims for the reason which they give, that Cartier was a citizen of their city; and they can only take cognizance of the fact that he was a citizen of theirs, and render him accordingly the praise which is his due.

Besides, Cartier in the voyage which he made never passed the great Fall of St. Louis, and made no discoveries north or south of the river St. Lawrence. His narratives give no evidence of it, in which he speaks only of the river Saguenay, the Trois Rivières and St. Croix, where he spent the winter in a fort near our settlement. Had he done so, he would not have failed to mention it, any more than what he has mentioned, which shows that he left all the upper part of the St. Lawrence, from Tadoussac to the great Fall, being a territory difficult to explore, and that he was unwilling to expose himself or let his barques engage in the venture.[1] So that what he did has borne no fruit until four years ago, when we made

---

[1] This is a mistake. Cartier went as far as the present city of Montreal, though he does not describe in detail the country between Montreal and Quebec. See *Early English and French Voyages*, pp. 54–71.

our settlement at Quebec, after which I ventured to pass the
Fall to help the savages in their wars, and send among them
men to make the acquaintance of the people, to learn their
mode of living, and the character and extent of their territory.
After devoting ourselves to labors which have been so successful, is it not just that we should enjoy their fruits, His Majesty
not having contributed anything to aid those who have assumed the responsibilities of these undertakings up to the
present time? I hope that God will at some time incline him to
do so much for His service, his own glory and the welfare of his
subjects, as to bring many new peoples to the knowledge of our
faith, that they may at last enjoy the heavenly kingdom.[1]

[1] The two general maps mentioned on the title-page of the *Voyages of*
1613 are inserted by Champlain at this point. At the end of the *Voyages*
proper, just before the *Quatriesme Voyage,* under the heading "Explanation
of two Geographical Maps of New France," he says: "The smallest is in its
true meridian, in accordance with the directions of the Sieur de Castelfranc
in his book on the mecometry of the magnetic needle [*Mécométrie de*
l'Eymant, c'est a dire la Manière de mesurer les Longitudes par le moyen de
l'Eymant (Toulouse, 1603). See p. 27, note 3], where I have noted, as will
be seen on the map, several declinations, which have been of much service
to me, so also all the altitudes, latitudes and longitudes, from the forty-first
degree of latitude to the fifty-first, in the direction of the North Pole, which
are the confines of Canada, or the Great Bay, where more especially the
Basques and Spaniards engage in the whale fishery." This was the first
attempt to lay down the latitude and longitude on any map of the coast.
Different "states" of the map vary in minor particulars.

FOURTH VOYAGE OF SIEUR DE CHAM-
PLAIN MADE IN THE YEAR 1613

FOURTH VOYAGE OF SIEUR DE CHAMPLAIN

CAPTAIN IN ORDINARY TO THE KING IN THE MARINE, AND LIEUTENANT OF MONSEIGNEUR LE PRINCE DE CONDÉ IN NEW FRANCE

MADE IN THE YEAR 1613

To the very high, powerful, and excellent Henri de Bourbon, Prince de Condé, First Prince of the Blood, First Peer of France, Governor and Lieutenant of His Majesty in Guienne.[1]

MONSEIGNEUR,

The honor that I have received from your Highness in being intrusted with the discovery of New France has inspired in me the desire to pursue with still greater pains and zeal than ever the search for the North Sea. With this object in view I have made a voyage during the past year, 1613, relying on a man whom I had sent there and who assured me he had seen it, as you will perceive in this brief narrative, which I venture to present to your Excellence, and in which are particularly described all the toils and sufferings I have had in the undertaking. But although I regret having lost this year so far as the main object is concerned, yet my expectation, as in the first voyage, of obtaining more definite information respecting the subject from the savages, has been fulfilled. They have told me about various lakes and rivers in the north, in view of which, aside from their assurance

---

[1] The third prince of Condé was appointed in 1612 protector of the Company of New France, whose formation ended the four-years' period of free trade on the upper St. Lawrence. Though Condé was a man of little ability, his rank as first prince of the blood was of service to the company amid the maze of court and commercial intrigues.

that they know of this sea, it seems to me easy to conclude from the maps that it cannot be far from the farthest discoveries I have hitherto made. Awaiting a favorable time and opportunity to prosecute my plans, and praying God to preserve you, most happy Prince, in all prosperity, wherein consists my highest wish for your greatness, I remain in the quality of

Your most humble and devoted servant,

SAMUEL DE CHAMPLAIN.

Chapter 1

What led me to seek for terms of regulation. A commission obtained. Oppositions to the same. Publication at last in all the ports of France.

THE desire which I have always had of making new discoveries in New France, for the good, profit, and glory of the French name, and at the same time to lead the poor natives to the knowledge of God, has led me to seek more and more for the greater facility of this undertaking, which can only be secured by means of good regulations. For, since individuals desire to gather the fruits of my labor without contributing to the expenses and great outlays requisite for the support of the settlements necessary to a successful result, this branch of trade is ruined by the greediness of gain, which is so great that it causes merchants to set out prematurely in order to arrive first in this country. By this means they not only become involved in the ice, but also in their own ruin, for, from trading with the savages in a secret manner and offering through rivalry with each other more merchandise than is necessary, they get the worst of the bargain. Thus, while purposing to deceive their associates, they generally deceive themselves.

For this reason, when I returned to France on the 10th

of September, 1611, I spoke to Sieur de Monts about the matter, who approved of my suggestions; but his engagements not allowing him to prosecute the matter at court, he left to me its whole management.

I then drew up a statement, which I presented to President Jeannin,[1] who, being a man desirous of seeing good undertakings prosper, commended my project, and encouraged me in its prosecution.

But feeling assured that those who love to fish in troubled waters would be vexed at such regulations and seek means to thwart them, it seemed advisable to throw myself into the hands of some power whose authority would prevail over their jealousy.

Now, knowing Monseigneur le Comte de Soissons [2] to be a prince devout and well disposed to all holy undertakings, I addressed myself to him through Sieur de Beaulieu, councillor and almoner in ordinary to the King, and urged upon him the importance of the matter, setting forth the means of regulating it, the harm which disorder had heretofore produced, and the total ruin with which it was threatened, to the great dishonor of the French name, unless God should raise up some one who would reanimate it and give promise of securing for it some day the success which had hitherto been little anticipated. After he had been informed in regard to all the details of the scheme and seen the map of the country which I had made, he promised me, under the sanction of the King, to undertake the protectorate of the enterprise.

I immediately after presented to His Majesty, and to the gentlemen of his council, a petition accompanied by articles, to the end that it might please him to issue regulations for the undertaking, without which, as I have said, it would fail.

[1] President Jeannin (1540–1622) was one of the most important lawyers and statesmen of the reigns of Henry III. and Henry IV., and of the regency which followed, and took a great interest in all schemes of colonization. Lescarbot dedicates to him his *Histoire de la Nouvelle France*.

[2] Charles de Bourbon, Count de Soissons, a prince of the blood, youngest son of the first Condé. He preceded the third Condé as lieutenant-general for the king in New France. He died November 1, 1612.

Accordingly his Majesty gave the direction and control to the before-mentioned count, who then honored me with the lieutenancy.

Now as I was preparing to publish the commission [1] of the King in all the ports and harbors of France, there occurred the sickness and greatly lamented death of the count, which postponed somewhat the undertaking. But his Majesty at once committed the direction to Monseigneur le Prince, [2] who proceeded in the execution of its duties, and, having in like manner honored me with the lieutenancy, directed me to go on with the publication of the commission. But as soon as this was done, some marplots, who had no interest in the matter, importuned him to annul it, representing to him, as they claimed, the interests of all the merchants of France, who had no cause for complaint, since all were received into the association and could not therefore justly be aggrieved. Accordingly, their evil intention being recognized, they were dismissed, with permission only to enter into the association.

During these altercations, it was impossible for me, as the time of my departure was very near at hand, to do anything for the habitation at Quebec, for repairing and enlarging which I desired to take out some workmen. It was accordingly necessary to go out this year without any farther organization. The passports of Monseigneur le Prince were made out for four vessels, which were already in readiness for the voyage, viz. three from Rouen and one from La Rochelle, on condition that each should furnish four men for my assistance, not only in my discoveries but in war, as I desired to keep the promise which I had made to the Ochataiguins in the year 1611, to assist them in their wars at the time of my next voyage.

As I was preparing to set out, I was informed that the Parliamentary Court of Rouen would not permit the publication of the commission of the King, because his Majesty

---

[1] This commission, dated October 15, 1612, is given in Champlain's *Voyages* of 1632, Bourne's ed., II. 45–51.

[2] *I.e.*, Condé (see p. 227, note 1), nephew of Soissons.

had reserved to himself and his council the sole cognizance of the differences which might arise in this matter; added to which was the fact that the merchants of St. Malo were also opposed to it. This greatly embarrassed me, and obliged me to make three journeys to Rouen, with orders of his Majesty, in consideration of which the Court desisted from their inhibition, and the assumptions of the opponents were overruled. The commission was then published in all the ports of Normandy.

Chapter 2

Departure from France. What took place up to our arrival at the Falls.

I set out from Rouen on the 5th of March for Honfleur, accompanied by Sieur L'Ange, to assist me in my explorations, and in war if occasion should require.

On the next day, the 6th of the month, we embarked in the vessel of Sieur de Pont Gravé, immediately setting sail, with a favorable wind.

On the 10th of April we sighted the Grand Bank, where we several times tried for fish, but without success.

On the 15th we had a violent gale, accompanied by rain and hail, which was followed by another, lasting forty-eight hours, and so violent as to cause the loss of several vessels on the island of Cape Breton.

On the 21st we sighted the island[1] and Cap de Raye. On the 29th the Montagnais savages, perceiving us from All Devils' Point,[2] threw themselves into their canoes and came to meet us, being so thin and hideous-looking that I did not recognize them. At once they began crying for bread, saying that they were dying of hunger. This led us to conclude that the winter had not been severe, and consequently the hunting poor, which matter we have alluded to in previous voyages.

Having arrived on board of our vessel they examined the

---

[1] Newfoundland. [2] See p. 125, note 2.

faces of all, and as I was not to be seen anywhere they asked where Monsieur de Champlain was, and were answered that I had remained in France. But this they would not think of believing, and an old man among them came to me in a corner where I was walking, not desiring to be recognized as yet, and taking me by the ear, for he suspected who it was, saw the scar of the arrow wound which I received at the defeat of the Iroquois. At this he cried out, and all the others after him, with great demonstrations of joy, saying, Your people are awaiting you at the harbor of Tadoussac.

The same day we arrived at Tadoussac, and although we had set out last, nevertheless arrived first, Sieur Boyer [1] of Rouen arriving with the same tide. From this it is evident that to set out before the season is simply rushing into the ice. When we had anchored, our friends came out to us, and, after informing us how everything was at the habitation, began to dress three *outardes* [2] and two hares, which they had brought, throwing the entrails overboard, after which the poor savages rushed, and, like famished beasts, devoured them without drawing. They also scraped off with their nails the fat with which our vessel had been coated, eating it gluttonously as if they had found some great delicacy.

The next day two vessels arrived from St. Malo, which had set out before the oppositions had been settled and the commission been published in Normandy. I proceeded on board, accompanied by L'Ange. The Sieurs de la Moinerie and la Tremblaye were in command, to whom I read the commission of the King, and the prohibition against violating it on penalties attached to the same. They replied that they were subjects and faithful servants of His Majesty, and that they would obey his commands; and I then had attached to a post in the port the arms and commission of His Majesty, that no ground for ignorance might be claimed.

[1] An old free-trader, long a thorn in the side of the companies of de Monts and his associates. See pp. 214–216.

[2] In Europe the *outarde* is the bustard. Champlain and other early writers on Canada apply the term to a species of wild goose, probably the brant.

On the 2d of May, seeing two shallops equipped to go
to the Falls, I embarked with the before-mentioned L'Ange
in one of them. We had very bad weather, so that the masts
of our shallop were broken, and had it not been for the preserving hand of God we should have been lost, as was before
our eyes a shallop from St. Malo, which was going to the
Isle d'Orleans, those on board of which, however, were saved.

On the 7th we arrived at Quebec, where we found in good
condition those who had wintered there, they not having
been sick; they told us that the winter had not been severe,
and that the river had not frozen. The trees also were beginning to put forth leaves and the fields to be decked with
flowers.

On the 13th we set out from Quebec for the Falls of St.
Louis, where we arrived on the 21st, finding there one of
our barques which had set out after us from Tadoussac, and
which had traded somewhat with a small troop of Algonquins,
who came from the war with the Iroquois, and had with them
two prisoners. Those in the barque gave them to understand
that I had come with a number of men to assist them in their
wars, according to the promise I had made them in previous
years; also that I desired to go to their country and enter
into an alliance with all their friends, at which they were greatly
pleased. And, inasmuch as they were desirous of returning to
their country to assure their friends of their victory, see their
wives, and put to death their prisoners in a festive *tabagie*,[1]
they left as pledges of their return, which they promised should
be before the middle of the first moon, according to their reckoning, their shields made of wood and elk leather, and a part
of their bows and arrows. I regretted very much that I was
not prepared to go with them to their country.

Three days after, three canoes arrived with Algonquins,
who had come from the interior, with some articles of merchandise which they bartered. They told me that the bad
treatment which the savages had received the year before
had discouraged them from coming any more, and that they

[1] Banquet.

did not believe that I would ever return to their country on account of the wrong impressions which those jealous of me had given them respecting me; wherefore twelve hundred men had gone to the war, having no more hope from the French, who they did not believe would return again to their country.

This intelligence greatly disheartened the merchants, as they had made a great purchase of merchandise, with the expectation that the savages would come, as they had been accustomed to. This led me to resolve, as I engaged in my explorations, to pass through their country, in order to encourage those who had stayed back, with an assurance of the good treatment they would receive, and of the large amount of good merchandise at the Fall, and also of the desire I had to assist them in their war. For carrying out this purpose I requested three canoes and three savages to guide us, but after much difficulty obtained only two and one savage, and this by means of some presents made them.

Chapter 3

Departure to discover the North Sea, on the ground of the report made me in regard to it. Description of several rivers, lakes, and islands; the Falls of the Chaudière and other falls.

Now, as I had only two canoes, I could take with me but four men, among whom was one named Nicholas de Vignau, the most impudent liar that has been seen for a long time, as the sequel of this narrative will show. He had formerly spent the winter with the savages, and I had sent him on explorations the preceding years. He reported to me, on his return to Paris in 1612, that he had seen the North Sea; that the river of the Algonquins came from a lake which emptied into it; and that in seventeen days one could go from the Falls of St. Louis to this sea and back again; that he had seen the

wreck and *débris* of an English ship that had been wrecked,
on board of which were eighty men, who had escaped to the
shore, and whom the savages killed because the English endeavored to take from them by force their Indian corn and
other necessaries of life; and that he had seen the scalps
which these savages had flayed off, according to their custom, which they would show me, and that they would likewise give me a young English boy whom they had kept for
me.[1] This intelligence had greatly pleased me, for I thought
that I had almost found that for which I had for a long time
been searching. Accordingly I enjoined upon him to tell me
the truth, in order that I might inform the King, and warned
him that if he gave utterance to a lie he was putting the
rope about his neck, assuring him on the other hand that,
if his narrative were true, he could be certain of being well
rewarded. He again assured me, with stronger oaths than
ever; and in order to play his *rôle* better he gave me a description of the country, which he said he had made as well
as he was able. Accordingly the confidence which I saw in
him, his entire frankness as it seemed, the description which
he had prepared, the wreck and *débris* of the ship, and the
things above mentioned, had an appearance of probability,
in connection with the voyage of the English to Labrador in
1612, where they found a strait, in which they sailed as far
as the 63d degree of latitude and the 290th[2] of longitude,
wintering at the 53d degree and losing some vessels, as their
report proves. Their circumstances inducing me to believe
that what he said was true, I made a report of the same to the
Chancellor,[3] which I showed to Marshal de Brissac,[4] President

[1] Vignau had evidently heard rumors of the expedition of Hudson
of 1610–1611.

[2] Longitude at that time was reckoned from the island of Ferro, one of
the Canaries. Reckoning eastward from that island, the 290th meridian
would pass through Hudson's Bay. (Slafter.) The voyage of 1612 to
Hudson's Bay was that of Sir Thomas Button.

[3] Nicolas Brûlart de Sillery (1544–1624).

[4] Charles de Cosse-Brissac (d. 1621), who had been a prominent member of the League in its wars with Henry IV.

Jeannin, and other seigneurs of the Court, who told me that
I ought to visit the place in person.   For this reason I requested
Sieur Georges, a merchant of La Rochelle, to give him a passage in his ship, which he willingly did, and during the voyage
he questioned him as to his object in making it; and, since
it was not of any profit to him, he asked if he expected any
pay, to which the young man answered that he did not, that
he did not expect anything from any one but the King, and
that he undertook the voyage only to show me the North Sea,
which he had seen.   He made an affidavit of this at La Rochelle
before two notaries.

Now, as I took leave on Whitsuntide,[1] of all the principal
men to whose prayers I commended myself, and also to those
of all others, I said to him in their presence that if what he had
previously said was not true he must not give me the trouble
to undertake the journey, which involved many dangers.
Again he affirmed all that he had said, on peril of his
life.

Accordingly, our canoes being laden with some provisions,
our arms, and a few articles of merchandise for making presents
to the savages, I set out on Monday the 27th of May, from
Isle St. Hélène with four Frenchmen and one savage, a parting
salute being given me with some rounds from small pieces.
This day we went only to the Falls of St. Louis, a league up
the river, the bad weather not allowing us to go any farther.

On the 29th we passed the Falls, partly by land, partly by
water, it being necessary for us to carry our canoes, clothes,
victuals, and arms on our shoulders, no small matter for persons not accustomed to it.   After going two leagues beyond
the Falls, we entered a lake,[2] about twelve leagues in circuit,
into which three rivers empty; one coming from the west,
from the direction of the Ochateguins, distant from one
hundred and fifty to two hundred leagues from the great
Falls;[3] another from the south and the country of the Iroquois, a like distance off;[4] and the other from the north

---

[1] May 26, 1613.   [3] The St. Lawrence.
[2] Lake St. Louis.   [4] The Chateauguay.

and the country of the Algonquins and Nebicerini,[1] also about
the same distance.[2] This river on the north, according to
the report of the savages, comes from a source more remote,
and passes by tribes unknown to them and about three hundred leagues distant.

This lake is filled with fine large islands, containing only
pasturage land, where there is fine hunting, deer and fowl
being plenty. Fish are abundant. The country bordering
the lake is covered with extensive forests. We proceeded
to pass the night at the entrance to this lake, making barricades against the Iroquois, who roam in these regions in order
to surprise their enemies; and I am sure that if they were
to find us they would give us as good a welcome as them,
for which reason we kept a good watch all night. On the next
day I took the altitude of the place, and found it in latitude
45° 18′. About three o'clock in the afternoon we entered the
river which comes from the north, and, passing a small fall
by land so as to favor our canoes, we proceeded to a little island,
where we spent the remainder of the night.

On the last day of May we passed another lake,[3] seven
or eight leagues long and three broad, containing several
islands. The neighboring country is very level, except in some
places, where there are pine-covered hills. We passed a
fall called by the inhabitants of the country Quenechouan,[4]
which is filled with stones and rocks, and where the water
runs with great velocity. We had to get into the water and
drag our canoes along the shore with a rope. Half a league
from there we passed another little fall by rowing, which
makes one sweat. Great skill is required in passing these
falls, in order to avoid the eddies and surf, in which they
abound; but the savages do this with the greatest possible
dexterity, winding about and going by the easiest places,
which they recognize at a glance.

On Saturday, the 1st of June, we passed two other falls;
the first half a league long, the second a league, in which we

[1] The Nipissings.   [2] The Ottawa.   [3] Lake of Two Mountains.
[4] The first of a series now known as the Long Sault.

had much difficulty; for the rapidity of the current is so great that it makes a frightful noise, and produces, as it descends from stage to stage, so white a foam everywhere that the water cannot be seen at all. This fall is strewn with rocks, and contains some islands here and there covered with pines and white cedars. This was the place where we had a hard time; for, not being able to carry our canoes by land on account of the density of the wood, we had to drag them in the water with ropes, and in drawing mine I came near losing my life, as it crossed into one of the eddies, and if I had not had the good fortune to fall between two rocks the canoe would have dragged me in, inasmuch as I was unable to undo quickly enough the rope which was wound around my hand, and which hurt me severely and came near cutting it off. In this danger I cried to God and began to pull my canoe, which was returned to me by the refluent water, such as occurs in these falls. Having thus escaped I thanked God, begging Him to preserve us. Later our savage came to help me, but I was out of danger. It is not strange that I was desirous of preserving my canoe, for if it had been lost it would have been necessary to remain, or wait until some savages came that way, a poor hope for those who have nothing to dine on, and who are not accustomed to such hardship. As for our Frenchmen, they did not have any better luck, and several times came near losing their lives; but the Divine Goodness preserved us all. During the remainder of the day we rested, having done enough.

The next day we fell in with fifteen canoes of savages called Quenongebin,[1] in a river, after we had passed a small lake, four leagues long and two broad. They had been informed of my coming by those who had passed the Falls of St. Louis, on their way from the war with the Iroquois. I was very glad to meet them, as were they also to meet me, but they were astonished to see me in this country with so few companions, and with only one savage. Accordingly, after saluting each other after the manner of the country, I desired them not to

_____

[1] An Algonquin nation situated south of Allumette Island. (Laverdière.)

go any farther until I had informed them of my plan. To
this they assented, and we encamped on an island.

The next day I explained to them that I was on my way
to their country to visit them, and fulfil the promise I had
previously made them, and that if they had determined to
go to the war it would be very agreeable to me, inasmuch as
I had brought some companions with this view, at which they
were greatly pleased; and having told them that I wished to
go farther in order to notify the other tribes, they wanted to
deter me, saying that the way was bad, and that we had seen
nothing up to this point. Wherefore I asked them to give me
one of their number to take charge of our second canoe, and
also to serve us as guide, since our conductors were not acquainted any farther. This they did willingly, and in return
I made them a present and gave them one of our Frenchmen,
the least indispensable, whom I sent back to the Falls with a
leaf of my note-book, on which for want of paper I made a
report of myself.

Thus we parted, and continuing our course up the river
we found another one, very fair, and broad, which comes
from a nation called Ouescharini,[1] who live north of it, a
distance of four days' journey from the mouth. This river
is very pleasant in consequence of the fine islands it contains,
and the fair and open woods with which its shores are bordered.
The land is very good for tillage.

On the fourth day we passed near another river coming
from the north, where tribes called Algonquins live. This
river falls into the great river St. Lawrence, three leagues
below the Falls of St. Louis, forming a large island of nearly
forty leagues.[2] This river is not broad, but filled with a

[1] Subsequently called the Little Nation of the Algonquins, living on
the *Rivière de la Petite Nation.* (Laverdière.)

[2] This passage as it stands in Champlain's text, here and in the edition
of 1632, cannot be squared with the facts of Canadian geography. Laverdière's conjecture, III. 299, note 3, is almost certainly correct. It is that
the original reading was not "laquelle [the Gatineau] va tomber," but,
"laquelle va *joindre dans les terres une autre rivière* [the St. Maurice] *qui va*
tomber 30 lieuës [instead of 3] aval le saut St. Louys," and that the com-

countless number of falls, very hard to pass. Sometimes these tribes go by way of this river in order to avoid encounters with their enemies, knowing that they will not try to find them in places so difficult of access.

Where this river has its debouchure is another coming from the south,[1] at the mouth of which is a marvellous fall. For it descends a height of twenty or twenty-five fathoms with such impetuosity that it makes an arch nearly four hundred paces broad. The savages take pleasure in passing under it, not wetting themselves, except from the spray that is thrown off. There is an island in the middle of the river which, like all the country round about, is covered with pines and white cedars. When the savages desire to enter the river they ascend the mountain, carrying their canoes, and go half a league by land. The neighboring country is filled with all sorts of game, so that the savages often make a stop here. The Iroquois also go there sometimes and surprise them while making the passage.

We passed a fall[2] a league from there, which is half a league broad, and has a descent of six or seven fathoms. There are many little islands, which are, however, nothing more than rough and dangerous rocks covered with a poor sort of brushwood. The water falls in one place with such force upon a rock that it has hollowed out in course of time a large and deep basin, in which the water has a circular motion and forms large eddies in the middle, so that the savages call it Asticou, which signifies boiler.[3] This cataract produces such a noise in this basin that it is heard for more than two leagues. The savages when passing here observe a ceremony which we shall speak of in its place. We had much

positor's eye passed from *va* to *va*, omitting the words italicized above or their equivalents. This would meet the geographical facts and make good sense, for the upper waters of the Gatineau connect closely with an affluent of the St. Maurice.

[1] The Rideau, at the mouth of which, close by Ottawa, is Green Island. The fall is really only 40 or 45 feet in height.

[2] The Chaudière Falls, just above the present city of Ottawa.

[3] The French name *Chaudière* has a similar meaning.

trouble in ascending by rowing against a strong current, in order to reach the foot of the fall. Here the savages took their canoes, my Frenchmen and myself our arms, provisions, and other necessaries, and we passed over the rough rocks for the distance of about a quarter of a league, the extent of the fall. Then we embarked, being obliged afterwards to land a second time and go about three hundred paces through copse-wood, after which we got into the water in order to get our canoes over the sharp rocks, the trouble attending which may be imagined. I took the altitude of this place, which I found to be in latitude 45° 38′.

In the afternoon we entered a lake,[1] five leagues long and two wide, in which there are very fine islands covered with vines, nut-trees, and other excellent kinds of trees. Ten or twelve leagues above we passed some islands covered with pines. The land is sandy, and there is found here a root which dyes a crimson color, with which the savages paint their faces, as also little gewgaws after their manner. There is also a mountain range along this river, and the surrounding country seems to be very unpromising. The rest of the day we passed on a very pleasant island.

The next day we proceeded on our course to a great fall, nearly three leagues broad, in which the water falls a height of ten or twelve fathoms in a slope, making a marvellous noise.[2] It is filled with a vast number of islands, covered with pines and cedars. In order to pass it we were obliged to give up our maize or Indian corn, and some few other provisions we had, together with our least necessary clothes, retaining only our arms and lines, to afford us means of support from hunting and fishing as place and luck might permit. Thus lightened we passed, sometimes rowing, sometimes carrying our canoes and arms by land, the fall, which is a league and a half long, and in which our savages, who are indefatigable in this work and accustomed to endure such hardships, aided us greatly.

[1] Chaudière Lake, an expansion of the Ottawa River.
[2] Rapide des Chats, from the raccoons (*chats sauvages*).

Continuing our course, we passed two other falls, one by land, the other with oar and poles standing up. Then we entered a lake,[1] six or seven leagues long, into which flows a river coming from the south,[2] on which at a distance of five days' journey from the other river live a people called Matou-oüescarini. The lands about the before-mentioned lake are sandy and covered with pines, which have been almost entirely burned down by the savages. There are some islands, in one of which we rested ourselves. Here we saw a number of fine red cypresses, the first I had seen in this country, out of which I made a cross, which I planted at one end of the island, on an elevated and conspicuous spot, with the arms of France, as I had done in other places where we had stopped. I called this island Sainte Croix.

On the 6th we set out from this island of St. Croix, where the river is a league and a half broad, and having made eight or ten leagues we passed a small fall by oar, and a number of islands of various sizes. Here our savages left the sacks containing their provisions and their less necessary articles, in order to be lighter for going overland and avoiding several falls which it was necessary to pass. There was a great dispute between our savages and our impostor, who affirmed that there was no danger by way of the falls, and that we ought to go that way. Our savages said to him, You are tired of living, and to me, that I ought not to believe him, and that he did not tell the truth. Accordingly, having several times observed that he had no knowledge of the places, I followed the advice of the savages, which was fortunate for me, for he sought for dangers in order to ruin me or to disgust me with the undertaking, as he has since confessed, a statement of which will be given hereafter. We crossed accordingly towards the west of the river, which extended northward. I took the altitude of this place and found it in latitude 46° 40'. We had much difficulty in going this distance overland. I, for my part, was loaded only with three arquebuses, as many oars, my cloak, and some small articles. I cheered on our

---

[1] Lake des Chats. [2] The Madawaska.

men, who were somewhat more heavily loaded, but more
troubled by the mosquitoes than by their loads. Thus after
passing four small ponds and having gone a distance of two
and a half leagues, we were so wearied that it was impossible
to go farther, not having eaten for twenty-four hours anything
but a little broiled fish without seasoning, for we had left our
provisions behind, as I mentioned before. Accordingly we
rested on the border of a pond, which was very pleasant,
and made a fire to drive away the mosquitoes, which annoyed
us greatly, whose persistency is so marvellous that one cannot
describe it. Here we cast our lines to catch some fish.

The next day we passed this pond, which was perhaps a
league long. Then we went by land three leagues through
a country worse than we had yet seen, since the winds had
blown down the pines on top of each other. This was no
slight inconvenience, as it was necessary to go now over, now
under, these trees. In this way we reached a lake, six leagues
long and two wide,[1] very abundant in fish, the neighboring
people doing their fishing there. Near this lake is a settlement of savages, who till the soil and gather harvests of maize.
Their chief is named Nibachis, who came to visit us with his
followers, astonished that we could have passed the falls and
bad roads in order to reach them. After offering us tobacco,
according to their custom, he began to address his companions,
saying, that we must have fallen from the clouds, for he knew
not how we could have made the journey, and that they who
lived in the country had much trouble in traversing these
bad ways: and he gave them to understand that I accomplished all that I set my mind upon ; in short, that he believed
respecting me all that the other savages had told him. Aware

---

[1] Muskrat Lake. In this neighborhood was found in 1867 an astrolabe with the date 1603, probably lost by Champlain during this expedition.
The astrolabe, an instrument for taking the altitude of the sun or stars, has
long since been superseded by the quadrant or sextant. It is observable
that after this point Champlain no longer states the latitude in degrees and
minutes, according to his previous custom, but only in degrees. His latitudes, it may be well to observe, are throughout this expedition overstated
bv somewhat more than a degree.

that we were hungry, he gave us some fish, which we ate, and after our meal I explained to him, through Thomas, our interpreter, the pleasure I had in meeting them, that I had come to this country to assist them in their wars, and that I desired to go still farther to see some other chiefs for the same object, at which they were glad and promised me assistance. They showed me their gardens and the fields, where they had maize. Their soil is sandy, for which reason they devote themselves more to hunting than to tillage, unlike the Ochateguins. When they wish to make a piece of land arable, they burn down the trees, which is very easily done, as they are all pines, and filled with rosin. The trees having been burned, they dig up the ground a little, and plant their maize kernel by kernel, like those in Florida. At the time I was there it was only four fingers high.

Chapter 4

Continuation. Arrival at the abode of Tessoüat, and his favorable reception of me. Character of their cemeteries. The savages promise me four canoes for continuing my journey; which they however shortly after refuse. Address of the savages to dissuade me from my undertaking, in which they represent its difficulties. My reply to these objections. Tessoüat accuses my guide of lying, and of not having been where he said he had. The latter maintains his veracity. I urge them to give me canoes. Several refusals. My guide convicted of falsehood, and his confession.

Nibachis had two canoes fitted out, to conduct me to another chief, named Tessoüat, who lived eight leagues from him, on the border of a great lake, through which flows the river which we had left, and which extends northward. Accordingly, we crossed the lake in a west-northwesterly direction, a distance of nearly seven leagues. Landing there, we went a league towards the northeast through a very fine country, where are small beaten paths, along which one can go easily. Thus we arrived on the shore of the lake,[1] where the dwelling of Tessoüat was. He was accompanied by a neighboring chieftain, and was greatly amazed to see me, saying that he thought I was a dream, and that he did not believe his eyes. Thence we crossed on to an island, where their cabins are, which are poorly constructed out of the bark of trees. The island is covered with oaks, pines, and elms, and is not subject to inundations, like the other islands in the lake.

This island is strongly situated; for at its two ends, and where the river enters the lake, there are troublesome falls, the roughness of which makes the island difficult of access. They have accordingly taken up their abode here in order to avoid the pursuit of their enemies. It is in latitude 47°, as also the lake, which is twenty leagues long,[2] and three or four wide. It abounds in fish; the hunting, however, is not especially good.

On visiting the island, I observed their cemeteries, and was struck with wonder as I saw sepulchres of a shape like shrines, made of pieces of wood fixed in the ground at a distance of about three feet from each other, and intersecting at the upper end. On the intersections above they place a large piece of wood, and in front another upright piece, on which is carved roughly, as would be expected, the figure of the male or female interred. If it is a man, they add a shield, a sword attached to a handle after their manner, a mace, and bow and arrows. If it is a chief, there is a plume on his head, and some other *matachia* or embellishment. If it is a child, they give it a bow and arrow; if a woman or girl, a boiler, an earthen vessel, a wooden spoon, and an oar. The entire sepulchre is six or seven feet long at most, and four wide; others

---

[1] Lake Allumette, an expansion of the Ottawa on the southern side of Allumette Island. The name Algonquin, afterwards applied in a generic sense to a large and scattered family of cognate tribes, seems originally to have been restricted to the inhabitants of this island, whose strategic position enabled them to play a large part in the early history of the colony.

[2] In his edition of 1632 Champlain alters this to ten. It is now about fifteen miles by four.

are smaller. They are painted yellow and red, with various
ornaments as neatly done as the carving. The deceased is
buried with his dress of beaver or other skins which he wore
when living, and they lay by his side all his possessions, as
hatchets, knives, boilers, and awls, so that these things may
serve him in the land whither he goes; for they believe in the
immortality of the soul, as I have elsewhere observed. These
carved sepulchres are only made for the warriors; for in respect
to others they add no more than in the case of women, who
are considered a useless class, accordingly but little is added
in their case.

Observing the poor quality of the soil, I asked them what
pleasure they took in cultivating land so unpromising, since
there was some much better, which they left barren and
waste, as at the Falls of St. Louis. They answered that they
were forced to do so in order to dwell in security, and that
the roughness of the locality served them as a defence against
their enemies. But they said that if I would make a settlement of French at the Falls of St. Louis, as I had promised,
they would leave their abode and go and live near us, confident that their enemies would do them no harm while we
were with them. I told them that we would this year collect wood and stone in order the coming year to build a fort
and cultivate the land; upon hearing which they raised a
great cry of applause. This conference having been finished,
I asked all the chiefs and prominent men among them to
assemble the next day on the main land, at the cabin of Tessoüat, who purposed to celebrate a *tabagie* in my honor, adding
that I would there tell them my plans. This they promised,
and sent word to their neighbors to convene at the appointed
place.

The next day all the guests came, each with his porringer
and wooden spoon. They seated themselves without order
or ceremony on the ground in the cabin of Tessoüat, who
distributed to them a kind of broth made of maize crushed
between two stones, together with meat and fish which was
cut into little pieces, the whole being boiled together without

salt. They also had meat roasted on coals, and fish boiled apart, which he also distributed. In respect to myself, as I did not wish any of their chowder, which they prepare in a very dirty manner, I asked them for some fish and meat, that I might prepare it my own way, which they gave me. For drink, we had fine clear water. Tessoüat, who gave the *tabagie*, entertained us without eating himself, according to their custom.

The *tabagie* being over, the young men, who are not present at the harangues and councils, and who during the *tabagies* remain at the door of the cabins, withdrew, when all who remained began to fill their pipes, one and another offering me one. We then spent a full half-hour in this occupation, not a word being spoken, as is their custom.

After smoking amply during so long a period of silence, I explained to them, through my interpreter, that the object of my journey was none other than to assure them of my friendship, and of the desire I had to assist them in their wars, as I had before done; that I had been prevented from coming the preceding year, as I had promised them, because the King had employed me in other wars, but that now he had ordered me to visit them and to fulfil my promises, and that for this purpose I had a number of men at the Falls of St. Louis. I told them that I was making an excursion in their territory to observe the fertility of their soil, their lakes and rivers, and the sea which they had told me was in their country; and that I desired to see a tribe distant six days' journey from them, called the Nebicerini,[1] in order to invite them also to the war, and accordingly I asked them to give me four canoes with eight savages to guide me to these lands. And since the Algonquins are not great friends of the Nebicerini, they seemed to listen to me with greater attention.

After I had finished my discourse, they began again to smoke, and to confer among themselves in a very low voice respecting my propositions. Then Tessoüat in behalf of all

[1] The Nipissings, on the border of Lake Nipissing, a tribe famed for sorcery.

the rest began and said, that they had always regarded me more friendly towards them than any Frenchman they had seen; that the proofs they had of this in the past made their confidence easier for the future: moreover, that I had shown myself in reality their friend, by encountering so many risks in coming to see them and invite them to the war, and that all these considerations obliged them to feel as kindly disposed towards me as towards their own children. But they said that I had the preceding year broken my promise, that two thousand savages had gone to the Falls with the expectation of finding me ready to go to the war, and making me presents, but that they had not found me and were greatly saddened, supposing that I was dead, as some persons had told them. He said also, that the French who were at the Falls did not want to help them in their wars, that they had been badly treated by certain ones, so that they had resolved among themselves not to go to the Falls again, and that this had caused them, as they did not expect to see me again, to go alone to the war, and that in fact twelve hundred of them had already gone. And since the greater part of their warriors were absent, they begged me to postpone the expedition to the following year, saying that they would communicate the matter to all the people of their country. In regard to the four canoes, which I asked for, they granted them to me, but with great reluctance, telling me that they were greatly displeased at the idea of such an undertaking, in view of the hardships which I would endure; that the people there were sorcerers, that they had caused the death of many of their own tribe by charms and poisoning, on which account they were not their friends: moreover they said that, as it regards war, I was not to think of them, as they were little-hearted. With these and many other considerations they endeavored to deter me from my purpose.

But my sole desire on the other hand was to see this people, and enter into friendship with them, so that I might visit the North Sea. Accordingly, with a view to lessening the force of their objections, I said to them, that it was not far to the country in question; that the bad roads could not be worse than those I had already passed; that their witchcraft would have no power to harm me, as my God would preserve me from them; that I was also acquainted with their herbs, and would therefore beware of eating them; that I desired to make the two tribes mutual friends, and that I would to this end make presents to the other tribe, being assured that they would do something for me. In view of these reasons they granted me, as I have said, four canoes, at which I was very happy, forgetting all past hardships in the hope of seeing this sea, as I so much desired.

For the remainder of the day, I went out walking in their gardens, which were filled with squashes, beans, and our peas, which they were beginning to cultivate, when Thomas, my interpreter, who understands the language very well, came to inform me that the savages, after I had left them, had come to the conclusion, that if I were to undertake this journey I should die and they also, and that they could not furnish the promised canoes, as there was no one of them who would guide me, but that they wished me to postpone the journey until the next year, when they would conduct me with a good train to protect me from that people, in case they should attempt to harm me, as they are evil-disposed.

This intelligence greatly disturbed me, and I at once went to them and told them, that up to this day I had regarded them as men and truthful persons, but that now they had shown themselves children and liars, and that if they would not fulfil their promises, they would fail to show me their friendship; that, however, if they felt it an inconvenience to give me four canoes, they should only furnish two and four savages.

They represented to me anew the difficulties attending the journey, the number of the falls, the bad character of the people, and that their reason for refusing my request was their fear of losing me.

I replied that I was sorry to have them show themselves to so slight an extent my friends, and that I should never have believed it; that I had a young man, showing them my impostor, who had been in their country, and had not found all these difficulties which they represented, nor the people in question so bad as they asserted. Then they began to look at him, in particular Tessoüat the old captain, with whom he had passed the winter, and calling him by name he said to him in his language: Nicholas, is it true that you said you were among the Nebicerini? It was long before he spoke, when he said to them in their language, which he spoke to a certain extent: Yes, I was there. They immediately looked at him awry, and throwing themselves upon him, as if they would eat him up or tear him in pieces, raised loud cries, when Tessoüat said to him: You are a downright liar, you know well that you slept at my side every night with my children, where you arose every morning; if you were among the people mentioned, it was while sleeping. How could you have been so bold as to lead your chief to believe lies, and so wicked as to be willing to expose his life to so many dangers? You are a worthless fellow, and he ought to put you to death more cruelly than we do our enemies. I am not astonished that he should so importune us on the assurance of your words.

I at once told him that he must reply to these people; and since he had been in the regions indicated, that he must give me proofs of it, and free me from the suspense in which he had placed me. But he remained silent and greatly terrified.

I immediately withdrew him from the savages, and conjured him to declare the truth of the matter, telling him that, if he had seen the sea in question, I would give him the reward which I had promised him, and that, if he had not seen it, he must tell me so without causing me farther trouble. Again he affirmed with oaths all he had before said, and that he would demonstrate to me the truth of it, if the savages would give us canoes.

Upon this, Thomas came and informed me, that the savages of the island had secretly sent a canoe to the Nebicerini, to notify them of my arrival. Thereupon, in order to profit

by the opportunity, I went to the savages to tell them, that
I had dreamed the past night that they purposed to send a
canoe to the Nebicerini without notifying me of it, at which
I was greatly surprised, since they knew that I was desirous
of going there.   Upon which they replied that I did them a
great wrong in trusting a liar, who wanted to cause my death,
more than so many brave chiefs, who were my friends and
who held my life dear.   I replied that my man, meaning our
impostor, had been in the aforesaid country with one of the
relatives of Tessoüat and had seen the sea, the wreck and ruins
of an English vessel, together with eighty scalps which the
savages had in their possession, and a young English boy whom
they held as prisoner, and whom they wished to give me as a
present.

When they heard me speak of the sea, vessels, scalps of
the English, and the young prisoner, they cried out more than
before that he was a liar, and thus they afterwards called him,
as if it were the greatest insult they could have done him,
and they all united in saying that he ought to be put to death,
or else that he should tell with whom he had gone to the place
indicated, and state the lakes, rivers, and roads, by which he
had gone.   To this he replied with assurance, that he had
forgotten the name of the savage, although he had stated to
me his name more than twenty times, and even on the previous
day.   In respect to the peculiarities of the country, he had
described them in a paper which he had handed me.   Then
I brought forward the map and had it explained to the savages,
who questioned him in regard to it.   To this end he made no
reply, but rather manifested by his sullen silence his perverse
nature.

As my mind was wavering in uncertainty, I withdrew by
myself, and reflected upon the above-mentioned particulars
of the voyage of the English, and how the reports of our liar
were quite in conformity with it, also that there was little
probability of this young man's having invented all that, in
which case he would not have been willing to undertake the
journey, but that it was more probable that he had seen these

things, and that his ignorance did not permit him to reply to the questions of the savages. To the above is to be added the fact that, if the report of the English be true, the North Sea cannot be farther distant from this region than a hundred leagues in latitude, for I was in latitude 47° and in longitude 296°. But it may be that the difficulties attending the passage of the falls, the roughness of the mountains covered with snows, is the reason why this people have no knowledge of the sea in question; indeed they have always said that from the country of the Ochateguins it is a journey of thirty-five or forty days to the sea, which they see in three places, a thing which they have again assured me of this year. But no one has spoken to me of this sea on the north, except this liar, who had given me thereby great pleasure in view of the shortness of the journey.

Now, when this canoe was ready, I had him summoned into the presence of his companions; and after laying before him all that had transpired, I told him that any further dissimulation was out of the question, and that he must say whether he had seen these things or not; that I was desirous of improving the opportunity that presented itself; that I had forgotten the past; but that, if I went farther, I would have him hung and strangled, which should be his sole reward. After meditating by himself, he fell on his knees and asked my pardon, declaring that all he had said, both in France and this country, in respect to the sea in question was false; that he had never seen it, and that he had never gone farther than the village of Tessoüat; that he had said these things in order to return to Canada. Overcome with wrath at this, I had him removed, being unable to endure him any longer in my presence, and giving orders to Thomas to inquire into the whole matter in detail; to whom he stated, that he did not believe that I would undertake the journey on account of the dangers, thinking that some difficulty would present itself to prevent me from going on, as in the case of these savages, who were not disposed to lend me canoes; and accordingly that the journey would be put off until another year, when he being in France would be rewarded for his discovery; but that, if I would leave him in this country, he would go until he found the sea in question, even if he should die in the attempt. These were his words as reported to me by Thomas, but they did not give me much satisfaction, astounded as I was at the effrontery and maliciousness of this liar: and I cannot imagine how he could have devised this imposition, unless that he had heard of the above-mentioned voyage of the English, and in the hope of some reward, as he said, had the temerity to venture on it.

Shortly after I proceeded to notify the savages, to my great regret, of the malignity of this liar, stating that he had confessed the truth; at which they were delighted, reproaching me with the little confidence I put in them, who were chiefs and my friends, and who always spoke the truth; and who said that this liar ought to be put to death, being extremely malicious; and they added, Do you not see that he meant to cause your death. Give him to us, and we promise you that he shall not lie any more. And as they all went after him shouting, their children also shouting still more, I forbade them to do him any harm, directing them to keep their children also from doing so, inasmuch as I wished to take him to the Falls to show him to the gentlemen there, to whom he was to bring some salt water; and I said that, when I arrived there, I would consult as to what should be done with him.

My journey having been in this manner terminated, and without any hope of seeing the sea in this direction, except in imagination, I felt a regret that I should not have employed my time better, and that I should have had to endure the difficulties and hardships, which however I was obliged patiently to submit to. If I had gone in another direction, according to the report of the savages, I should have made a beginning in a thing which must be postponed to another time. At present my only wish being to return, I desired the savages to go to the Falls of St. Louis, where there were four vessels loaded with all kinds of merchandise, and where they would be well treated. This they communicated to all their neighbors. Before setting out, I made a cross of white cedar, which I planted in a prominent place on the border of the lake, with the arms of France, and I begged the savages to have the kindness to preserve it, as also those which they would find along the ways we had passed; telling them that, if they broke them, misfortune would befall them, but that, if they preserved them, they would not be assaulted by their enemies. They promised to do so, and said that I should find them when I came to visit them again.

Chapter 5

Our return to the Falls. False alarm. Ceremony at the Chaudière Falls. Confession of our liar before all the chief men. Our return to France.

On the 10th of June I took leave of Tessoüat, a good old captain, making him presents, and promising him, if God preserved me in health, to come the next year, prepared to go to war. He in turn promised to assemble a large number by that time, declaring that I should see nothing but savages and arms which would please me; he also directed his son to go with me for the sake of company. Thus we set out with forty canoes, and passed by way of the river we had left, which extends northward, and where we went on shore in order to cross the lakes. On the way we met nine large canoes of the Ouescharini, with forty strong and power-ful men, who had come upon the news they had received; we also met others, making altogether sixty canoes; and we overtook twenty others, who had set out before us, each heavily laden with merchandise.

We passed six or seven falls between the island of the Algonquins and the little fall, where the country was very unpleasant. I readily realized that, if we had gone in that direction, we should have had much more trouble, and should with difficulty have succeeded in getting through: and it

was not without reason that the savages opposed our liar, as
his only object was to cause my ruin.

Continuing our course ten or twelve leagues below the
island of the Algonquins, we rested on a very pleasant island,
which was covered with vines and nut-trees, and where we
caught some fine fish. About midnight, there arrived two
canoes, which had been fishing farther off, and which reported
that they had seen four canoes of their enemies. At once three
canoes were despatched to reconnoitre, but they returned
without having seen anything. With this assurance all gave
themselves up to sleep, excepting the women, who resolved
to spend the night in their canoes, not feeling at ease on land.
An hour before daylight a savage, having dreamed that the
enemy were attacking them, jumped up and started on a run
towards the water, in order to escape, shouting, They are killing
me. Those belonging to his band all awoke dumfounded and,
supposing that they were being pursued by their enemies,
threw themselves into the water, as did also one of our Frenchmen, who supposed that they were being overpowered. At
this great noise, the rest of us, who were at a distance, were at
once awakened, and without making farther investigation ran
towards them: but as we saw them here and there in the
water, we were greatly surprised, not seeing them pursued
by their enemies, nor in a state of defence, in case of necessity,
but only ready to sacrifice themselves. After I had inquired
of our Frenchman about the cause of this excitement, he
told me that a savage had had a dream, and that he with the
rest had thrown themselves into the water in order to escape,
supposing that they were being attacked. Accordingly, the
state of the case being ascertained, it all passed off in a laugh.

Continuing our way, we came to the Chaudière Falls,
where the savages went through with the customary ceremony,
which is as follows. After carrying their canoes to the foot
of the Fall, they assembled in one spot, where one of them
takes up a collection with a wooden plate, into which each
one puts a bit of tobacco. The collection having been made,
the plate is passed in the midst of the troupe, and all dance

about it, singing after their style. Then one of the captains makes an harangue, setting forth that for a long time they have been accustomed to make this offering, by which means they are insured protection against their enemies, that otherwise misfortune would befall them, as they are convinced by the evil spirit; and they live on in this superstition, as in many others, as we have said in other places. This done, the maker of the harangue takes the plate, and throws the tobacco into the midst of the caldron, whereupon they all together raise a loud cry. These poor people are so superstitious that they would not believe it possible for them to make a prosperous journey without observing this ceremony at this place, since their enemies await them at this portage, not venturing to go any farther on account of the difficulty of the journey, whence they say they surprise them there, as they have sometimes done.

The next day we arrived at an island at the entrance to a lake, and seven or eight leagues distant from the great Falls of St. Louis. Here while reposing at night we had another alarm, the savages supposing that they had seen the canoes of their enemies. This led them to make several large fires, which I had them put out, representing to them the harm which might result, namely, that instead of concealing they would disclose themselves.

On the 17th of June, we arrived at the Falls of St. Louis, where I found L'Ange, who had come to meet me in a canoe to inform me, that Sieur de Maisonneuve of St. Malo had brought a passport from the Prince for three vessels. In order to arrange matters until I should see him, I assembled all the savages and informed them that I did not wish them to traffic in any merchandise until I had given them permission, and that I would furnish them provisions as soon as we should arrive; which they promised, saying that they were my friends. Thus, continuing our course, we arrived at the barques, where we were saluted by some discharges of cannon, at which some of our savages were delighted, and others greatly astonished, never having heard such music. After I

had landed, Maisonneuve [1] came to me with the passport of
the Prince. As soon as I had seen it, I allowed him and his
men to enjoy the benefits of it like the rest of us; and I sent
word to the savages that they might trade on the next day.

After seeing all the chief men and relating the particulars
of my journey and the malice of my liar, at which they were
greatly amazed, I begged them to assemble, in order that in
their presence, and that of the savages and his companions,
he might make declaration of his maliciousness; which they
gladly did. Being thus assembled, they summoned him, and
asked him, why he had not shown me the sea in the north,
as he had promised me at his departure. He replied that
he had promised something impossible for him, since he had
never seen the sea, and that the desire of making the journey
had led him to say what he did, also that he did not suppose
that I would undertake it; and he begged them to be pleased
to pardon him, as he also begged me again, confessing that he
had greatly offended, and if I would leave him in the country,
he would by his efforts repair the offence, and see this sea,
and bring back trustworthy intelligence concerning it the following year; and in view of certain considerations I pardoned
him on this condition.

After relating to them in detail the good treatment I had
received at the abodes of the savages, and how I had been
occupied each day, I inquired what they had done during
my absence, and what had been the result of their hunting
excursions, and they said they had had such success that they
generally brought home six stags. Once on St. Barnabas's
day,[2] Sieur du Parc, having gone hunting with two others,
killed nine. These stags are not at all like ours, and there
are different kinds of them, some larger, others smaller, which
resemble closely our deer. They had also a very large number of pigeons, and also fish, such as pike, carp, sturgeon,
shad, barbel, turtles, bass, and other kinds unknown to us,

---

[1] Paul de Chomedy, Sieur de Maisonneuve, founded Montreal on this
spot in 1642. His permit was from the Prince of Condé.

[2] June 11.

s

on which they dined and supped every day. They were also all in better condition than myself, who was reduced from work and the anxiety which I had experienced, not having eaten more than once a day, and that of fish badly cooked and half broiled.

On the 22d of June, about 8 o'clock in the evening, the savages sounded an alarm because one of them had dreamed he had seen the Iroquois. In order to content them, all the men took their arms, and some were sent to their cabins to reassure them, and into the approaches to reconnoitre, so that, finding it was a false alarm, they were satisfied with the firing of some two hundred musket and arquebus shots, after which arms were laid down, the ordinary guard only being left. This reassured them greatly, and they were very glad to see the French ready to help them.

After the savages had bartered their articles of merchandise and had resolved to return, I asked them to take with them two young men, to treat them in a friendly manner, show them the country, and bind themselves to bring them back. But they strongly objected to this, representing to me the trouble our liar had given me, and fearing that they would bring me false reports, as he had done. I replied that they were men of probity and truth, and that if they would not take them they were not my friends, whereupon they resolved to do so. As for our liar, none of the savages wanted him, notwithstanding my request to them to take him, and we left him to the mercy of God.

Finding that I had no further business in this country, I resolved to cross in the first vessel that should return to France. Sieur de Maisonneuve, having his ready, offered me a passage, which I accepted; and on the 27th of June I set out with Sieur L'Ange from the Falls, where we left the other vessels, which were awaiting the return of the savages who had gone to the war, and we arrived at Tadoussac on the 6th of July.

On the 8th of August [1] we were enabled by favorable weather to set sail. On the 18th we left Gaspé and Isle Percée.

---

[1] July must be meant.

On the 28th we were on the Grand Bank, where the green fishery is carried on, and where we took as many fish as we wanted.

On the 26th of August we arrived at St. Malo, where I saw the merchants, to whom I represented the ease of forming a good association in the future, which they resolved to do, as those of Rouen and La Rochelle had done, after recognizing the necessity of the regulations, without which it is impossible to hope for any profit from these lands. May God by His grace cause this undertaking to prosper to His honor and glory, the conversion of these poor benighted ones, and to the welfare and honor of France.

VOYAGES AND DISCOVERIES IN NEW FRANCE FROM THE YEAR 1615 TO THE END OF THE YEAR 1618

VOYAGES AND DISCOVERIES IN NEW FRANCE FROM THE YEAR 1615 TO THE END OF THE YEAR 1618

BY SIEUR DE CHAMPLAIN, CAPTAIN IN ORDINARY TO THE KING IN THE WESTERN SEA

WHERE ARE DESCRIBED THE MANNERS, CUS-
toms, dress, mode of warfare, hunting, dances, festivals,
and method of burial of various savage peoples, with
many remarkable experiences of the author in this coun-
try, and an account of the beauty, fertility, and temper-
ature of the same.
Paris: Claude Collet, in the Palace, at the Gallery of the Pris-
oners. MDCXIX. With authority of the King.[1]

TO THE KING

SIRE,

This is a third volume[2] containing a narrative of what
has transpired most worthy of note during the voyages I have
made to New France, and its perusal will, I think, afford your
Majesty greater pleasure than that of those preceding, which
only designate the ports, harbors, situations, declinations, and
other particulars, having more interest for navigators and
sailors than for other persons. In this narrative you will be
able to observe more especially the manners and mode of life
of these peoples both in particular and in general, their wars,

---

[1] This italic heading is a translation of the title-page of the original of
1619.

[2] Reckoning the *Sauvages* of 1604 as the first, the *Voyages* of 1613 as
the second. and this, the *Voyages et Descouvertures* of 1619, as the third.

ammunition, method of attack and of defence, their expeditions and retreats in various circumstances, matters about which those interested desire information. You will perceive also that they are not savages to such an extent that they could not in course of time and through association with others become civilized and cultivated. You will likewise perceive how great hopes we cherish from the long and arduous labors we have for the past fifteen years sustained, in order to plant in this country the standard of the cross, and to teach the people the knowledge of God and the glory of His holy name, it being our desire to cultivate a feeling of charity towards His unfortunate creatures, which it is our duty to practise more patiently than any other thing, especially as there are many who have not entertained such purposes, but have been influenced only by the desire of gain. Nevertheless, we may, I suppose, believe that these are the means which God makes use of for the greater promotion of the holy desire of others. As the fruits which the trees bear are from God, the Lord of the soil, who has planted, watered, and nourished them with an especial care, so your Majesty can be called the legitimate lord of our labors, and the good resulting from them, not only because the land belongs to you, but also because you have protected us against so many persons, whose only object has been by troubling us to prevent the success of so holy a determination, taking from us the power to trade freely in a part of your country, and striving to bring everything into confusion, which would be, in a word, preparing the way for the ruin of everything to the injury of your state. To this end your subjects have employed every conceivable artifice and all possible means which they thought could injure us. But all these efforts have been thwarted by your Majesty, assisted by your prudent council, who have given us the authority of your name, and supported us by your decrees rendered in our favor. This is an occasion for increasing in us our long-cherished desire to send communities and colonies there, to teach the people the knowledge of God, and inform them of the glory and triumphs of your Majesty, so that together with the French language they may also acquire a French heart and spirit, which, next to the fear of God, will be inspired with nothing so ardently as the desire to serve you. Should our design succeed, the glory of it will be due, after God, to your Majesty, who will receive a thousand benedictions from Heaven for so many souls saved by your instrumentality, and your name will be immortalized for carrying the glory and sceptre of the French as far to the Occident as your precursors have extended it to the Orient, and over the entire habitable earth. This will augment the quality of MOST CHRISTIAN belonging to you above all the kings of the earth, and show that it is as much your due by merit as it is your own of right, it having been transmitted to you by your predecessors, who acquired it by their virtues; for you have been pleased, in addition to so many other important affairs, to give your attention to this one, so seriously neglected hitherto, God's special grace reserving to your reign the publication of His gospel, and the knowledge of His holy name to so many tribes who had never heard of it. And some day may God's grace lead them, as it does us, to pray to Him without ceasing to extend your empire, and to vouchsafe a thousand blessings to your Majesty.

SIRE,
Your most humble, most faithful,
and most obedient servant and subject,
CHAMPLAIN.

PREFACE

As in the various affairs of the world each thing strives for its perfection and the preservation of its being, so on the other hand does man interest himself in the different concerns of others on some account, either for the public good, or to acquire, apart from the common interest, praise, and reputation with some profit. Wherefore many have pursued this course, but as for myself I have made choice of the most unpleasant and difficult one of the perilous navigation of the seas; with the purpose, however, not so much of gaining wealth, as the honor and glory of God in behalf of my King and country, and contributing by my labors something useful to the public good. And I make declaration that I have not been tempted by any other ambition, as can be clearly perceived, not only by my conduct in the past, but also by the narratives of my voyages, made by the command of His Majesty, in New France, contained in my first and second books, as may be seen in the same.

Should God bless our purpose, which aims only for His glory, and should any fruit result from our discoveries and arduous labors, I will return thanks to Him, and for Your Majesty's protection and assistance will continue my prayers for the aggrandizement and prolongation of your reign.

EXTRACT FROM THE LICENSE OF THE KING

By favor and license of the KING, permission is given to Claude Collet, merchant bookseller in our city of Paris, to print, or have printed by such printer as shall seem good to him, a book entitled, *Voyages and Discoveries in New France, from the Year 1615 to the End of the Year 1618. By Sieur de Champlain, Captain in Ordinary to the King in the Western Sea.* All booksellers and printers of our kingdom are forbidden to print or have printed, to sell wholesale or retail, said book, except with the consent of said Collet, for the time and term of six years, beginning with the day when said book is printed, on penalty of confiscation of the copies, and a fine of four hundred livres, a half to go to us and a half to said petitioner. It is our will, moreover, that this license should be placed at the commencement or end of said book. This is our pleasure.

Given at Paris, the 18th day of May, 1619, and of our reign the tenth.

By the Council,

DE CESCAUD.

VOYAGE OF SIEUR DE CHAMPLAIN
TO NEW FRANCE, MADE IN
THE YEAR 1615

VOYAGE OF SIEUR DE CHAMPLAIN TO NEW FRANCE, MADE IN THE YEAR 1615[1]

THE strong love, which I have always cherished for the exploration of New France, has made me desirous of extending more and more my travels over the country, in order, by means of its numerous rivers, lakes, and streams, to obtain at last a complete knowledge of it, and also to become acquainted with the inhabitants, with the view of bringing them to the knowledge of God. To this end I have toiled constantly for the past fourteen or fifteen years, yet have been able to advance my designs but little, because I have not received the assistance which was necessary for the success of such an undertaking. Nevertheless, without losing courage, I have not ceased to push on, and visit various nations of the savages; and, by associating familiarly with them, I have concluded, as well from their conversation as from the knowledge already attained, that there is no better way than, disregarding all storms and difficulties, to have patience until His Majesty shall give the requisite attention to the matter, and meanwhile, not only to continue the exploration of the country, but also to learn the language, and form relations and friendships with the leading men of the villages and tribes, in order to lay the foundations of a permanent edifice, as well for the glory of God as for the renown of the French.

And His Majesty having transferred and intrusted the superintendence of this work to Monseigneur the Prince de Condé, the latter has, by his management, under the authority of His Majesty, sustained us against all sorts of jealousies

---

[1] Much to the disappointment of the savages, Champlain did not visit Canada during 1614. This was probably due to the civil war which his patron Condé was carrying on against the Queen Mother.

and obstacles concerted by evil wishers.   This has, as it were,
animated me and redoubled my courage for the continuation
of my labors in the exploration of New France, and with increased effort I have pushed forward in my undertaking into
the mainland, and farther on than I had previously been,
as will be hereafter indicated in the course of this narrative.

But it is appropriate to state first that, as I had observed
in my previous journeys, there were in some places people
permanently settled, who were fond of the cultivation of the
soil, but who had neither faith nor law, and lived without
God and religion, like brute beasts.   In view of this, I felt
convinced that I should be committing a grave offence if I
did not take it upon myself to devise some means of bringing
them to the knowledge of God.   To this end I exerted myself
to find some good friars, with zeal and affection for the glory
of God, that I might persuade them to send some one, or go
themselves, with me to these countries, and try to plant there
the faith, or at least do what was possible according to their
calling, and thus to observe and ascertain whether any good
fruit could be gathered there.   But since to attain this object
an expenditure would be required exceeding my means, and
for other reasons, I deferred the matter for a while, in view
of the difficulties there would be in obtaining what was necessary and requisite in such an enterprise; and since, furthermore, no persons offered to contribute to it.   Nevertheless,
while continuing my search, and communicating my plan to
various persons, a man of distinction chanced to present himself, whose intimate acquaintance I enjoyed.   This was Sieur
Hoüel, secretary of the King and controller-general of the salt
works at Brouage,[1] a man of devoted piety, and of great
zeal and love for the honor of God and the extension of His
religion.   He gave me the following information, which afforded
me great pleasure.   He said that he was acquainted with some
good religious fathers, of the order of the Recollects,[2] in whom
he had confidence; and that he enjoyed such intimacy and

[1] The salt marshes in this district are still worked.
[2] A branch of the Franciscans.

confidence with them that he could easily induce them to consent to undertake the voyage; and that, as to the necessary
means for sending out three or four friars, there would be no
lack of people of property who would give them what they
needed, offering for his part to assist them to the extent of
his ability; and, in fact, he wrote in relation to the subject
to Father du Verger, who welcomed with joy the undertaking,
and, in accordance with the recommendation of Sieur Hoüel,
communicated it to some of his brethren, who, burning with
charity, offered themselves freely for this holy undertaking.

Now he was at that time in Saintonge, whence he sent
two men to Paris with a commission, though not with absolute power, reserving the rest to the nuncio [1] of our Holy
Father the Pope, who was at that time, in 1614, in France.
He called upon these friars at their house in Paris, and was
greatly pleased with their resolution. We then went all together to see the Sieur Nuncio, in order to communicate to
him the commission, and entreat him to interpose his authority in the matter. But he, on the contrary, told us that he
had no power whatever in such matters, and that it was to
their General that they were to address themselves. Notwithstanding this reply, the Recollects, in consideration of
the difficulty of the mission, were unwilling to undertake
the journey on the authority of Father du Verger, fearing
that it might not be sufficient, and that the commission
might not be valid, on which account the matter was postponed to the following year. Meanwhile they took counsel,
and came to a determination, according to which all
arrangements were made for the undertaking, which was to
be carried out in the following spring; awaiting which the
two friars returned to their convent at Brouage.

I for my part improved the time in arranging my affairs
in preparation for the voyage.

Some months after the departure of the two friars, the
Reverend Father Chapoüin, Provincial of the Recollect Fathers,
a man of great piety, returned to Paris. Sieur Hoüel called on

[1] Roberto Ubaldini by name.

him, and narrated what had taken place respecting the authority of Father du Verger, and the mission he had given to the
Recollect Fathers. After which narrative the Provincial
Father proceeded to extol the plan, and to interest himself
with zeal in it, promising to promote it with all his power,
and adding that he had not before well comprehended the subject of this mission; and it is to be believed that God inspired
him more and more to prosecute the matter. Subsequently,
he spoke of it to Monseigneur the Prince de Condé, and to all
the cardinals and bishops who were then assembled at Paris
for the session of the Estates.[1] All of them approved and
commended the plan; and to show that they were favorably
disposed towards it, they assured the Sieur Provincial that
they would devise among themselves and the members of the
court means for raising a small fund, and that they would collect some money for assisting four friars to be chosen, and who
were then chosen for the execution of so holy a work. And
in order to facilitate the undertaking, I visited at the Estates
the cardinals and bishops, and urgently represented to them
the advantage and usefulness which might one day result, in
order by my entreaties to move them to give, and cause others
who might be stimulated by their example to give, contributions and presents, leaving all to their good will and judgment.

The contributions which were made for the expenses of
this expedition amounted to nearly fifteen hundred livres,
which were put into my hands, and then employed, according to the advice and in the presence of the fathers, for the
purchase of what was necessary, not only for the mainte-
nance of the fathers who should undertake the journey into
New France, but also for their clothing, and the attire and
ornaments necessary for performing divine service. The
friars were sent on in advance to Honfleur, where their embarkation was to take place.

Now the fathers who were appointed for this holy enterprise were Father Denis [2] as commissary, Jean d'Olbeau,

---

[1] The great sitting of the States General in 1614, the last before the
gathering of 1789 which brought on the Revolution.   [2] Denis Jamay.

Joseph le Caron, and Pacifique du Plessis,[1] each of whom was moved by a holy zeal and ardor to make the journey, through God's grace, in order to see if they might produce some good fruit, and plant in these regions the standard of Jesus Christ, determined to live and to die for His holy name, should it be necessary to do so and the occasion require it. Everything having been prepared, they provided themselves with church ornaments, and we with what was necessary for our voyage.

I left Paris the last day of February to meet at Rouen our associates, and represent to them the will of Monseigneur the Prince, and also his desire that these good fathers should make the journey, since he recognized the fact that the affairs of the country could hardly reach any perfection or advancement, if God should not first of all be served; with which our associates were highly pleased, promising to assist the fathers to the extent of their ability, and provide them with the support they might need.

The fathers arrived at Rouen the twentieth of March following, where we stayed some time. Thence we went to Honfleur to embark, where we also stayed some days, waiting for our vessel to be got ready, and loaded with the necessaries for so long a voyage. Meanwhile preparations were made in matters of conscience, so that each one of us might examine himself, and cleanse himself from his sins by penitence and confession, in order to celebrate the sacrament and attain a state of grace, so that, being thereby freer in conscience, we might, under the guidance of God, expose ourselves to the mercy of the waves of the great and perilous sea.

This done, we embarked on the vessel of the association, which was of three hundred and fifty tons burden, and was called the *Saint Étienne,* commanded by Sieur de Pont Gravé.

---

[1] Pacifique du Plessis was a lay-brother, though sometimes given the title of Father. For further information concerning the Recollect mission, consult Laverdière, especially IV. 7, 10, and the *Histoire du Canada* (1636, reprinted by Tross, 1866) by Gabriel Sagard, himself a Recollect friar.

T

We departed from Honfleur on the twenty-fourth day of August,[1] in the above-mentioned year, and set sail with a very favorable wind. We continued on our voyage without encountering ice or other dangers, through the mercy of God, and in a short time arrived off the place called Tadoussac, on the twenty-fifth day of May, when we rendered thanks to God for having conducted us so favorably to the harbor of our destination.

Then we began to set men at work to fit up our barques in order to go to Quebec, the place of our abode, and to the great Falls of St. Louis, the rendezvous of the savages, who come there to traffic.

The barques having been fitted up, we went on board with the fathers, one of whom, named Father Joseph, desired, without stopping or making any stay at Quebec, to go directly to the great Falls, where he saw all the savages and their mode of life. This induced him to go and spend the winter in their country and that of other tribes who have a fixed abode, not only in order to learn their language, but also to see what the prospect was of their conversion to Christianity. This resolution having been formed, he returned to Quebec the twentieth day of June for some church ornaments and other necessaries. Meanwhile I had stayed at Quebec in order to arrange matters relating to our habitation, as the lodgings of the fathers, church ornaments, the construction of a chapel for the celebration of the mass, as also the employment of persons for clearing up lands. I embarked for the Falls together with Father Denis, who had arrived the same day from Tadoussac with Sieur de Pont Gravé.

As to the other friars, viz., Fathers Jean and Pacifique, they stayed at Quebec in order to fit up their chapel and arrange their lodgings. They were greatly pleased at seeing the place so different from what they had imagined, which increased their zeal.

We arrived at the Rivière des Prairies, five leagues below the Falls of St. Louis, whither the savages had come down.

---

[1] Sagard says April, which is certainly correct.

I will not attempt to speak of the pleasure which our fathers experienced at seeing, not only so long and large a river, filled with many fine islands and bordered by a region apparently so fertile, but also a great number of strong and robust men, with natures not so savage as their manners, nor as they acknowledged they had conceived them to be, and very different from what they had been given to understand, owing to their lack of cultivation. I will not enter into a description of them, but refer the reader to what I have said about them in my preceding books, printed in the year 1614.[1]

To continue my narrative: We met Father Joseph, who was returning to Quebec in order to make preparations, and take what he needed for wintering in their country. This I did not think advisable at this season, but counselled him rather to spend the winter at our settlement as being more for his comfort, and undertake the journey when spring came or at least in summer, offering to accompany him, and adding that by doing so he would not fail to see what he might have seen by going, and that by returning and spending the winter at Quebec he would have the society of his brothers and others who remained at the settlement, by which he would be more profited than by staying alone among these people, with whom he could not, in my opinion, have much satisfaction. Nevertheless, in spite of all that could be said to him and all representations, he would not change his purpose, being urged by a godly zeal and love for this people, and hoping to make known to them their salvation.

His motive in undertaking this enterprise, as he stated to us, was that he thought it was necessary for him to go there not only in order to become better acquainted with the characteristics of the people, but also to learn more easily their language. In regard to the difficulties which it was represented to him that he would have to encounter in his intercourse with them, he felt assured that he could bear and overcome them, and that he could adapt himself very well and

[1] The volume bears date 1613, but may not have been actually issued till 1614.

cheerfully to the manner of living and the inconveniences he would find, through the grace of God, of whose goodness and help he felt clearly assured, being convinced that, since he went on His service, and since it was for the glory of His name, and the preaching of His holy gospel that he undertook freely this journey, He would never abandon him in his undertaking. And in regard to temporal provisions very little was needed to satisfy a man who demands nothing but perpetual poverty, and who seeks for nothing but heaven, not only for himself but also for his brethren, it being inconsistent with his rule of life to have any other ambition than the glory of God, and it being his purpose to endure to this end all the hardships, sufferings, and labors which might offer.

Seeing him impelled by so holy a zeal and so ardent a charity, I was unwilling to try any more to restrain him. Thus he set out with the purpose of being the first to announce through His holy favor to this people the name of God, having the great satisfaction that an opportunity presented itself for suffering something for the name and glory of our Saviour Jesus Christ.

As soon as I had arrived at the Falls, I visited the people, who were very desirous of seeing us and delighted at our return. They hoped that we would furnish them some of our number to assist them in their wars against our enemies, representing to us that they could with difficulty come to us if we should not assist them; for the Iroquois, they said, their old enemies, were always on the road obstructing their passage. Moreover, I had constantly promised to assist them in their wars, as they gave us to understand by their interpreter. Whereupon Sieur Pont Gravé and myself concluded that it was very necessary to assist them, not only in order to put them the more under obligations to love us, but also to facilitate my undertakings and explorations which, as it seemed, could only be accomplished by their help, and also as this would be a preparatory step to their conversion to Christianity. Therefore I resolved to go and explore their country and assist

them in their wars, in order to oblige them to show me what
they had so many times promised to do.

We accordingly caused them all to assemble together, that
we might communicate to them our intention. When they
had heard it, they promised to furnish us two thousand five
hundred and fifty men of war, who would do wonders, with
the understanding that I with the same end in view should
furnish as many men as possible. This I promised to do, being very glad to see them decide so well. Then I proceeded
to make known to them the methods to be adopted for fighting,
in which they took especial pleasure, manifesting a strong
hope of victory. Everything having been decided upon, we
separated with the intention of returning for the execution
of our undertaking. But before entering upon this journey,
which would require not less than three or four months, it
seemed desirable that I should go to our settlement to make
the necessary arrangements there for my absence.

On the —— day of —— following I set out on my
return to the Rivière des Prairies.¹ While there with two
canoes of savages I met Father Joseph, who was returning
from our settlement with some church ornaments for celebrating the holy sacrifice of the mass, which was chanted on
the border of the river with all devotion by the Reverend
Fathers Denis and Joseph, in presence of all the people, who
were amazed at seeing the ceremonies observed and the
ornaments which seemed to them so handsome. It was
something which they had never before seen, for these Fathers
were the first who celebrated here the holy mass.

To return and continue the narrative of my journey: I
arrived at Quebec on the 26th, where I found the Fathers
Jean and Pacifique in good health. They on their part did

He probably left the falls on June 23. The first celebration of the mass
in New France took place on June 24, the festival of St. John the Baptist.
(Laverdière.) It may be safer, despite Champlain's statement below, to
say the first celebration of the mass since Cartier's time; for Cartier seems
to have had priests with him upon his second voyage. *Early English and
French Voyages*, p. 53.

their duty at that place in getting all things ready. They celebrated the holy mass, which had never been said there before,
nor had there ever been any priest in this region.

Having arranged all matters at Quebec, I took with me
two men and returned to the Rivière des Prairies, in order
to go with the savages. I left Quebec on the fourth day of
July, and on the eighth of the month while *en route* I met
Sieur du Pont Gravé and Father Denis, who were returning
to Quebec, and who told me that the savages had departed
greatly disappointed at my not going with them; and that
many of them declared that we were dead or had been taken
by the Iroquois, since I was to be gone only four or five days,
but had been gone ten. This made them and even our own
Frenchmen give up hope, so much did they long to see us
again. They told me that Father Joseph had departed with
twelve Frenchmen, who had been furnished to assist the
savages. This intelligence troubled me somewhat; since, if I
had been there, I should have arranged many things for the
journey, which I could not now do. I was troubled not only
on account of the small number of men, but also because
there were only four or five who were acquainted with the hand-
ling of arms, while in such an expedition the best are not too
good in this particular. All this, however, did not cause me
to lose courage at all for going on with the expedition, on
account of the desire I had of continuing my explorations.
I separated accordingly from Sieurs du Pont Gravé and Father
Denis, determined to go on in the two canoes which I had, and
follow after the savages, having provided myself with what
I needed.

On the 9th of the month I embarked with two others,
namely, one of our interpreters and my man, accompanied
by ten savages in the two canoes, these being all they could
carry, as they were heavily loaded and encumbered with
clothes, which prevented me from taking more men.

We continued our voyage up the River St. Lawrence some
six leagues, and then went by the Rivière des Prairies, which
discharges into that river. Leaving on the left the Falls of

St. Louis, which are five or six leagues higher up, and passing
several small falls on this river, we entered a lake, after passing
which we entered the river where I had been before, which
leads to the Algonquins, a distance of eighty-nine leagues [1]
from the Falls of St. Louis. Of this river I have made an
ample description, with an account of my explorations, in
my preceding book, printed in 1614. For this reason I shall
not speak of it in this narrative, but pass on directly to the
lake of the Algonquins.[2] Here we entered a river [3] which
flows into this lake, up which we went some thirty-five leagues,
passing a large number of falls both by land and water, the
country being far from attractive, and covered with pines,
birches, and some oaks, being also very rocky, and in many
places somewhat hilly. Moreover, it was very barren and ster-
ile, being but thinly inhabited by certain Algonquin savages,
called Otaguottouemin, who dwell in the country, and live
by hunting and the fish they catch in the rivers, ponds, and
lakes, with which the region is well provided. It seems indeed
that God has been pleased to give to these forbidding and
desert lands some things in their season for the refreshment
of man and the inhabitants of these places. For I assure you
that there are along the rivers many strawberries, also a marvellous quantity of blueberries, a little fruit very good to eat,
and other small fruits. The people here dry these fruits for
the winter, as we do plums in France for Lent. We left this
river,[4] which comes from the north, and by which the savages
go to the Saguenay [5] to barter their furs for tobacco. This

---

[1] If this refers to the distance from the Algonquins (*i.e.*, Allumette
Island) to the Lachine Rapids, he is very nearly correct, as it is just over
200 miles; if to that between the rapids and the mouth of the Ottawa, or
the spot where they struck that river after crossing the Lake of Two Mountains, 89 must be a misprint for 8 or 9. The former explanation is the more
probable, though Laverdière and apparently Slafter adopt the latter.

[2] Allumette Lake.

[3] The Ottawa.

[4] They left the Ottawa, at its junction with the Mattawa.

[5] *I.e.*, by ascending the Ottawa and then making a series of short
portages to the Chamouchouan, which flows into Lake St. John.

place is situated in latitude 46°, and is very pleasant, but otherwise of little account.

Continuing our journey by land, after leaving the river of the Algonquins, we passed several lakes where the savages carry their canoes, and entered the lake of the Nipissings, in latitude 46° 15′, on the twenty-sixth day of the month, having gone by land and the lakes twenty-five leagues, or thereabouts. We then arrived at the cabins of the savages, with whom we stayed two days. There was a large number of them, who gave us a very welcome reception. They are a people who cultivate the land but little. A shows the dress of these people as they go to war; B that of the women,[1] which differs in nowise from that of the Montagnais and the great people of the Algonquins, extending far into the interior.

During the time that I was with them the chief of this tribe and their most prominent men entertained us with many banquets according to their custom, and took the trouble to go fishing and hunting with me, in order to treat me with the greatest courtesy possible. These people are very numerous, there being from seven to eight hundred souls, who live in general near the lake. This contains a large number of very pleasant islands, among others one more than six leagues long, with three or four fine ponds and a number of fine meadows; it is bordered by very fine woods, that contain an abundance of game, which frequent the little ponds, where the savages also catch fish. The northern side of the lake is very pleasant, with fine meadows for the grazing of cattle, and many little streams, discharging into the lake.

They were fishing at that time in a lake very abundant in various kinds of fish, among others one a foot long that was very good. There are also other kinds which the savages catch for the purpose of drying and storing away. The lake is some eight leagues broad and twenty-five long,[2] into which a river[3] flows from the northwest, along which they go to barter the merchandise, which we give them in exchange for

---

[1] References to illustrations not reproduced in this volume.
[2] Really about 50 miles by 14.   [3] Sturgeon River.

their peltry, with those who live on it, and who support themselves by hunting and fishing, their country containing great
quantities of animals, birds, and fish.

After resting two days with the chief of the Nipissings
we re-embarked in our canoes, and entered a river,[1] by which
this lake discharges itself. We proceeded down it some
thirty-five leagues, and descended several little falls by land
and by water, until we reached Lake Attigouautan.[2] All
this region is still more unattractive than the preceding, for
I saw along this river only ten acres of arable land, the rest
being rocky and very hilly. It is true that near Lake Attigouautan we found some Indian corn, but only in small quantity. Here our savages proceeded to gather some squashes,
which were acceptable to us, for our provisions began to give
out in consequence of the bad management of the savages,
who ate so heartily at the beginning that towards the end
very little was left, although we had only one meal a day.
But, as I have mentioned before, we did not lack for blueberries and strawberries; otherwise we should have been in
danger of being reduced to straits.

We met three hundred men of a tribe we named *Cheveux
Relevés*,[3] since their hair is very high and carefully arranged,
and better dressed beyond all comparison than that of our
courtiers, in spite of their irons and refinements. This gives
them a handsome appearance. They have no breeches, and
their bodies are very much pinked [4] in divisions of various

---

[1] French River.

[2] Lake Huron. To connect it with Ottawa by canals and by deepen-
ing the channel of French River is a project long discussed in Canada. The
route which Champlain had just followed to it "continued to be the fur
traders' highroad to the west until the days of steamboat navigation. In
the early years of the colony it was beyond the usual reach of Iroquois war
parties, and it is, in fact, the shortest and most direct course to Lake Superior,
for from the Strait of Michilimackinac to the head of tide water, at Lake
St. Peter, below Montreal, is an absolutely due east line — the parallel of
46° N." Dawson, *The St. Lawrence*, p. 273.

[3] Their place of abode lay between Georgian Bay and Lake Huron.

[4] *Decouppez; i.e.*, with the skin punctured or cut away to form a
pattern.

shapes. They paint their faces in various colors, have their nostrils pierced, and their ears adorned with beads. When they go out of their houses they carry a club. I visited them, became somewhat acquainted, and formed a friendship with them. I gave a hatchet to their chief, who was as much pleased and delighted with it as if I had given him some rich present. Entering into conversation with him, I inquired in regard to the extent of his country, which he pictured to me with coal on the bark of a tree. He gave me to understand that he had come into this place for drying the fruit called *bluës*,[1] to serve for manna in winter, and when they can find nothing else. A and C show the manner in which they arm themselves when they go to war.[2] They have as arms only the bow and arrow, made in the manner you see depicted, and which they regularly carry; also a round shield of dressed leather made from an animal like the buffalo.

The next day we separated, and continued our course along the shore of the lake of the Attigouautan, which contains a large number of islands. We went some forty-five leagues, all the time along the shore of the lake. It is very large, nearly four hundred leagues long from east to west, and fifty leagues broad, and in view of its great extent I have named it the *Mer Douce*.[3] It is very abundant in various sorts of very good fish, both those which we have and those we do not, but especially in trout, which are enormously large, some of which I saw as long as four feet and a half, the least being two feet and a half. There are also pike of like size, and a certain kind of sturgeon, a very large fish and of remarkable excellence. The country bordering this lake is partly hilly, as on the north side, and partly flat, inhabited by savages, and thinly covered with wood, including oaks. After crossing a bay, which forms one of the extremities of the lake,[4] we went

---

[1] Blueberries.

[2] References to illustrations not reproduced in the present volume.

[3] *I.e.*, the Fresh-water Sea. Its greatest dimensions are 186 miles north to south, and 220 east to west.

[4] They were really coasting the eastern shore of the Georgian Bay. The bay here referred to is Matchedash.

some seven leagues until we arrived in the country of the Attigouautan [1] at a village called Otoüacha, on the first day of
August. Here we found a great change in the country. It
was here very fine, the largest part being cleared up, and
many hills and several rivers rendering the region agreeable.
I went to see their Indian corn, which was at that time far
advanced for the season.

These localities seemed to me very pleasant, in comparison with so disagreeable a region as that from which we had
come. The next day I went to another village, called Car-
maron, a league distant from this, where they received us in
a very friendly manner, making for us a banquet with their
bread, squashes, and fish. As to meat, that is very scarce
there. The chief of this village earnestly begged me to stay,
to which I could not consent, but returned to our village,
where on the next night but one, as I went out of the cabin
to escape the fleas, of which there were large numbers and
by which we were tormented, a girl of little modesty came
boldly to me and offered to keep me company, for which
I thanked her, sending her away with gentle remonstrances,
and spent the night with some savages.

The next day I departed from this village to go to another, called Touaguainchain, and to another, called Teque-
nonquiaye, in which we were received in a very friendly manner by the inhabitants, who showed us the best cheer they
could with their Indian corn served in various styles. This
country is very fine and fertile, and travelling through it is
very pleasant.

Thence I had them guide me to Carhagouha, which was
fortified by a triple palisade of wood thirty-five feet high for
its defence and protection. In this village Father Joseph
was staying, whom we saw and were very glad to find well.
He on his part was no less glad, and was expecting nothing
so little as to see me in this country. On the twelfth day of
August the Recollect Father celebrated the holy mass, and

---

[1] They were a principal tribe of the Hurons, living within the limits
of the present county of Simcoe. (Slafter.)

a cross was planted near a small house apart from the village, which the savages built while I was staying there, awaiting the arrival of our men and their preparation to go to the war, in which they had been for a long time engaged.

Finding that they were so slow in assembling their army, and that I should have time to visit their country, I resolved to go by short days' journeys from village to village as far as Cahiagué,[1] where the rendezvous of the entire army was to be, and which was fourteen leagues distant from Carhagouha, from which village I set out on the fourteenth of August with ten of my companions. I visited five of the more important villages, which were enclosed with palisades of wood, and reached Cahiagué, the principal village of the country, where there were two hundred large cabins and where all the men of war were to assemble. Now in all these villages they received us very courteously with their simple welcome. All the country where I went contains some twenty to thirty leagues, is very fine, and situated in latitude 44° 30′. It is very extensively cleared up. They plant in it a great quantity of Indian corn, which grows there finely. They plant likewise squashes, and sunflowers, from the seed of which they make oil, with which they anoint the head. The region is extensively traversed with brooks, discharging into the lake. There are many very good vines and plums, which are excellent, raspberries, strawberries, little wild apples, nuts, and a kind of fruit of the form and color of small lemons, with a similar taste, but having an interior which is very good and almost like that of figs. The plant which bears this fruit is two and a half feet high, with but three or four leaves at most, which are of the shape of those of the fig-tree, and each plant bears but two pieces of fruit. There are many of these plants in various places, the fruit being very good and savory.[2] Oaks, elms, and beeches are numerous here, as also forests of fir, the regular retreat of partridges and hares. There are also quantities of small cherries and black cherries, and the

---

[1] Near the lower end of Lake Simcoe, in Ontario.
[2] The May-apple. (Slafter.)

same varieties of wood that we have in our forests in France. The soil seems to me indeed a little sandy, yet it is for all that good for their kind of cereal. The small tract of country which I visited is thickly settled with a countless number of human beings, not to speak of the other districts where I did not go, and which, according to general report, are as thickly settled or more so than those mentioned above. I reflected what a great misfortune it is that so many poor creatures live and die without the knowledge of God, and even without any religion or law established among them, whether divine, political, or civil; for they neither worship, nor pray to any object, at least so far as I could perceive from their conversation. But they have, however, some sort of ceremony, which I shall describe in its proper place, in regard to the sick, or in order to ascertain what is to happen to them, and even in regard to the dead. These, however, are the works of certain persons among them, who want to be confidentially consulted in such matters, as was the case among the ancient pagans, who allowed themselves to be carried away by the persuasions of magicians and diviners. Yet the greater part of the people do not believe at all in what these charlatans do and say. They are very generous to one another in regard to provisions, but otherwise very avaricious. They do not give in return. They are clothed with deer and beaver skins, which they obtain from the Algonquins and Nipissings in exchange for Indian corn and meal.

On the 17th of August I arrived at Cahiagué, where I was received with great joy and gladness by all the savages of the country, who had abandoned their undertaking, in the belief that they would see me no more, and that the Iroquois had captured me, as I have before stated. This was the cause of the great delay experienced in this expedition, they even having postponed it to the following year. Meanwhile they received intelligence that a certain nation of their allies,[1]

---

[1] The Andastes, Conestogas, or Susquehannocks. "This tribe was probably situated on the upper waters of the Susquehanna, and consequently south of the Five Nations." (Slafter.)

dwelling three good days' journeys beyond the Entouhonorons,[1] on whom the Iroquois also make war, desired to assist them in this expedition with five hundred good men; also to form an alliance and establish a friendship with us, that we might all engage in the war together; moreover that they greatly desired to see us and give expression to the pleasure they would have in making our acquaintance.

I was glad to find this opportunity for gratifying my desire of obtaining a knowledge of their country.[2] It is situated only seven days from where the Dutch [3] go to traffic on the fortieth degree. The savages there, assisted by the Dutch, make war upon them, take them prisoners, and cruelly put them to death; and indeed they told us that the preceding year, while making war, they captured three of the Dutch, who were assisting their enemies, as we do the Attigouautans, and while in action one of their own men was killed. Nevertheless they did not fail to send back the three Dutch prisoners, without doing them any harm, supposing that they belonged to our party, since they had no knowledge of us except by hearsay, never having seen a Christian; otherwise, they said, these three prisoners would not have got off so easily, and would not escape again should they surprise and take them. This nation is very warlike, as those of the nation of the Attigouautans maintain. They have only three villages, which are in the midst of more than twenty others, on which they make war without assistance from their friends; for they are obliged to pass through the thickly settled country of the Chouontouaroüon,[4] or else they would have to make a very long circuit.

[1] Champlain appears to apply the name Iroquois only to the Eastern portion of the Confederacy of the Five Nations, giving this Indian name to those farther west.

[2] *I.e.*, the middle portions of the present state of New York.

[3] In 1609 Hudson, then in the Dutch service, sailed up the river which bears his name, and from that time desultory trading was carried on at Manhattan Island. In 1615 a trading fort was built at Fort Nassau, afterwards Orange, the modern Albany.

[4] *I.e.*, the Entouhonorons, previously mentioned. From this is derived the modern word Ontario.

After arriving at the village, it was necessary for me to remain until the men of war should come from the surrounding villages, so that we might be off as soon as possible. During this time there was a constant succession of banquets and dances on account of the joy they experienced at seeing me so determined to assist them in their war, just as if they were already assured of victory.

The greater portion of our men having assembled, we set out from the village on the first day of September, and passed along the shore of a small lake[1] distant three leagues from the village, where they catch large quantities of fish, which they preserve for the winter. There is another lake,[2] closely adjoining, which is twenty-five leagues in circuit, and flows into the small one by a strait, where the above-mentioned extensive fishing is carried on. This is done by means of a large number of stakes which almost close the strait, only some little openings being left where they place their nets, in which the fish are caught. These two lakes discharge into the *Mer Douce*. We remained some time in this place to await the rest of our savages. When they were all assembled, with their arms, meal, and necessaries, it was decided to choose some of the most resolute men to compose a party to go and give notice of our departure to those who were to assist us with five hundred men, that they might join us, and that we might appear together before the fort of the enemy. The decision having been made, they dispatched two canoes, with twelve of the most stalwart savages, and also with one of our interpreters, who asked me to permit him to make the journey, which I readily accorded, inasmuch as he was led to do so of his own will, and as he might in this way see their country and get a knowledge of the people living there. The danger, however, was not small, since it was necessary to pass through the midst of enemies. They set out on the 8th of the month, and on the 10th following there was a heavy white frost.

We continued our journey towards the enemy, and went some five or six leagues through these lakes, where the

---

[1] Lake Couchiching.   [2] Lake Simcoe.

savages carried their canoes about ten leagues by land. We then came to another lake,[1] six to seven leagues in length and three broad. From this flows a river which discharges into the great lake of the Entouhonorons. After traversing this lake we passed a fall, and continuing our course down this river for about sixty-four leagues entered the lake of the Entouhonorons, having passed, on our way by land, five falls, some being from four to five leagues long. We also passed several lakes of considerable size, through which the river passes.[2] The latter is large and very abundant in good fish.

It is certain that all this region is very fine and pleasant. Along the banks it seems as if the trees had been set out for ornament in most places, and that all these tracts were in former times inhabited by savages, who were subsequently compelled to abandon them from fear of their enemies. Vines and nut-trees are here very numerous. Grapes mature, yet there is always a very pungent tartness which is felt remaining in the throat when one eats them in large quantities, arising from defect of cultivation. These localities are very pleasant when cleared up.

Stags and bears are here very abundant. We tried the hunt and captured a large number as we journeyed down. It was done in this way. They place four or five hundred savages in line in the woods, so that they extend to certain points on the river; then marching in order with bow and arrow in hand, shouting and making a great noise in order to frighten the beasts, they continue to advance until they come to the end of the point. Then all the animals between the point and the hunters are forced to throw themselves into the water, as many at least as do not fall by the arrows shot at them by the hunters. Meanwhile the savages, who are

---

[1] Sturgeon Lake.

[2] The route, here described as consisting of the course of one river, would now be defined as passing successively down the Otonabee River, through Rice Lake, and down the River Trent. It entered Lake Ontario through the Bay of Quinte. Coming thus into Lake Ontario at its north-eastern corner, the war party skirted the east shore of the lake, and left it at its southeastern corner.

expressly arranged and posted in their canoes along the shore, easily approach the stags and other animals, tired out and greatly frightened in the chase, when they readily kill them with the spear-heads attached to the extremity of a piece of wood of the shape of a half-pike. This is the way they engage in the chase; and they do likewise on the islands where there are large quantities of game. I took especial pleasure in seeing them hunt thus and in observing their dexterity. Many animals were killed by the shot of the arquebus, at which the savages were greatly surprised. But it unfortunately happened that, while a stag was being killed, a savage, who chanced to come in range, was wounded by a shot of an arquebus. Thence a great commotion arose among them, which however subsided when some presents were given to the wounded. This is the usual manner of allaying and settling quarrels, and, in case of the death of the wounded, presents are given to the relatives of the one killed.

As to smaller game there is a large quantity of it in its season. There are also many cranes, white as swans, and other varieties of birds like those in France.

We proceeded by short days' journeys as far as the shore of the lake of the Entouhonorons, constantly hunting as before mentioned. Here at its eastern extremity, which is the entrance to the great River St. Lawrence, we made the traverse, in latitude 43°, where in the passage there are very large beautiful islands. We went about fourteen leagues in passing to the southern side of the lake towards the territory of the enemy. The savages concealed all their canoes in the woods near the shore. We went some four leagues over a sandy strand, where I observed a very pleasant and beautiful country, intersected by many little streams and two small rivers, which discharge into the before-mentioned lake, also many ponds and meadows, where there was an endless amount of game, many vines, fine woods, and a large number of chestnut trees, whose fruit was still in the burr. The chestnuts are small, but of a good flavor. The country is covered with forests, which over its greater portion have not been cleared up. All the canoes being thus hidden, we left the border of the lake, which is some eighty leagues long and twenty-five wide.[1] The greater portion of its shores is inhabited by savages. We continued our course by land for about twenty-five or thirty leagues. In the space of four days we crossed many brooks, and a river which proceeds from a lake that discharges into that of the Entouhonorons.[2] This lake is twenty-five or thirty leagues in circuit, contains some fine islands, and is the place where our enemies, the Iroquois, catch their fish, in which it abounds.

On the 9th of the month of October, our savages going out to reconnoitre met eleven savages, whom they took prisoners. They consisted of four women, three boys, one girl, and three men, who were going fishing and were distant some four leagues from the fort of the enemy. Now it is to be noted that one of the chiefs, on seeing the prisoners, cut off the finger of one of these poor women as a beginning of their usual punishment; upon which I interposed and reprimanded the chief, Iroquet, representing to him that it was not the act of a warrior, as he declared himself to be, to conduct himself with cruelty towards women, who have no defence but their tears, and that one should treat them with humanity on account of their helplessness and weakness; and I told him that on the contrary this act would be deemed to proceed from a base and brutal courage, and that if he committed any more of these cruelties he would not give me heart to assist them or favor them in the war. To which the only answer he gave me was that their enemies treated them in the same manner, but that, since this was displeasing to me, he would not do anything more to the women, although he would to the men.

The next day, at three o'clock in the afternoon, we arrived before the fort[3] of their enemies, where the savages made

---

[1] About 180 miles by 50.

[2] Oneida River, flowing from Oneida Lake into Lake Ontario.

[3] Some miles south of Oneida Lake. It was probably situated on Nichols's Pond and on two streams which enter and leave it, in the township of Fenner, in Madison County, New York.

some skirmishes with each other, although our design was
not to disclose ourselves until the next day, which however
the impatience of our savages would not permit, both on account of their desire to see fire opened upon their enemies,
and also that they might rescue some of their own men who
had become too closely engaged, and were hotly pressed. Then
I approached the enemy, and although I had only a few men,
yet we showed them what they had never seen nor heard
before; for, as soon as they saw us and heard the arquebus
shots and the balls whizzing in their ears, they withdrew speedily to their fort, carrying the dead and wounded in this charge.
We also withdrew to our main body, with five or six wounded,
one of whom died.

This done, we withdrew to the distance of cannon range,
out of sight of the enemy, but contrary to my advice and to
what they had promised me. This moved me to address
them very rough and angry words in order to incite them to
do their duty, foreseeing that if everything should go according to their whim and the guidance of their council, their
utter ruin would be the result. Nevertheless I did not fail
to send to them and propose means which they should use in
order to get possession of their enemies.

These were, to make with certain kinds of wood a *cavalier*[1] which should be higher than the palisades. Upon this
were to be placed four or five of our arquebusiers, who should
keep up a constant fire over their palisades and galleries,
which were well provided with stones, and by this means dislodge the enemy who might attack us from their galleries.
Meanwhile orders were to be given to procure boards for making a sort of mantelet [2] to protect our men from the arrows
and stones of which the savages generally make use. These
instruments, namely the cavalier and mantelets, were capable
of being carried by a large number of men. One mantelet was

---

[1] A wooden framework with an enclosed platform on top. In the
original Champlain gives a very spirited drawing of the siege; it is reproduced
in this volume.
[2] A large wooden shield.

so constructed that the water could not extinguish the fire, which might be set to the fort, under cover of the arquebusiers who were doing their duty on the cavalier. In this manner, I told them, we might be able to defend ourselves so that the enemy could not approach to extinguish the fire which we should set to their ramparts.

This proposition they thought good and very seasonable, and immediately proceeded to carry it out as I directed. In fact the next day they set to work, some to cut wood, others to gather it, for building and equipping the cavalier and mantelets. The work was promptly executed and in less than four hours, although the amount of wood they had collected for burning against the ramparts, in order to set fire to them, was very small. Their expectation was that the five hundred men who had promised to come would do so on this day, but doubt was felt about them, since they had not appeared at the rendezvous, as they had been charged to do, and as they had promised. This greatly troubled our savages; but seeing that they were sufficiently numerous to take the fort without other assistance, and thinking for my part that delay, if not in all things at least in many, is prejudicial, I urged them to attack it, representing to them that the enemy, having become aware of their force and our arms, which pierced whatever was proof against arrows, had begun to barricade themselves and cover themselves with strong pieces of wood, with which they were well provided and their village filled. I told them that the least delay was the best, since the enemy had already strengthened themselves very much; for their village was enclosed by four good palisades, which were made of great pieces of wood, interlaced with each other, with an opening of not more than half a foot between two, and which were thirty feet high, with galleries after the manner of a parapet, which they had furnished with double pieces of wood that were proof against our arquebus shots. Moreover it was near a pond where the water was abundant, and was well supplied with gutters, placed between each pair of palisades, to throw out water, which they had also under cover inside, in order to extinguish fire. Now this is the character of their fortifications and defences, which are much stronger than the villages of the Attigouautan and others.

We approached to attack the village, our cavalier being carried by two hundred of the strongest men, who put it down before the village at a pike's length off. I ordered three arquebusiers to mount upon it, who were well protected from the arrows and stones that could be shot or hurled at them. Meanwhile the enemy did not fail to send a large number of arrows which did not miss, and a great many stones, which they hurled from their palisades. Nevertheless a hot fire of arquebusiers forced them to dislodge and abandon their galleries, in consequence of the cavalier which uncovered them, they not venturing to show themselves, but fighting under shelter. Now when the cavalier was carried forward, instead of bringing up the mantelets according to order, including that one under cover of which we were to set the fire, they abandoned them and began to scream at their enemies, shooting arrows into the fort, which in my opinion did little harm to the enemy.

But we must excuse them, for they are not warriors, and besides will have no discipline nor correction, and will do only what they please. Accordingly one of them set fire inconsiderately to the wood placed against the fort of the enemy, quite the wrong way and in the face of the wind, so that it produced no effect.

This fire being out, the greater part of the savages began to carry wood against the palisades, but in so small quantity that the fire could have no great effect. There also arose such disorder among them that one could not understand another, which greatly troubled me. In vain did I shout in their ears and remonstrate to my utmost with them as to the danger to which they exposed themselves by their bad behavior, but on account of the great noise they made they heard nothing. Seeing that shouting would only burst my head, and that my remonstrances were useless for putting a stop to the disorder, I did nothing more, but determined together with my men to do what we could, and fire upon such as we could see.

Meanwhile the enemy profited by our disorder to get water and pour it so abundantly that you would have said brooks were flowing through their spouts, the result of which was that the fire was instantly extinguished, while they did not cease shooting their arrows, which fell upon us like hail. But the men on the cavalier killed and maimed many. We were engaged in this combat about three hours, in which two of our chiefs and leading warriors were wounded, namely, one called Ochateguain and another Orani, together with some fifteen common warriors. The others, seeing their men and some of the chiefs wounded, now began to talk of a retreat without farther fighting, in expectation of the five hundred men, whose arrival could not be much delayed. Thus they retreated, a disorderly rabble.

Moreover the chiefs have in fact no absolute control over their men, who are governed by their own will and follow their own fancy, which is the cause of their disorder and the ruin of all their undertakings; for, having determined upon anything with their leaders, it needs only the whim of a villain, or nothing at all, to lead them to break it off and form a new plan. Thus there is no concert of action among them, as can be seen by this expedition.

Now we withdrew into our fort, I having received two arrow wounds, one in the leg, the other in the knee, which caused me great inconvenience, aside from the severe pain. When they were all assembled, I addressed them some words of remonstrance on the disorder that had occurred. But all I said availed nothing, and had no effect upon them. They replied that many of their men had been wounded, like myself, so that it would cause the others much trouble and inconvenience to carry them as they retreated, and that it was not possible to return again against their enemies, as I told them it was their duty to do. They agreed, however, to wait four days longer for the five hundred men who were to come; and, if they came, to make a second effort against their enemies, and execute better what I might tell them than they had done in the past. With this I had to content myself, to my great regret.

Herewith is indicated the manner in which they fortify their towns, from which representation it may be inferred that those of their friends and enemies are fortified in like manner.[1]

The next day there was a violent wind, which lasted two days, and was very favorable for setting fire anew to the fort of the enemy, which, although I urged them strongly, they were unwilling to do, as if they were afraid of getting the worst of it, and besides they pleaded their wounded as an excuse.

We remained in camp until the 16th of the month,[2] during which time there were some skirmishes between the enemy and our men, who were very often surrounded by the former, rather through their imprudence than from lack of courage; for I assure you that every time we went to the charge it was necessary for us to go and disengage them from the crowd, since they could only retreat under cover of our arquebusiers, whom the enemy greatly dreaded and feared; for as soon as they perceived any one of the arquebusiers they withdrew speedily, saying in a persuasive manner that we should not interfere in their combats, and that their enemies had very little courage to require us to assist them, with many other words of like tenor, in order to prevail upon us.

I have represented by figure E the manner in which they arm themselves in going to war.

After some days, seeing that the five hundred men did not come,[3] they determined to depart, and enter upon their retreat as soon as possible. They proceeded to make a kind of basket for carrying the wounded, who are put into it crowded up in a heap, being bound and pinioned in such a manner that it is as impossible for them to move as for an infant in its swaddling clothes; but this is not without causing the wounded

---

[1] This paragraph refers to a drawing of the Iroquois fort, not reproduced in this volume.

[2] October.   [3] They arrived two days later. See p. 353.

much extreme pain. This I can say with truth from my
own experience, having been carried some days, since I could
not stand up, particularly on account of an arrow-wound which
I had received in the knee. I never found myself in such a
gehenna as during this time, for the pain which I suffered in
consequence of the wound in my knee was nothing in comparison with that which I endured while I was carried bound
and pinioned on the back of one of our savages; so that I lost
my patience, and as soon as I could sustain myself, got out of
this prison, or rather *gehenna*.

The enemy followed us about half a league, though at a
distance, with the view of trying to take some of those com-
posing the rear guard; but their efforts were vain, and they
retired.

Now the only good point that I have seen in their mode
of warfare is that they make their retreat very securely, placing all the wounded and aged in their centre, being well armed
on the wings and in the rear, and continuing this order without
interruption until they reach a place of security.

Their retreat was very long, being from twenty-five to
thirty leagues, which caused the wounded much fatigue, as
also those who carried them, although the latter relieved
each other from time to time.

On the 18th day of the month there fell much snow and
hail, accompanied by a strong wind, which greatly incom-
moded us. Nevertheless we succeeded in arriving at the
shore of the lake of the Entouhonorons, at the place where
our canoes were concealed, which we found all intact, for we
had been afraid lest the enemy might have broken them up.

When they were all assembled, and I saw that they were
ready to depart to their village, I begged them to take me to
our settlement, which, though unwilling at first, they finally
concluded to do, and sought four men to conduct me. Four
men were found, who offered themselves of their own accord;
for, as I have before said, the chiefs have no control over their
men, in consequence of which they are often unable to do
as they would like. Now the men having been found, it was

necessary also to find a canoe, which was not to be had, each one needing his own, and there being no more than they required. This was far from being pleasant to me, but on the contrary greatly annoyed me, since it led me to suspect some evil purpose, inasmuch as they had promised to conduct me to our settlement after their war. Moreover I was poorly prepared for spending the winter with them, or else should not have been concerned about the matter. But not being able to do anything, I was obliged to resign myself in patience. Now after some days I perceived that their plan was to keep me and my companions, not only as a security for themselves, for they feared their enemies, but also that I might listen to what took place in their councils and assemblies, and determine what they should do in the future against their enemies for their security and preservation.

The next day, the 28th of the month, they began to make preparations; some to go deer-hunting, others to hunt bears and beavers, others to go fishing, others to return to their villages. An abode and lodging were furnished me by one of the principal chiefs, called D'Arontal, with whom I already had some acquaintance. Having offered me his cabin, provisions, and accommodations, he set out also for the deer-hunt, which is esteemed by them the greatest and most noble one. After crossing, from the island, the end of the lake, we entered a river [1] some twelve leagues in extent. They then carried their canoes by land some half a league, when we entered a lake [2] which was some ten or twelve leagues in circuit, where there was a large amount of game, as swans, white cranes, *outardes*, ducks, teal, song-thrush, larks, snipe, geese, and several other kinds of fowl too numerous to mention. Of these I killed a great number, which stood us in good stead while waiting for the capture of a deer. From there we proceeded to a certain place some ten leagues distant, where our savages thought there were deer in abundance. Assembled there were some twenty-five savages, who set to building two

---

[1] Probably Cataraqui Creek, in the province of Ontario.
[2] Probably Loughborough Lake.

or three cabins out of pieces of wood fitted to each other, the chinks of which they stopped up by means of moss to prevent the entrance of the air, covering them with the bark of trees.

When they had done this they went into the woods to a small forest of firs, where they made an enclosure in the form of a triangle, closed up on two sides and open on one. This enclosure was made of great stakes of wood closely pressed together, from eight to nine feet high, each of the sides being fifteen hundred paces long. At the extremity of this triangle there was a little enclosure, constantly diminishing in size, covered in part with boughs and with only an opening of five feet, about the width of a medium-sized door, into which the deer were to enter. They were so expeditious in their work, that in less than ten days they had their enclosure in readiness. Meanwhile other savages had gone fishing, catching trout and pike of prodigious size, and enough to meet all our wants.

All preparations being made, they set out half an hour before day to go into the wood, some half a league from the before-mentioned enclosure, separated from each other some eighty paces. Each had two sticks, which they struck together, and they marched in this order at a slow pace until they arrived at their enclosure. The deer hearing this noise flee before them until they reach the enclosure, into which the savages force them to go. Then they gradually unite on approaching the bay and opening of their triangle, the deer skirting the sides until they reach the end, to which the savages hotly pursue them, with bow and arrow in hand ready to let fly. On reaching the end of the triangle they begin to shout and imitate wolves, which are numerous, and which devour the deer. The deer, hearing this frightful noise, are constrained to enter the retreat by the little opening, whither they are very hotly pursued by arrow shots. Having entered this retreat, which is so well closed and fastened that they can by no possibility get out, they are easily captured. I assure you that there is a singular pleasure in this chase, which took place every two days, and was so successful that, in the thirty-eight days during which we were there, they captured one hundred and twenty deer, which they make good use of, reserving the fat for winter, which they use as we do butter, and taking away to their homes some of the flesh for their festivities.

They have other contrivances for capturing the deer; as snares, with which they kill many. You see depicted opposite the manner of their chase, enclosure, and snare. Out of the skins they make garments. Thus you see how we spent the time while waiting for the frost, that we might return the more easily, since the country is very marshy.

When they first went out hunting, I lost my way in the woods, having followed a certain bird that seemed to me peculiar. It had a beak like that of a parrot, and was of the size of a hen. It was entirely yellow, except the head which was red, and the wings which were blue, and it flew by intervals like a partridge. The desire to kill it led me to pursue it from tree to tree for a very long time, until it flew away in good earnest. Thus losing all hope, I desired to retrace my steps, but found none of our hunters, who had been constantly getting ahead, and had reached the enclosure. While trying to overtake them, and going, as it seemed to me, straight to where the enclosure was, I found myself lost in the woods, going now on this side now on that, without being able to recognize my position. The night coming on, I was obliged to spend it at the foot of a great tree, and in the morning set out and walked until three o'clock in the afternoon, when I came to a little pond of still water. Here I noticed some game, which I pursued, killing three or four birds, which were very acceptable, since I had had nothing to eat. Unfortunately for me there had been no sunshine for three days, nothing but rain and cloudy weather, which increased my trouble. Tired and exhausted I prepared to rest myself and cook the birds in order to alleviate the hunger which I began painfully to feel, and which by God's favor was appeased.

When I had made my repast I began to consider what I should do, and to pray God to give me the will and courage to sustain patiently my misfortune if I should be obliged to

remain abandoned in this forest without counsel or consola-
tion except the Divine goodness and mercy, and at the same
time to exert myself to return to our hunters.   Thus committing all to His mercy I gathered up renewed courage, going
here and there all day, without perceiving any foot-print or
path, except those of wild beasts, of which I generally saw a
good number.   I was obliged to pass here this night also.
Unfortunately I had forgotten to bring with me a small compass which would have put me on the right road, or nearly so.
At the dawn of day, after a brief repast, I set out in order to
find, if possible, some brook and follow it, thinking that it
must of necessity flow into the river on the border of which
our hunters were encamped.   Having resolved upon this
plan, I carried it out so well that at noon I found myself on
the border of a little lake, about a league and a half in extent,
where I killed some game, which was very timely for my wants;
I had likewise remaining some eight or ten charges of powder,
which was a great satisfaction.

I proceeded along the border of this lake to see where
it discharged, and found a large brook, which I followed until
five o'clock in the evening, when I heard a great noise, but on
carefully listening failed to perceive clearly what it was.   On
hearing the noise, however, more distinctly, I concluded that
it was a fall of water in the river which I was searching for.
I proceeded nearer, and saw an opening, approaching which
I found myself in a great and far-reaching meadow, where there
was a large number of wild beasts, and looking to my right
I perceived the river, broad and long.   I looked to see if I
could not recognize the place, and walking along on the
meadow I noticed a little path where the savages carried their
canoes.   Finally, after careful observation, I recognized it
as the same river, and that I had gone that way before.

I passed the night in better spirits than the previous ones,
supping on the little I had.   In the morning I re-examined
the place where I was, and concluded from certain mountains on the border of the river that I had not been deceived,
and that our hunters must be lower down by four or five good

leagues. This distance I walked at my leisure along the border of the river, until I perceived the smoke of our hunters, where I arrived to the great pleasure not only of myself but of them, who were still searching for me, but had about given up all hopes of seeing me again. They begged me not to stray off from them any more, or never to forget to carry with me my compass, and they added: If you had not come, and we had not succeeded in finding you, we should never have gone again to the French, for fear of their accusing us of having killed you. After this he was very careful of me when I went hunting, always giving me a savage as companion, who knew how to find again the place from which he started so well that it was something very remarkable.

To return to my subject: they have a kind of superstition in regard to this hunt; namely, they believe that if they should roast any of the meat taken in this way, or if any of the fat should fall into the fire, or if any of the bones should be thrown into it, they would not be able to capture any more deer. Accordingly they begged me to roast none of this meat, but I laughed at this and their way of doing. Yet, in order not to offend them, I cheerfully desisted, at least in their presence; though when they were out of sight I took some of the best and roasted it, attaching no credit to their superstitions. When I afterwards told them what I had done, they would not believe me, saying that they could not have taken any deer after the doing of such a thing.

On the fourth day of December we set out from this place, walking on the river, lakes, and ponds, which were frozen, and sometimes through the woods. Thus we went for nineteen days, undergoing much hardship and toil, both the savages, who were loaded with a hundred pounds, and myself, who carried a burden of twenty pounds, which in the long journey tired me very much. It is true that I was sometimes relieved by our savages, but nevertheless I suffered great discomfort. The savages, in order to go over the ice more easily, are accustomed to make a kind of wooden sledge, on which they put their loads, which they easily and swiftly drag along.

Some days after there was a thaw, which caused us much trouble and annoyance; for we had to go through pine forests full of brooks, ponds, marshes, and swamps, where many trees had been blown down upon each other. This caused us a thousand troubles and embarrassments, and great discomfort, as we were all the time wet to above our knees. We were four days in this plight, since in most places the ice would not bear. At last, on the 20th[1] of the month, we succeeded in arriving at our village. Here the Captain Yroquet had come to winter with his companions, who are Algonquins, also his son, whom he brought for the sake of treatment, since while hunting he had been seriously injured by a bear which he was trying to kill.

After resting some days I determined to go and visit Father Joseph, and to see in winter the people where he was, whom the war had not permitted me to see in the summer. I set out from this village on the 14th[2] of January following, thanking my host for the kindness he had shown me, and, taking formal leave of him, as I did not expect to see him again for three months.

The next day I saw Father Joseph, in his small house where he had taken up his abode, as I have before stated. I stayed with him some days, finding him deliberating about making a journey to the Petun people, as I had also thought of doing, although it was very disagreeable travelling in winter. We set out together on the fifteenth of February[3] to go to that nation, where we arrived on the seventeenth of the month. These Petun[4] people plant the maize, called by us *blé de Turquie*, and have fixed abodes like the rest. We went to seven other villages of their neighbors and allies, with whom we contracted friendship, and who promised to come in good numbers to our settlement. They welcomed us with good cheer, making a banquet with meat and fish, as is their custom. To this the people from all quarters flocked

---

[1] The edition of 1632 says 23d.   [2] Probably a misprint for 4th.
[3] Almost certainly January.
[4] *I.e.*, the Tobacco Nation, about twenty miles west of the Hurons.

in order to see us, showing many manifestations of friendship, and accompanying us on the greater part of our way back. The country is diversified with pleasant slopes and plains. They were beginning to build two villages, through which we passed, and which were situated in the midst of the woods, because of the convenience of building and fortifying their towns there. These people live like the Attignouaatitans, and have the same customs. They are situated near the Neutral Nation,[1] which are powerful and occupy a great extent of country. After visiting these people, we set out from that place, and went to a nation of savages, whom we named *Cheveux Relevés*. They were very happy to see us again, and we entered into friendship with them, while they in return promised to come and see us, namely at the habitation in this place.

It has seemed to me desirable to describe them and their country, their customs and mode of life. In the first place they are at war with another nation of savages, called Asistagueroüon, which means *Gens de Feu*,[2] who are distant from them ten days' journey. I informed myself accordingly very particularly in regard to their country and the tribes living there, as also to their character and numbers. The people of this nation are very numerous, and are for the most part great warriors, hunters, and fishermen. They have several chiefs, each ruling in his own district. In general they plant Indian corn, and other cereals. They are hunters who go in troops to various regions and countries, where they traffic with other nations, distant four or five hundred leagues. They are the cleanest savages in their household affairs that I have ever seen, and are very industrious in making a kind of mat, which constitutes their Turkish carpets. The women have the body covered, but the men go uncovered, with the exception of a fur robe in the form of a cloak, which they usually leave off in summer. The women and girls are not more moved at seeing them thus, than if they saw nothing unusual. The

---

[1] These lived near the north shore of Lake Erie. They were finally exterminated by the Iroquois.

[2] *I.e.*, the Race of Fire.

women live very happily with their husbands. They have the following custom when they have their catamenia: the wives withdraw from their husbands, or the daughter from her father and mother and other relatives, and go to certain small houses. There they remain in retirement, awaiting their time, without any company of men, who bring them food and necessaries until their return. Thus it is known who have their catamenia and who have not. This tribe is accustomed more than others to celebrate great banquets. They gave us good cheer and welcomed us very cordially, earnestly begging me to assist them against their enemies, who dwell on the banks of the *Mer Douce,* two hundred leagues distant; to which I replied that they must wait until another time, as I was not provided with the necessary means. They were at a loss how to welcome us. I have represented them in figure C as they go to war.

There is, also, at a distance of a two days' journey from them, in a southerly direction, another savage nation, that produces a large amount of tobacco. This is called the Neutral Nation. They number four thousand warriors, and dwell westward of the lake of the Entouhonorons, which is from eighty to a hundred leagues in extent. They, however, assist the *Cheveux Relevés* against the *Gens de Feu.* But with the Iroquois and our allies they are at peace, and preserve a neutrality. There is a cordial understanding towards both of these nations, and they do not venture to engage in any dispute or quarrel, but on the contrary often eat and drink with them like good friends. I was very desirous of visiting this nation, but the people where we were dissuaded me from it, saying that the year before one of our men had killed one of them, when we were at war with the Entouhonorons, which offended them; and they informed us that they are much inclined to revenge, not concerning themselves as to who struck the blow, but inflicting the penalty upon the first one they meet of the nation, even though one of their friends, when they succeed in catching him, unless harmony has been previously restored between them, and gifts and presents bestowed upon the rela-

tives of the deceased.   Thus I was prevented for the time
being from going, although some of this nation assured us that
they would do us no harm for the reason assigned above.

Thus we were led to return the same way we had come,
and continuing my journey, I reached the nation of the Pisie-
rinii,[1] who had promised to conduct me farther on in the prosecution of my plans and explorations.   But I was prevented
by the intelligence which came from our great village and
the Algonquins, where Captain Yroquet was, namely, that the
people of the nation of the Atignouaatitans had placed in his
hands a prisoner of a hostile nation, in the expectation that
this Captain Yroquet would exercise on the prisoner the revenge usual among them.   But they said that, instead of
doing so, he had not only set him at liberty, but, having found
him apt, and an excellent hunter, had treated him as his son,
on account of which the Atignouaatitans had become jealous
and resolved upon vengeance, and had in fact appointed a
man to go and kill this prisoner, allied as he was.   As he was
put to death in the presence of the chiefs of the Algonquin
nation, they, indignant at such an act and moved to anger,
killed on the spot this rash murderer; whereupon the Atignouaatitans feeling themselves insulted, seeing one of their
comrades dead, seized their arms and went to the tents of the
Algonquins, who were passing the winter near the above-
mentioned village, and belabored them severely, Captain
Yroquet receiving two arrow wounds.   At another time they
pillaged some of the cabins of the Algonquins before the latter
could place themselves in a state of defence, so that they had
not an equal chance.   Notwithstanding this they were not
reconciled to the Algonquins, who for securing peace had
given the Atignouaatitans fifty necklaces of porcelain[2] and

---

[1] This relates to those Nipissings who had accompanied Champlain on
the expedition against the Iroquois, and who were passing the winter among
the Hurons.   (Laverdière.)

[2] Wampum, made of shells and held in great esteem by the Indians.
For "branches" read fathoms.   On wampum see W. B. Weeden in *Johns
Hopkins Studies*, II. 389–400, and Laverdière, IV. 62, note 1.   There were

a hundred branches of the same which they value highly, and likewise a number of kettles and axes, together with two female prisoners in place of the dead man. They were, in a word, still in a state of violent animosity. The Algonquins were obliged to suffer patiently this great rage, and feared that they might all be killed, not feeling any security, notwithstanding their gifts, until they should be differently situated. This intelligence greatly disturbed me, when I considered the harm that might arise not only to them, but to us as well, who were in their country.

I then met two or three savages of our large village, who earnestly entreated me to go to them in order to effect a reconciliation, declaring that if I did not go none of them would come to us any more, since they were at war with the Algonquins and regarded us as their friends. In view of this I set out as soon as possible, and visited on my way the Nipissings to ascertain when they would be ready for the journey to the north, which I found broken off on account of these quarrels and hostilities, as my interpreter gave me to understand, who said that Captain Yroquet had come among all these tribes to find and await me. He had requested them to be at the habitation of the French at the same time with himself to see what agreement could be made between them and the Atignouaatitans, and to postpone the journey to the north to another time. Moreover, Yroquet had given porcelain to break off this journey. They promised us to be at our habitation at the same time as the others.

If ever there was one greatly disheartened it was myself, since I had been waiting to see this year what during many preceding ones I had been seeking for with great toil and effort, through so many fatigues and risks of my life. But realizing that I could not help the matter, and that everything depended on the will of God, I comforted myself, resolving to see it in a short time. I had such sure information that I could not doubt the report of these people, who

two kinds, white and black or violet, the latter the more valued. Necklaces were made of this; the white was made up into fathoms.

go to traffic with others dwelling in those northern regions, a great part of whom live in a place very abundant in the chase, and where there are great numbers of large animals, the skins of several of which I saw, and which I concluded were buffaloes, from their representation of their form.   Fishing is also very abundant there.   This journey requires forty days, as well in returning as in going.

I set out towards our above-mentioned village on the 15th of February, taking with me six of our men.   Having arrived at that place the inhabitants were greatly pleased, as also the Algonquins, whom I sent our interpreter to visit in order to ascertain how everything had taken place on both sides, for I did not wish to go myself that I might give no ground for suspicion to either party.

Two days were spent in hearing from both sides how everything had taken place.   After this the principal men and seniors of the place came away with us, and we all together went to the Algonquins.   Here in one of their cabins, where several of the leading men were assembled, they all, after some talk, agreed to come and accept all that might be said by me as arbiter in the matter, and to carry out what I might propose.

Then I gathered the views of each one, obtaining and investigating the wishes and inclinations of both parties, and ascertained that all they wanted was peace.

I set forth to them that the best course was to become reconciled and remain friends, since being united and bound together they could the more easily withstand their enemies; and as I went away I begged them not to ask me to effect their reconciliation if they did not intend to follow in all respects the advice I should give them in regard to this dispute, since they had done me the honor to request my opinion. Whereupon they told me anew that they had not desired my return for any other reason.   I for my part thought that if I should not reconcile and pacify them they would separate ill disposed towards each other, each party thinking itself in the right.   I reflected, also, that they would not have gone to their cabins if I had not been with them, nor to the French if I had not interested myself and taken, so to speak, the charge and conduct of their affairs.   Upon this I said to them that as for myself I proposed to go with my host, who had always treated me well, and that I could with difficulty find one so good; for it was on him that the Algonquins laid the blame, saying that he was the only captain who had caused the taking up of arms.   Much was said by both sides, and finally it was concluded that I should tell them what seemed to me best, and give them my advice.

Since I saw now from what was said that they referred the whole matter to my own decision as to that of a father, and promised that in the future I might dispose of them as I thought best, referring the whole matter to my judgment for settlement, I replied that I was very glad to see them so inclined to follow my advice, and assured them that it should be only for the best interests of the tribes.

Moreover I told them, I had been greatly disturbed at hearing the further sad intelligence, namely the death of one of their relatives and friends, whom we regarded as one of our own, which might have caused a great calamity resulting in nothing but perpetual wars between both parties, with various and serious disasters and a rupture of their friendship, in consequence of which the French would be deprived of seeing them and of intercourse with them, and be obliged to enter into alliance with other nations; since we loved each other as brothers, leaving to God the punishment of those meriting it.

I proceeded to say to them, that this mode of action between two nations, who were, as they acknowledged, friendly to each other, was unworthy of reasoning men, but rather characteristic of brute beasts.   I represented to them, moreover, that they were enough occupied in repelling their enemies who pursued them, in routing them as often as possible, in pursuing them to their villages and taking them prisoners; and that these enemies, seeing divisions and wars among them, would be delighted and derive great advantage therefrom, and be led to lay new and pernicious plans, in the hope

of soon being able to see their ruin, or at least their enfeebling
through one another, which would be the truest and easiest
way for them to conquer and become masters of their territories, since they did not assist each other.

I told them likewise that they did not realize the harm
that might befall them from thus acting; that on account of
the death of one man they hazarded the lives of ten thousand, and ran the risk of being reduced to perpetual slavery;
that, although in fact one man was of great value, yet they
ought to consider how he had been killed, and that it was
not with deliberate purpose, nor for the sake of inciting a civil
war, it being only too evident that the dead man had first
offended, since with deliberate purpose he had killed the
prisoner in their cabins, a most audacious thing, even if the
latter were an enemy. This aroused the Algonquins, who,
seeing a man that had been so bold as to kill in their own
cabins another to whom they had given liberty and treated
as one of themselves, were carried away with passion; and
some, more excited than the rest, advanced, and, unable to
restrain or control their wrath, killed the man in question.
Nevertheless they had no ill feeling at all towards the nation
as a whole, and did not extend their purposes beyond the
audacious one, who, they thought, fully deserved what he
had wantonly earned.

And besides I told them they must consider that the En-
touhonoron, finding himself wounded by two blows in the
stomach, tore from his wound the knife which his enemy
had left there, and gave the latter two blows, as I had been
informed; so that in fact one could not tell whether it was
really the Algonquins who had committed the murder. And
in order to show to the Attigouantans that the Algonquins
did not love the prisoner, and that Yroquet did not bear
towards him the affection which they were disposed to think,
I reminded them that they had eaten him, as he had inflicted
blows with a knife upon his enemy; a thing, however, unworthy of a human being, but rather characteristic of brute
beasts.

I told them also that the Algonquins very much regretted all that had taken place, and that, if they had supposed such a thing would have happened, they would have sacrificed this Iroquois for their satisfaction. I reminded them likewise that they had made recompense for this death and offence, if so it should be called, by large presents and two prisoners, on which account they had no reason at present to complain, and ought to restrain themselves and act more mildly towards the Algonquins, their friends. I told them that, since they had promised to submit every thing to arbitration, I entreated them to forget all that had passed between them and never to think of it again, nor bear any hatred or ill will on account of it to each other, but to live good friends as before, by doing which they would constrain us to love them and assist them as I had done in the past. But in case they should not be pleased with my advice, I requested them to come, in as large numbers as possible, to our settlement, so that there, in the presence of all the captains of vessels, our friendship might be ratified anew, and measures taken to secure them from their enemies, a thing which they ought to consider.

Then they began to say that I had spoken well, and that they would adhere to what I had said, and all went away to their cabins, apparently satisfied, excepting the Algonquins, who broke up and proceeded to their village, but who, as it seemed to me, appeared to be not entirely satisfied, since they said among themselves that they would not come to winter again in these places, the death of these two men having cost them too dearly. As for myself, I returned to my host, in whom I endeavored to inspire all the courage I could, in order to induce him to come to our settlement, and bring with him all those of his country.

During the winter, which lasted four months, I had suffi-cient leisure to observe their country, customs, dress, manner of living, the character of their assemblies, and other things which I should like to describe. But it is necessary first to speak of the situation of the country in general and its divisions, also of the location of the tribes and the distances between them.

The country extends in length, in the direction from east
to west, nearly four hundred and fifty leagues, and some
eighty or a hundred leagues in breadth from north to south,
from latitude 41° to 48° or 49°. This region is almost an
island, surrounded by the great river Saint Lawrence, which
passes through several lakes of great extent, on the shores of
which dwell various tribes speaking different languages,
having fixed abodes, and all fond of the cultivation of the soil,
but with various modes of life, and customs, some better
than others. On the shore north of this great river, extending
westerly some hundred leagues towards the Attigouantans,
there are very high mountains, and the air is more temperate
than in any other part of these regions, the latitude being 41°.
All these places abound in game, such as stags, caribous, elks,
does, buffaloes, bears, wolves, beavers, foxes, minxes, weasels,
and many other kinds of animals which we do not have in
France. Fishing is abundant, there being many varieties,
both those which we have in France, as also others which we
have not. There are likewise many birds in their time and
season. The country is traversed by numerous rivers, brooks,
and ponds, connecting with each other and finally emptying
into the river St. Lawrence and the lakes through which it
passes. The country is very pleasant in spring, is covered
with extensive and lofty forests, and filled with wood similar
to that which we have in France, although in many places
there is much cleared land, where they plant Indian corn.
This region also abounds in meadows, lowlands, and marshes,
which furnish food for the animals before mentioned.

The country north of the great river is very rough and
mountainous, and extends in latitude from 47° to 49°, and
in places abounds in rocks. So far as I could make out,
these regions are inhabited by savages, who wander through
the country, not engaging in the cultivation of the soil, nor
doing anything, or at least as good as nothing. But they
are hunters, now in one place, now in another, the region
being very cold and disagreeable. This land on the north is
in latitude 49° and extends over six hundred leagues in breadth

from east to west, of parts of which we have full knowledge. There are also many fine large rivers rising in this region and discharging into the before-mentioned river, together with an infinite number of fine meadows, lakes, and ponds, through which they pass, where there is an abundance of fish. There are likewise numerous islands which are for the most part cleared up and very pleasant, the most of them containing great quantities of vines and wild fruits.

With regard to the regions further west, we cannot well determine their extent, since the people here have no knowledge of them except for two or three hundred leagues or more westerly, from whence comes the great river, which passes, among other places, through a lake having an extent of nearly thirty days' journey by canoe, namely that which we have called the *Mer Douce*. This is of great extent, being nearly four hundred leagues long. Inasmuch as the savages, with whom we are on friendly terms, are at war with other nations on the west of this great lake, we cannot obtain a more complete knowledge of them, except as they have told us several times that some prisoners from the distance of a hundred leagues had reported that there were tribes there like ourselves in color and in other respects. Through them they have seen the hair of these people, which is very light, and which they esteem highly, saying that it is like our own. I can only conjecture in regard to this, that the people they say resemble us were those more civilized than themselves. It would require actual presence to ascertain the truth in regard to this matter. But assistance is needed, and it is only men of means, leisure, and energy, who could or would undertake to promote this enterprise so that a full exploration of these places might be made, affording us a complete knowledge of them.

In regard to the region south of the great river it is very thickly settled, much more so than that on the north, and by tribes who are at war with each other. The country is very pleasant, much more so than that on the northern border, and the air is more temperate. There are many kinds of trees and fruits not found north of the river, while there are many things on the north side, in compensation, not found on the south. The regions towards the east are sufficiently well known, inasmuch as the ocean borders these places. These are the coasts of Labrador, Newfoundland, Cape Breton, La Cadie, and the Almouchiquois,[1] places well known, as I have treated of them sufficiently in the narrative of my previous voyages, as likewise of the people living there, on which account I shall not speak of them in this treatise, my object being only to make a succinct and true report of what I have seen in addition.

The country of the nation of the Attigouantans is in latitude 44° 30′, and extends two hundred and thirty leagues[2] in length westerly, and ten in breadth. It contains eighteen villages, six of which are enclosed and fortified by palisades of wood in triple rows, bound together, on the top of which are galleries, which they provide with stones and water; the former to hurl upon their enemies and the latter to extinguish the fire which their enemies may set to the palisades. The country is pleasant, most of it cleared up. It has the shape of Brittany, and is similarly situated, being almost surrounded by the *Mer Douce*.[3] They assume that these eighteen villages are inhabited by two thousand warriors, not including the common mass, which amounts to perhaps thirty thousand souls.

Their cabins are in the shape of tunnels or arbors, and are covered with the bark of trees. They are from twenty-five to thirty fathoms long, more or less, and six wide, having a passage-way through the middle from ten to twelve feet wide, which extends from one end to the other. On the two sides there is a kind of bench, four feet high, where they sleep in summer, in order to avoid the annoyance of the fleas, of which there were great numbers. In winter they sleep on the ground

---

[1] *I.e.*, the New England coast.

[2] Probably a misprint for twenty-three, or twenty to thirty. (Laverdière.)

[3] *I.e.*, by Lake Huron, and the waters connected with it, the River Severn and Lake Simcoe.

on mats near the fire, so as to be warmer than they would be on the platform. They lay up a stock of dry wood, with which they fill their cabins, to burn in winter. At the extremity of the cabins there is a space, where they preserve their Indian corn, which they put into great casks made of the bark of trees and placed in the middle of their encampment. They have pieces of wood suspended, on which they put their clothes, provisions, and other things, for fear of the mice, of which there are great numbers. In one of these cabins there may be twelve fires, and twenty-four families. It smokes excessively, from which it follows that many receive serious injury to the eyes, so that they lose their sight towards the close of life. There is no window nor any opening, except that in the upper part of their cabins for the smoke to escape.

This is all that I have been able to learn about their mode of life; and I have described to you fully the kind of dwelling of these people, as far as I have been able to learn it, which is the same as that of all the tribes living in these regions. They sometimes change their villages at intervals of ten, twenty, or thirty years,[1] and transfer them to a distance of one, two, or three leagues from the preceding situation, except when compelled by their enemies to dislodge, in which case they retire to a greater distance, as the Antouhonorons, who went some forty to fifty leagues. This is the form of their dwellings, which are separated from each other some three or four paces, for fear of fire, of which they are in great dread.

Their life is a miserable one in comparison with our own; but they are happy among themselves, not having experienced anything better, and not imagining that anything more excellent is to be found. Their principal articles of food are Indian corn and Brazilian beans, which they prepare in various ways. By braying in a wooden mortar they reduce the corn to meal. They remove the bran by means of fans made of the bark of trees. From this meal they make bread, using also beans which they first boil, as they do the Indian

_____

[1] When the wood in the neighborhood became exhausted.

corn for soup, so that they may be more easily crushed. Then
they mix all together, sometimes adding blueberries or dry raspberries, and sometimes pieces of deer's fat, though not often,
as this is scarce with them. After steeping the whole in luke-
warm water, they make bread in the form of bannocks or pies,
which they bake in the ashes. After they are baked they
wash them, and from these they often make others by wrapping
them in corn leaves, which they fasten to them, and then putting them in boiling water.

But this is not their most common kind. They make another, which they call *migan*, which is as follows: They take
the pounded Indian corn, without removing the bran, and
put two or three handfuls of it in an earthen pot full of water.
This they boil, stirring it from time to time, that it may not
burn nor adhere to the pot. Then they put into the pot a
small quantity of fish, fresh or dry, according to the season,
to give a flavor to the *migan*, as they call it. They make it
very often, although it smells badly, especially in winter,
either because they do not know how to prepare it rightly,
or do not wish to take the trouble to do so. They make two
kinds of it, and prepare it very well when they choose. When
they use fish the *migan* does not smell badly, but only when
it is made with venison. After it is all cooked, they take out
the fish, pound it very fine, and then put it all together into
the pot, not taking the trouble to remove the appendages,
scales, or inwards, as we do, which generally causes a bad taste.
It being thus prepared, they deal out to each one his portion.
This *migan* is very thin, and without much substance, as may
be well supposed. As for drink, there is no need of it, the
migan being sufficiently thin of itself.

They have another kind of *migan*, namely, they roast new
corn before it is ripe, which they preserve and cook whole
with fish, or flesh when they have it. Another way is this:
they take Indian corn, which is very dry, roast it in the ashes,
then bray it and reduce it to meal as in the former case. This
they lay up for the journeys which they undertake here and
there. The *migan* made in the latter manner is the best

according to my taste. Figure H shows the women braying
their Indian corn. In preparing it, they cook a large quantity of fish and meat, which they cut into pieces and put into
great kettles, which they fill with water and let it all boil well.
When this is done, they gather with a spoon from the surface
the fat which comes from the meat and fish. Then they
put in the meal of the roasted corn, constantly stirring it until
the *migan* is cooked and thick as soup. They give to each one
a portion, together with a spoonful of the fat. This dish they
are accustomed to prepare for banquets, but they do not generally make it.

Now the corn freshly roasted, as above described, is highly
esteemed among them. They eat also beans, which they boil
with the mass of the roasted flour, mixing in a little fat and
fish. Dogs are in request at their banquets, which they
often celebrate among themselves, especially in winter, when
they are at leisure. In case they go hunting for deer or go
fishing, they lay aside what they get for celebrating these
banquets, nothing remaining in their cabins but the usual
thin *migan*, resembling bran and water, such as is given to
hogs to eat.

They have another way of eating the Indian corn. In
preparing it, they take it in the ear and put it in water under
the mud, leaving it two or three months in this state until
they think it is putrefied. Then they remove it, and eat it
boiled with meat or fish. They also roast it, and it is better
so than boiled. But I assure you that there is nothing that
smells so badly as this corn as it comes from the water all
muddy. Yet the women and children take it and suck it
like sugar-cane, nothing seeming to them to taste better, as
they show by their manner. In general they have two meals
a day. As for ourselves, we fasted all of Lent and longer,
in order to influence them by our example. But it was time
lost.

They also fatten bears, which they keep two or three
years, for the purpose of their banquets. I observed that if
this people had domestic animals they would be interested

in them and care for them very well, and I showed them the
way to keep them, which would be an easy thing for them,
since they have good grazing grounds in their country, and
in large quantities, for all kinds of animals, horses, oxen,
cows, sheep, swine, and other kinds, for lack of which one
would consider them badly off, as they seem to be. Yet
with all their drawbacks they seem to me to live happily
among themselves, since their only ambition is to live and
support themselves, and they lead a more settled life than
those who wander through the forests like brute beasts. They
eat many squashes, which they boil, and roast in the ashes.

In regard to their dress, they have various kinds and styles
made of the skins of wild beasts, both those which they capture themselves, and others which they get in exchange for
their Indian corn, meal, porcelain, and fishing-nets from the
Algonquins, Nipissings, and other tribes, which are hunters
having no fixed abodes. All their clothes are of one uniform
shape, not varied by any new styles. They prepare and fit
very well the skins, making their breeches of deer-skin rather
large, and their stockings of another piece, which extend up
to the middle and have many folds. Their shoes are made
of the skins of deer, bears, and beaver, of which they use
great numbers. Besides, they have a robe of the same fur,
in the form of a cloak, which they wear in the Irish or Egyp-
tian style, with sleeves which are attached with a string behind. This is the way they are dressed in winter, as is seen
in figure D. When they go into the fields, they gird up their
robe about the body; but when in the village, they leave
off their sleeves and do not gird themselves. The Milan trim-
mings for decorating their garments are made of glue and the
scrapings of the before-mentioned skins, of which they make
bands in various styles according to their fancy, putting in
places bands of red and brown color amid those of the glue,
which always keep a whitish appearance, not losing at all
their shape, however dirty they may get. There are those
among these nations who are much more skilful than others
in fitting the skins, and ingenious in inventing ornaments

to put on their garments. It is our Montagnais and Algonquins, above all others, who take more pains in this matter.
They put on their robes bands of porcupine quills, which they
dye a very fine scarlet color. They value these bands very
highly, and detach them so that they may serve for other robes
when they wish to make a change. They also make use of
them to adorn the face, in order to give it a more graceful
appearance whenever they wish particularly to decorate
themselves.

Most of them paint the face black and red. These colors
they mix with oil made from the seed of the sun-flower, or with
bear's fat or that of other animals. They also dye their
hair, which some wear long, others short, others on one side
only. The women and girls always wear their hair in one
uniform style. They are dressed like men, except that they
always have their robes girt about them, which extend down
to the knee. They are not at all ashamed to expose the body
from the middle up and from the knees down, unlike the men,
the rest being always covered. They are loaded with quantities of porcelain, in the shape of necklaces and chains, which
they arrange in the front of their robes and attach to their
waists. They also wear bracelets and earrings. They have
their hair carefully combed, dyed, and oiled. Thus they go
to the dance, with a knot of their hair behind bound up with
eel-skin, which they use as a cord. Sometimes they put on
plates a foot square, covered with porcelain, which hang on
the back. Thus gaily dressed and habited, they delight to
appear in the dance, to which their fathers and mothers send
them, forgetting nothing that they can devise to embellish
and set off their daughters. I can testify that I have seen at
dances a girl who had more than twelve pounds of porcelain
on her person, not including the other bagatelles with which
they are loaded and bedecked. In the illustration already
cited, F shows the dress of the women, G that of the girls
attired for the dance.

All these people have a very[1] jovial disposition, although

---

[1] Fr. *assez, i.e.,* somewhat.

there are many of them who have a sad and gloomy look. Their bodies are well proportioned. Some of the men and women are well formed, strong, and robust. There is a moderate number of pleasing and pretty girls, in respect to figure, color, and expression, all being in harmony. Their blood is but little deteriorated, except when they are old. There are among these tribes powerful women of extraordinary height. These have almost the entire care of the house and work; namely, they till the land, plant the Indian corn, lay up a store of wood for the winter, beat the hemp and spin it, making from the thread fishing-nets and other useful things. The women harvest the corn, house it, prepare it for eating, and attend to household matters. Moreover they are expected to attend their husbands from place to place in the fields, filling the office of pack-mule in carrying the baggage, and to do a thousand other things. All the men do is to hunt for deer and other animals, fish, make their cabins, and go to war. Having done these things, they then go to other tribes with which they are acquainted to traffic and make exchanges. On their return, they give themselves up to festivities and dances, which they give to each other, and when these are over they go to sleep, which they like to do best of all things.

They have some sort of marriage, which is as follows: when a girl has reached the age of eleven, twelve, thirteen, fourteen, or fifteen years she has suitors, more or less according to her attractions, who woo her for some time. After this, the consent of their fathers and mothers is asked, to whose will the girls often do not submit, although the most discreet and considerate do so. The lover or suitor presents to the girl some necklaces, chains, and bracelets of porcelain. If the girl finds the suitor agreeable, she receives the present. Then the lover comes and remains with her three or four nights, without saying anything to her during the time. They receive thus the fruit of their affections. Whence it happens very often that, after from eight to fifteen days, if they cannot agree, she quits her suitor, who forfeits his necklaces and other presents that he has made, having received in return only a meagre satisfaction. Being thus disappointed in his hopes, the man seeks another woman, and the girl another suitor, if it seems to them desirable. Thus they continue to do until a favorable union is formed. It sometimes happens that a girl thus passes her entire youth, having more than twenty mates, which twenty are not alone in the enjoyment of the creature, mated though they are; for when night comes the young women run from one cabin to another, as do also the young men on their part, going where it seems good to them, but always without any violence, referring the whole matter to the pleasure of the woman. Their mates will do likewise to their women-neighbors, no jealousy arising among them on that account, nor do they incur any reproach or insult, such being the custom of the country.

Now the time when they do not leave their mates is when they have children. The preceding mate returns to her, renews the affection and friendship which he had borne her in the past, asserting that it is greater than that of any other one, and that the child she has is his and of his begetting. The next says the same to her. In fine, the victory is with the stronger, who takes the woman for his wife. Thus it depends upon the choice of the woman to take and accept him who shall please her best, having meantime in her searching and loves gained much porcelain and, besides, the choice of a husband. The woman remains with him without leaving him; or if she do leave him, for he is on trial, it must be for some good reason other than impotence. But while with this husband, she does not cease to give herself free rein, yet remains always at home, keeping up a good appearance. Thus the children which they have together, born from such a woman, cannot be sure of their legitimacy. Accordingly, in view of this uncertainty, it is their custom that the children never succeed to the property and honors of their fathers, there being doubt, as above indicated, as to their paternity. They make, however, the children of their sisters, from whom they are known to have issued, their successors and heirs.

The following is the way they nourish and bring up their

children: they place them during the day on a little wooden board, wrapping them up in furs or skins. To this board they bind them, placing them in an erect position, and leaving a little opening for the child to do its necessities. If it is a girl, they put a leaf of Indian corn between the thighs, which presses against its privates. The extremity of the leaf is carried outside in a turned position, so that the water of the child runs off on it without inconvenience. They put also under the children the down of certain reeds that we call hare's-foot, on which they rest very softly. They also clean them with the same down. As an ornament for the child, they adorn the board with beads, which they also put on its neck, however small it may be. At night they put it to bed, entirely naked, between the father and mother. It may be regarded as a great miracle that God should thus preserve it so that no harm befalls it, as might be expected, from suffocation, while the father and mother are in deep sleep, but that rarely happens. The children have great freedom among these tribes. The fathers and mothers indulge them too much, and never punish them. Accordingly they are so bad and of so vicious a nature, that they often strike their mothers and others. The most vicious, when they have acquired the strength and power, strike their fathers. They do this whenever the father or mother does anything that does not please them. This is a sort of curse that God inflicts upon them.

In respect to laws, I have not been able to find out that they have any, or anything that approaches them, inasmuch as there is not among them any correction, punishment, or censure of evil-doers, except in the way of vengeance when they return evil for evil, not by rule but by passion, which produces among them conflicts and differences, which occur very frequently.

Moreover, they do not recognize any divinity, or worship any God and believe in anything whatever, but live like brute beasts.[1] They have, however, some respect for the devil, or something so called, which is a matter of uncertainty,

---

[1] See p. 96, note 1, and Sagard, *Histoire du Canada*, p. 494.

since the word which they use thus has various significations and comprises in itself various things. It is accordingly difficult to determine whether they mean the devil or something else, but what especially leads to the belief that what they mean is the devil is this: whenever they see a man doing something extraordinary, or who is more capable than usual, or is a valiant warrior, or furthermore who is in a rage as if out of his reason and senses, they call him *oqui*, or, as we should say, a great knowing spirit, or a great devil. However this may be, they have certain persons, who are the *oqui*, or, as the Algonquins and Montagnais call them, *manitous*; and persons of this kind are the medicine-men, who heal the sick, bind up the wounded, and predict future events, who in fine practice all abuses and illusions of the devil to deceive and delude them. These *oquis* or conjurers persuade their patients and the sick to make, or have made banquets and ceremonies that they may be the sooner healed, their object being to participate in them finally themselves and get the principal benefit therefrom. Under the pretence of a more speedy cure, they likewise cause them to observe various other ceremonies, which I shall hereafter speak of in the proper place. These are the people in whom they put especial confidence, but it is rare that they are possessed of the devil and tormented like other savages living more remote than themselves.

This gives additional reason and ground to believe that their conversion to the knowledge of God would be more easy, if their country were inhabited by persons who would take the trouble and pains to instruct them. But it is not enough to send to them friars, unless there are those to support and assist them. For although these people have the desire to-day to know what God is, to-morrow this disposition will change when they are obliged to lay aside and bring under their foul ways, their dissolute manners, and their savage indulgences. So that there is need of people and families to keep them in the way of duty, to constrain them through mildness to do better, and to move them by good example to mend their lives. Father Joseph and myself have many times conferred with them in regard to our belief, laws, and customs. They listen attentively in their assemblies, sometimes saying to us:

> You say things that pass our knowledge, and which we cannot understand by words, being beyond our comprehension; but if you would do us a service come and dwell in this country, bringing your wives and children, and when they are here we shall see how you serve the God you worship, and how you live with your wives and children, how you cultivate and plant the soil, how you obey your laws, how you take care of animals, and how you manufacture all that we see proceeding from your inventive skill. When we see all this, we shall learn more in a year than in twenty by simply hearing you discourse; and if we cannot then understand, you shall take our children, who shall be as your own. And thus being convinced that our life is a miserable one in comparison with yours, it is easy to believe that we shall adopt yours, abandoning our own.

Their words seemed to me good common sense, showing the desire they have to get a knowledge of God. It is a great wrong to let so many men be lost, and see them perish at our door, without rendering them the succor which can only be given through the help of kings, princes, and ecclesiastics, who alone have the power to do this. For to them alone belongs the honor of so great a work; namely, planting the Christian faith in an unknown region and among savage nations, since we are well informed about these people, that they long for and desire nothing so much as to be clearly instructed as to what they should do and avoid. It is accordingly the duty of those who have the power, to labor there and contribute of their abundance, for one day they must answer before God for the loss of the souls which they allowed to perish through their negligence and avarice;[1] and these are not few but very numerous. Now this will be done when it shall please God to give them grace to this end. As for myself, I desire

---

[1] Lescarbot also complains of the indifference of the French ecclesiastics. The zeal of the Recollects, and still more of the Jesuits, was soon to blot out the reproach. See Parkman, *The Jesuits in North America.*

this result rather to-day than to-morrow, from the zeal which I have for the advancement of God's glory, for the honor of my King, and for the welfare and renown of my country.

When they are sick the man or woman who is attacked with any disease sends for the *oqui*, who visits the patient and informs himself about the malady and the suffering. After this, the *oqui* sends for a large number of men, women, and girls, including three or four old women. These enter the cabin of the sick, dancing, each one having on his head the skin of a bear or some other wild beast, that of the bear being the most common as it is the most frightful. There are three or four other old women about the sick or suffering, who for the most part feign sickness, or are sick merely in imagination. But they are soon cured of this sickness, and generally make banquets at the expense of their friends or relatives, who give them something to put into their kettle, in addition to the presents which they receive from the dancers, such as porcelain and other bagatelles, so that they are soon cured; for when they find that they have nothing more to look for, they get up with what they have secured. But those who are really sick are not readily cured by plays, dances, and such proceedings.

To return to my narrative: the old women near the sick person receive the presents each singing and pausing in turn. When all the presents have been made, they proceed to lift up their voices with one accord, all singing together and keeping time with sticks on pieces of dry bark. Then all the women and girls proceed to the end of the cabin, as if they were about to begin a ballet or masquerade. The old women walk in front with their bearskins on their heads, all the others following them, one after the other. They have only two kinds of dances with regular time, one of four steps and the other of twelve, as in the *trioli* of Brittany. They exhibit much grace in dancing. Young men often take part with them. After dancing an hour or two, the old women lead out the sick person to dance, who gets up dolefully and prepares to dance, and after a short time she dances and enjoys as much as the

others. I leave it to you to consider how sick she was. Below
is represented the mode of their dances.

The medicine-man thus gains honor and credit, his patient
being so soon healed and on her feet. This treatment, however, does nothing for those who are dangerously ill and reduced by weakness, but causes their death rather than their
cure; for I can testify that they sometimes make such a noise
and hubbub from morning until two o'clock at night that it
is impossible for the patient to endure it without great pain.
Sometimes the patient is seized with the desire to have the
women and girls dance all together, which is done in accordance with the direction of the *oqui*. But this is not all, for
he and the *manitou*, accompanied by some others, make
grimaces, perform magic arts, and twist themselves about so
that they generally end in being out of their senses, seemingly
crazy, throwing the fire from one side of the cabin to the other,
eating burning coals, holding them in their hands for a while,
and throwing red-hot ashes into the eyes of the spectators.
Seeing them in this condition, one would say that the devil,
the *oqui*, or *manitou*, if he is thus to be called, possesses and
torments them. This noise and hubbub being over, they
retire each to his own cabin.

But those who suffer especially during this time are the
wives of those possessed, and all the inmates of their cabins,
from the fear they have lest the raging ones burn up all that
is in their homes. This leads them to remove everything that
is in sight; for as soon as he arrives he is all in a fury, his eyes
flashing and frightful, sometimes standing up, sometimes
seated, as his fancy takes him. Suddenly a fit seizes him,
and laying hold of everything he finds in his way he throws
them to one side and the other. Then he lies down and sleeps
for some time. Waking up with a jump, he seizes fire and
stones, which he throws about recklessly on all sides. This
rage passes off with the sleep which seizes him again. Then
he rages and calls several of his friends to sweat with him.
The latter is the best means they have for preserving themselves
in health. While they are sweating, the kettle boils to prepare

them something to eat. They remain, two or three hours or
so, covered up with great pieces of bark and wrapped in their
robes, with a great many stones about them which have been
heated red-hot in the fire. They sing all the time while they
are in the rage, occasionally stopping to take breath. Then
they give them many draughts of water to drink, since they
are very thirsty, when the demoniac, who was crazy or possessed of an evil spirit, becomes sober.

Thus it happens that three or four of these sick persons
get well, rather by a happy coincidence and chance than in
consequence of any intelligent treatment, and this confirms
their false belief that they are healed by means of these ceremonies, not considering that, for two who are thus cured,
ten others die on account of the noise, great hubbub and hiss-
ing, which are rather calculated to kill than cure a sick person.
But that they expect to recover their health by this noise,
and we on the contrary by silence and rest, shows how the devil
does everything in hostility to the good.

There are also women who go into these rages, but they
do not do so much harm. They walk on all fours like beasts.
Seeing this, the magician, called *oqui*, begins to sing; then,
with some contortions of the face, he blows upon her, directing her to drink certain waters, and make at once a banquet
of fish or flesh, which must be procured although very scarce
at the time. When the shouting is over and the banquet
ended, they return each to her own cabin. At another time
he comes back and visits her, blowing upon her and singing
in company with several others, who have been summoned
for this purpose, and who hold in the hand a dry tortoise-shell
filled with little pebbles, which they cause to resound in the
ears of the sick woman. They direct her to make at once
three or four banquets with singing and dancing, when all
the girls appear adorned and painted as I have represented
in figure G. The *oqui* orders masquerades, and directs them
to disguise themselves, as those do who run along the streets
in France on Mardi-gras.[1] Thus they go and sing near the

[1] Shrove Tuesday.

bed of the sick woman and promenade through the village while the banquet is preparing to receive the maskers, who return very tired, having taken exercise enough to be able to empty the kettle of its *migan*.

According to their custom each household lives on what it gets by fishing and planting, improving as much land as it needs.   They clear it up with great difficulty, since they do not have the implements adapted to this purpose.   A party strip the trees of all their branches, which they burn at their base in order to kill them.   They clear carefully the land between the trees, and then plant their corn at distances of a pace, putting in each place some ten kernels, and so on until they have made provision for three or four years, fearing that a bad year may befall them.   The women attend to the planting and harvesting, as I have said before, and to procuring a supply of wood for winter.   All the women aid each other in procuring this provision of wood, which they do in the month of March or April, in the order of two days for each. Every household is provided with as much as it needs; and if a girl marries, each woman and girl is expected to carry to the newly married one a parcel of wood for her provision, since she could not procure it alone, and at a season when she has to give her attention to other things.

The following is their mode of government: the older and leading men assemble in a council, in which they settle upon and propose all that is necessary for the affairs of the village. This is done by a plurality of voices, or in accordance with the advice of some one among them whose judgment they consider superior: such a one is requested by the company to give his opinion on the propositions that have been made, and this opinion is minutely obeyed.   They have no particular chiefs with absolute command, but they show honor to the older and more courageous men, whom they name captains, as a mark of honor and respect, of which there are several in a village.   But, although they confer more honor upon one than upon others, yet he is not on that account to bear sway, nor esteem himself higher than his companions, unless he does so from vanity. They make no use of punishments nor arbitrary command, but accomplish everything by the entreaties of the seniors, and by means of addresses and remonstrances. Thus and not otherwise do they bring everything to pass.

They all deliberate in common, and whenever any member of the assembly offers to do anything for the welfare of the village, or to go anywhere for the service of the community, he is requested to present himself, and if he is judged capable of carrying out what he proposes, they exhort him, by fair and favorable words, to do his duty. They declare him to be an energetic man, fit for undertakings, and assure him that he will win honor in accomplishing them. In a word, they encourage him by flatteries, in order that this favorable disposition of his for the welfare of his fellow-citizens may continue and increase. Then, according to his pleasure, he refuses the responsibility, which few do, or accepts, since thereby he is held in high esteem.

When they engage in wars or go to the country of their enemies, two or three of the older or valiant captains make a beginning in the matter, and proceed to the adjoining villages to communicate their purpose, and make presents to the people of these villages, in order to induce them to accompany them to the wars in question. In so far they act as generals of armies. They designate the place where they desire to go, dispose of the prisoners who are captured, and have the direction of other matters of especial importance, of which they get the honor, if they are successful; but, if not, the disgrace of failure in the war falls upon them. These captains alone are looked upon and considered as chiefs of the tribes.

They have, moreover, general assemblies, with representatives from remote regions. These representatives come every year, one from each province, and meet in a town designated as the rendezvous of the assembly. Here are celebrated great banquets and dances, for three weeks or a month, according as they may determine. Here they renew their friendship, resolve upon and decree what they think best for the preser-

vation of their country against their enemies, and make each
other handsome presents, after which they retire each to his
own district.

In burying the dead, they take the body of the deceased,
wrap it in furs, and cover it very carefully with the bark of
trees.   Then they place it in a cabin, of the length of the body,
made of bark and erected upon four posts.   Others they place
in the ground, propping up the earth on all sides, that it may
not fall on the body, which they cover with the bark of trees,
putting earth on top.   Over this trench they also make a little
cabin.   Now it is to be understood that the bodies remain in
these places, thus inhumed, but for a period of eight or ten
years, when the men of the village recommend the place where
their ceremonies are to take place; or, to speak more precisely,
they hold a general council, in which all the people of the country are present, for the purpose of designating the place where
a festival is to be held.   After this they return each to his
own village, where they take all the bones of the deceased,
strip them and make them quite clean.   These they keep
very carefully, although they smell like bodies recently interred.   Then all the relatives and friends of the deceased
take these bones, together with their necklaces, furs, axes,
kettles, and other things highly valued, and carry them,
with a quantity of edibles, to the place assigned.   Here,
when all have assembled, they put the edibles in a place designated by the men of the village, and engage in banquets and
continual dancing.   The festival continues for the space of
ten days, during which time other tribes, from all quarters,
come to witness it and the ceremonies.   The latter are attended
with great outlays.

Now, by means of these ceremonies, including dances,
banquets, and assemblies, as above stated, they renew their
friendship to one another, saying that the bones of their relatives and friends are to be all put together, thus indicating
by a figure that, as their bones are gathered together, and
united in one and the same place, so ought they also, during
their life, to be united in one friendship and harmony, like rela-

tives and friends, without separation.   Having thus mingled together the bones of their mutual relatives and friends, they pronounce many discourses on the occasion.   Then, after various grimaces or exhibitions, they make a great trench, ten fathoms square, in which they put the bones, together with the necklaces, chains of porcelain, axes, kettles, sword-blades, knives, and various other trifles, which, however, are of no slight account in their estimation.   They cover the whole with earth, putting on top several great pieces of wood, and placing around many posts, on which they put a covering. This is their manner of proceeding with regard to the dead, and it is the most prominent ceremony they have.   Some of them believe in the immortality of the soul, while others have only a presentiment of it, which, however, is not so very different; for they say that after their decease they will go to a place where they will sing like crows, a song, it must be confessed, quite different from that of angels.   On the following page are represented their sepulchres and manner of interment.

It remains to describe how they spend their time in winter; namely, from the month of December to the end of March, or the beginning of our spring, when the snow melts.   All that they might do during autumn, as I have before stated, they postpone to be done during winter; namely, their banquetings, and usual dances for the sake of the sick, which I have already described, and the assemblages of the inhabitants of various villages, where there are banquetings, singing, and dances, which they call *tabagies*, and where sometimes five hundred persons are collected, both men, women, and girls. The latter are finely decked and adorned with the best and most costly things they have.

On certain days they make masquerades, and visit each other's cabins, asking for the things they like, and if they meet those who have what they want, these give it to them freely.   Thus they go on asking for many things without end; so that a single one of those soliciting will have robes of beaver, bear, deer, lynxes, and other furs, also fish, Indian corn, tobacco, or boilers, kettles, pots, axes, pruning-knives, knives, and other like things. They go to the houses and cabins of the village, singing these words, That one gave me this, another gave that, or like words, by way of commendation. But if one gives them nothing they get angry, and show such spite towards him that when they leave they take a stone and put it near this man or that woman who has not given them anything. Then, without saying a word, they return singing, which is a mark of insult, censure, and ill-will. The women do so as well as the men, and this mode of proceeding takes place at night, and the masquerade continues seven or eight days. There are some of their villages which have maskers or merry-makers, as we do on the evening of Mardi-gras, and they invite the other villages to come and see them and win their utensils, if they can. Meanwhile banquets are not wanting. This is the way they spend their time in winter.

Moreover, the women spin, and pound meal for the journeys of their husbands in summer, who go to other tribes to trade, as they decide to do at the above-mentioned councils, in which it is determined what number of men may go from each village, that it may not be deprived of men of war for its protection; and nobody goes from the country without the general consent of the chiefs, or if they should go they would be regarded as behaving improperly. The men make nets for fishing, which they carry on in summer, but generally in winter, when they capture the fish under the ice with the line or with the seine.

The following is their manner of fishing. They make several holes in a circular form in the ice, the one where they are to draw the seine being some five feet long and three wide. Then they proceed to place their net at this opening, attaching it to a rod of wood from six to seven feet long, which they put under the ice. This rod they cause to pass from hole to hole, when one or more men, putting their hands in the holes, take hold of the rod to which is attached an end of the net, until they unite at the opening of five to six feet. Then they let the net drop to the bottom of the water, it being sunk by little stones attached to the end. After it is down they draw it up again with their arms at its two ends, thus capturing the fish that are in it. This is, in brief, their manner of fishing in winter.

The winter begins in the month of November and continues until the month of April, when the trees begin to send forth the sap and show their buds.

On the 22d of the month of April we received news from our interpreter, who had gone to Carantoüan, through those who had come from there. They told us that they had left him on the road, he having returned to the village for certain reasons.

Now, resuming the thread of my narrative, our savages assembled to come with us, and conduct us back to our habitation, and for this purpose we set out from their country on the 20th of the month,[1] and were forty days on the way. We caught a large number of fish and animals of various kinds, together with small game, which afforded us especial pleasure, in addition to the provisions thus furnished us for our journey. Upon our arrival among the French, towards the end of the month of June, I found Sieur du Pont Gravé, who had come from France with two vessels, and who had almost despaired of seeing me again, having heard from the savages the bad news, that I was dead.

We also saw all the holy fathers who had remained at our settlement. They too were very happy to see us again, and we none the less so to see them. Welcomes and felicitations on all sides being over, I made arrangements to set out from the Falls of St. Louis for our settlement, taking with me my host D'Arontal. I took leave also of all the other savages, assuring them of my affection, and that, if I could, I would see them in the future, to assist them as I had already done in the past, bringing them valuable presents to secure their friendship with one another, and begging them to forget all the disputes which they had had when I reconciled them, which they promised to do.

[1] Of May.

Then we set out, on the 8th of July, and arrived at our settlement on the 11th of that month. Here I found everybody in good health, and we all, in company with our holy fathers, who chanted the Divine service, returned thanks to God for His care in preserving us, and protecting us amid the many perils and dangers to which we had been exposed.

After this, and when everything had become settled, I proceeded to show hospitalities to my host, D'Arontal, who admired our building, our conduct, and mode of living. After carefully observing us, he said to me, in private, that he should never die contented until he had seen all of his friends, or at least a good part of them, come and take up their abode with us, in order to learn how to serve God, and our way of living, which he esteemed supremely happy in comparison with their own. Moreover he said that, if he could not learn it by word of mouth, he would do so much better and more easily by sight and by frequent intercourse, and that, if their minds could not comprehend our arts, sciences, and trades, their children who were young could do so, as they had often represented to us in their country in conversation with Father Joseph. He urged us, for the promotion of this object, to make another settlement at the Falls of St. Louis, so as to secure them the passage of the river against their enemies, assuring us that, as soon as we should build a house, they would come in numbers to live as brothers with us. Accordingly I promised to make a settlement for them as soon as possible.

After we had remained four or five days together, I gave him some valuable presents, with which he was greatly pleased, and I begged him to continue his affection for us, and come again to see our settlement with his friends. Then he returned happy to the Falls of St. Louis, where his companions awaited him.

When this Captain D'Arontal had departed, we enlarged our habitation by a third at least in buildings and fortifications, since it was not sufficiently spacious, nor convenient for receiving the members of our own company and likewise the strangers that might come to see us. We used, in building, lime and sand entirely, which we found very good there in a spot near the habitation. This is a very useful material for building for those disposed to adapt and accustom themselves to it.

The Fathers Denis and Joseph determined to return to France, in order to testify there to all they had seen, and to the hope they could promise themselves of the conversion of these people, who awaited only the assistance of the holy fathers in order to be converted and brought to our faith and the Catholic religion.

During my stay at the settlement I had some common grain cut; namely, French grain, which had been planted there and which had come up very finely, that I might take it to France, as evidence that the land is good and fertile. In another part, moreover, there was some fine Indian corn, also scions and trees which had been given us by Sieur du Monts in Normandy. In a word, all the gardens of the place were in an admirably fine condition, being planted with peas, beans, and other vegetables, also squashes and very superior radishes of various sorts, cabbages, beets, and other kitchen vegetables. When on the point of departure, we left two of our fathers at the settlement; namely, Fathers Jean d'Olbeau and Pacifique, who were greatly pleased with all the time spent at that place, and resolved to await there the return of Father Joseph, who was expected to come back in the following year, which he did.

We sailed in our barques the 20th day of July, and arrived at Tadoussac the 23d day of the month, where Sieur du Pont Gravé awaited us with his vessel ready and equipped. In this we embarked and set out the 3d day of the month of August. The wind was so favorable that we arrived in health by the grace of God, at Honfleur,[1] on the 10th day of September, one thousand six hundred and sixteen, and upon our

---

[1] On his return Champlain found that the turbulent Condé had been flung into the Bastille, whence he did not emerge till 1619. See the edition of 1632.

arrival rendered praise and thanks to God for his great care in preserving our lives, and delivering and even snatching us, as it were, from the many dangers to which we had been exposed, and for bringing and conducting us in health to our country; we besought Him also to move the heart of our King and the gentlemen of his council, to contribute their assistance so far as necessary to bring these poor savages to the knowledge of God, whence honor will redound to his Majesty, grandeur and growth to his realm, profit to his subjects, and the glory of all these undertakings and toils to God, the sole author of all excellence, to whom be honor and glory. Amen.

CONTINUATION OF THE VOYAGES AND DISCOVERIES MADE IN NEW FRANCE

BY SIEUR DE CHAMPLAIN, CAPTAIN FOR THE KING IN THE WESTERN MARINE, IN THE YEAR 1618

At the beginning of the year one thousand six hundred and eighteen, on the twenty-second of March, I set out from Paris [1] together with my brother-in-law,[2] for Honfleur, our usual port of embarkation. There we were obliged to make a long stay on account of contrary winds. But when they had become favorable, we embarked on the large vessel of the Association,[3] which Sieur du Pont Gravé commanded. There was also on board a nobleman, named De la Mothe,[4] who had previously made a voyage with the Jesuits to the regions of La Cadie, where he was taken prisoner by the English, and by them carried to the Virginias, the place of their settlement. Some time after, they transferred him to England and from there to France, where there arose in him an increased desire to make another voyage to New France, which led him to seek the opportunity presented by me. I had assured him, accordingly, that I would use my influence and assistance with our associates, as it seemed to me that they would find

[1] Champlain made a voyage to New France in 1617, but published no record of its events, which were apparently unimportant. See Biggar, *Early Trading Companies of New France*, pp. 104–106.

[2] Eustache Boullé, son of Nicolas Boullé, secretary of the king's chamber.

[3] Champlain's Company of New France.

[4] Nicolas de la Mothe, who had been lieutenant to the Sieur de la Saussaye in the founding of Madame de Guercheville's colony on Mt. Desert, destroyed by Argall in 1613.

such a person desirable, since he would be very useful in those regions.

Our embarkation being made, we took our departure from Honfleur on the 24th day of May following, in the year 1618. The wind was favorable for our voyage, but continued so only a very few days, when it suddenly changed, and we had all the time head winds up to our arrival, on the 3d day of June following, on the Grand Bank, where the fresh fishery is carried on. Here we perceived to the windward of us some banks of ice, which came down from the north. While waiting for a favorable wind we engaged in fishing, which afforded us great pleasure, not only on account of the fish but also of a kind of bird called *fauquets*,[1] and other kinds that are caught on the line like fish. For, on throwing the line, with its hook baited with cod liver, these birds made for it with a rush, and in such numbers that you could not draw it out in order to throw it again, without capturing them by the beak, feet, and wings as they flew and fell upon the bait, so great were the eagerness and voracity of these birds. This fishing afforded us great pleasure, not only on account of the sport, but on account of the infinite number of birds and fish that we captured, which were very good eating, and made a very desirable change on shipboard.

Continuing on our route, we arrived on the 15th of the month off Isle Percée, and on St. John's day [2] following entered the harbor of Tadoussac, where we found our small vessel, which had arrived three weeks before us. The men on her told us that Sieur des Chesnes, the commander, had gone to our settlement at Quebec. Thence he was to go to the Trois Rivières to meet the savages, who were to come there from various regions for the purpose of trade, and likewise to determine what was to be done on account of the death of two of our men, who had been treacherously and perfidiously killed by two vicious young men of the Montagnais. These two unfortunate victims, as the men on the

---

[1] Probably the common tern, or sea swallow. (Slafter.)   [2] June 24.

vessel informed us, had been killed while out hunting nearly two years [1] before. Those in the settlement had always supposed that they had been drowned from the upsetting of their canoe, until a short time before, one of the men, conceiving an animosity against the murderers, made a disclosure and communicated the fact and cause of the murder to the men of our settlement. For certain reasons it has seemed to me well to give an account of the matter and of what was done in regard to it. But it is almost impossible to obtain the exact truth in the case, on account, not only of the small amount of testimony at hand, but of the diversity of the statements made, the most of which were presumptive. I will, however, give an account of the matter here, following the statement of the greater number as being nearer the truth, and relating what I have found to be the most probable.

The following is the occasion of the murder of the two unfortunate deceased. One of the two murderers paid frequent visits to our settlement, receiving there a thousand kindnesses and favors, among other persons from Sieur du Parc, a nobleman from Normandy, in command at the time at Quebec, in the service of the King and in behalf of the merchants of this Association in the year 1616. This savage, while on one of his customary visits, received one day, on account of some jealousy, ill treatment from one of the two murdered men, who was by profession a locksmith, and who after some words beat the savage so soundly as to impress it well upon his memory. And not satisfied with beating and misusing the savage he incited his companions to do the same, which aroused still more the hatred and animosity of the savage towards this locksmith and his companions, and led him to seek an opportunity to revenge himself. He accordingly watched for a time and opportunity for doing so, acting however cautiously

---

[1] This would make the murder take place in August or September, 1616. Sagard (*Histoire du Canada*, p. 42) places it in the middle of April, 1617. Champlain's date is the more probable, as there would be little game in April.

and appearing as usual, without showing any sign of resentment.

Some time after, the locksmith and a sailor named Charles Pillet, from the island of Ré,[1] arranged to go hunting and stay away three or four nights. For this purpose they got ready a canoe, and embarking departed from Quebec for Cape Tourmente. Here there were some little islands where a great quantity of game and birds resorted, near Isle d'Orleans, and distant seven leagues from Quebec. The departure of our men became at once known to the two savages, who were not slow in starting to pursue them and carry out their evil design. They sought for the place where the locksmith and his companion went to sleep, in order to surprise them. Having ascertained it at evening, at break of day on the following morning the two savages slipped quietly along certain very pleasant meadows. Arriving at a point near the place in question, they moored their canoe, landed and went straight to the cabin, where our men had slept. But they found only the locksmith, who was preparing to go hunting with his companion, and who thought of nothing less than of what was to befall him. One of these savages approached him, and with some pleasant words removed from him all suspicion of anything wrong in order that he might the better deceive him. But as he saw him stoop to adjust his arquebus, he quickly drew a club that he had concealed on his person, and gave the locksmith so heavy a blow on his head, that it sent him staggering and completely stunned. The savage, seeing that the locksmith was preparing to defend himself, repeated his blow, struck him to the ground, threw himself upon him, and with a knife gave him three or four cuts in the stomach, killing him in this horrible manner.

In order that they might also get possession of the sailor, the companion of the locksmith who had started early in the morning to go hunting, not because they bore any special hatred towards him, but that they might not be discovered nor accused by him, they went in all directions searching for

[1] Off Rochelle.

him. At last, from the report of an arquebus which they
heard, they discovered where he was, in which direction they
rapidly hastened, so as to give no time to the sailor to reload
his arquebus and put himself in a state of defence. Approaching, they fired their arrows at him, by which having pros-
trated him, they ran upon him and finished him with the
knife.

Then the assassins carried off the body, together with the
other, and, binding them so firmly together that they would
not come apart, attached to them a quantity of stones and
pebbles, together with their weapons and clothes, so as not
to be discovered by any sign, after which they carried them
to the middle of the river, threw them in, and they sank to
the bottom. Here they remained a long time until, through
the will of God, the cords broke, and the bodies were washed
ashore and thrown far up on the bank, to serve as accusers
and incontestable witnesses of the attack of these two cruel
and treacherous assassins. For the two bodies were found at a
distance of more than twenty feet from the water in the woods,
but had not become separated in so long a time, being still
firmly bound, the bones, stripped of the flesh like a skeleton,
alone remaining. For the two victims, contrary to the expectation of the two murderers, who thought they had done
their work so secretly that it would never be known, were
found a long time after their disappearance by the men of
our settlement, who, pained at their absence, searched for
them along the banks of the river. But God in his justice
would not permit so enormous a crime, and had caused it
to be exposed by another savage, their companion, in retalia-
tion for an injury he had received from them. Thus their
wicked acts were disclosed.

The holy fathers and the men of the settlement were greatly
surprised at seeing the bodies of these two unfortunates, with
their bones all bare, and their skulls broken by the blows
received from the club of the savages. The fathers and others
at the settlement advised to preserve them in some portion
of the settlement until the return of our vessels, in order to

consult with all the French as to the best course to pursue
in the matter. Meanwhile our people at the settlement resolved to be on their guard, and no longer allow so much freedom to these savages as they had been accustomed to, but on
the contrary require reparation for so cruel a murder by a
process of justice, or some other way, or let things in the meantime remain as they were, in order the better to await our
vessels and our return, that we might all together consult what
was to be done in the matter.

But the savages seeing that this iniquity was discovered,
and that they and the murderer were obnoxious to the French,
were seized with despair, and, fearing that our men would
exercise vengeance upon them for this murder, withdrew for
a while from our settlement.[1] Not only those guilty of the
act but the others also being seized with fear came no longer
to the settlement, as they had been accustomed to do, but
waited for greater security for themselves.

Finding themselves deprived of intercourse with us, and
of their usual welcome, the savages sent one of their companions, named by the French *La Ferrière*, to make their excuses
for this murder; namely, they asserted they had never been
accomplices in it, and had never consented to it, and that
if it was desired to have the two murderers for the sake of
inflicting justice, the other savages would willingly consent
to it, unless the French should be pleased to take as reparation and restitution for the dead some valuable presents of
skins, as they are accustomed to do in return for a thing that
cannot be restored. They earnestly entreated the French
to accept this rather than require the death of the accused,
which they anticipated would be hard for them to execute,
and so doing to forget everything as if it had not occurred.[2]

To this, in accordance with the advice of the holy fathers,

---

[1] Sagard (*Histoire du Canada*, p. 42) says that the Indians gathered
at Three Rivers to the number of 800, and assumed a threatening attitude.

[2] Sagard, pp. 44, 45, tells us that the majority of the laity were in favor
of accepting this offer, especially as famine was threatening the settlement,
but that the clergy held out against it.

it was decided to reply that the savages should bring and deliver up the two malefactors, in order to ascertain from them their accomplices, and who had incited them to do the deed. This they communicated to La Ferrière for him to report to his companions.

This decision having been made, La Ferrière withdrew to his companions, who upon hearing the decision of the French found this procedure and mode of justice very strange and difficult; since they have no established law among themselves, but only vengeance and restitution by presents. After considering the whole matter and deliberating with one another upon it, they summoned the two murderers and set forth to them the unhappy position into which they had been thrown by the event of this murder, which might cause a perpetual war with the French, from which their women and children would suffer. However much trouble they might give us, and although they might keep us shut up in our settlement and prevent us from hunting, cultivating and tilling the soil, and although we were in too small numbers to keep the river blockaded, as they persuaded themselves to believe in their consultations; still, after all their deliberations, they concluded that it was better to live in peace with the French than in war and perpetual distrust.

Accordingly the savages thus assembled, after finishing their consultation and representing the situation to the accused, asked them if they would not have the courage to go with them to the settlement of the French and appear before them; promising them that they should receive no harm, and assuring them that the French were lenient and disposed to pardon, and would in short go so far in dealing with them as to overlook their offence on condition of their not returning to such evil ways.

The two criminals, finding themselves convicted in conscience, yielded to this proposition and agreed to follow this advice. Accordingly one of them made preparations, arraying himself in such garments and decorations as he could procure, as if he had been invited to go to a marriage or some great festivity. Thus attired, he went to the settlement, accompanied by his father, some of the principal chiefs, and the captain of their company. As to the other murderer, he excused himself from this journey, realizing his guilt of the heinous act and fearing punishment.

When now they had entered the habitation, which was forthwith surrounded by a multitude of the savages of their company, the bridge was drawn up, and all of the French put themselves on guard, arms in hand. They kept a strict watch, sentinels being posted at the necessary points, for fear of what the savages outside might do, since they suspected that it was intended actually to inflict punishment upon the guilty one, who had so freely offered himself to our mercy, and not upon him alone, but upon those also who had accompanied him inside, who likewise were not too sure of their persons, and who, seeing matters in this state, did not expect to get out with their lives. The whole matter was very well managed and carried out, so as to make them realize the magnitude of the crime and have fear for the future. Otherwise there would have been no security with them, and we should have been obliged to live with arms in hand and in perpetual distrust.

After this, the savages suspecting lest something might happen contrary to what they hoped from us, the holy fathers proceeded to make them an address on the subject of this crime. They set forth to them the friendship which the French had shown them for ten or twelve years back, when we began to know them, during which time we had continually lived in peace and intimacy with them, nay even with such freedom as could hardly be expressed. They added moreover that I had in person assisted them several times in war against their enemies, thereby exposing my life for their welfare; while we were not under any obligations to do so, being impelled only by friendship and good will towards them, and feeling pity at the miseries and persecutions which their enemies caused them to endure and suffer. This is why we were unable to believe, they said, that this murder had been committed

without their consent, and especially since they had taken it
upon themselves to favor those who committed it.

Speaking to the father of the criminal, they represented to
him the enormity of the deed committed by his son, saying
that as reparation for it he deserved death, since by our law
so wicked a deed did not go unpunished, and that whoever
was found guilty and convicted of it deserved to be condemned to death as reparation for so heinous an act; but,
as to the other inhabitants of the country, who were not
guilty of the crime, they said no one wished them any harm
or desired to visit upon them the consequences of it.

All the savages, having clearly heard this, said, as their
only excuse, but with all respect, that they had not consented
to this act; that they knew very well that these two criminals
ought to be put to death, unless we should be disposed to pardon them; that they were well aware of their wickedness, not
before but after the commission of the deed; that they had
been informed of the death of the two ill-fated men too late
to prevent it. Moreover, they said that they had kept it
secret, in order to preserve constantly an intimate relation-
ship and confidence with us, and declared that they had ad-
ministered to the evil-doers severe reprimands, and set forth
the calamity which they had not only brought upon themselves, but upon all their tribe, relatives, and friends; and
they promised that such a calamity should never occur again
and begged us to forget this offence, and not visit it with
the consequences it deserved, but rather go back to the
primary motive which induced the two savages to go there,
and have regard for that. Furthermore they said that the
culprit had come freely and delivered himself into our
hands, not to be punished but to receive mercy from the
French.

But the father, turning to the friar, said with tears, there
is my son, who committed the supposed crime; he is worthless, but consider that he is a young, foolish, and inconsiderate
person, who has committed this act through passion, impelled
by vengeance rather than by premeditation: it is in your

power to give him life or death; you can do with him what you please, since we are both in your hands.

After this address, the culprit son, presenting himself with assurance, spoke these words. Fear has not so seized my heart as to prevent my coming to receive death according to my deserts and your law, of which I acknowledge myself guilty. Then he stated to the company the cause of the murder, and the planning and execution of it, just as I have related and here set forth.

After his recital he addressed himself to one of the agents and clerks of the merchants of our Association, named Beauchaine, begging him to put him to death without further formality.

Then the holy fathers spoke, and said to them, that the French were not accustomed to put their fellow-men to death so suddenly, and that it was necessary to have a consultation with all the men of the settlement, and bring forward this affair as the subject of consideration. This being a matter of great consequence, it was decided that it should be carefully conducted and that it was best to postpone it to a more favorable occasion, which would be better adapted to obtain the truth, the present time not being favorable for many reasons.

In the first place, we were weak in numbers in comparison with the savages without and within our settlement, who, resentful and full of vengeance as they are, would have been capable of setting fire on all sides and creating disorder among us. In the second place, there would have been perpetual distrust, and no security in our intercourse with them. In the third place, trade would have been injured, and the service of the King impeded.

In view of these and other urgent considerations, it was decided that we ought to be contented with their putting themselves in our power and their willingness to give satisfaction submissively, the father of the criminal on the one hand presenting and offering him to the company, and he, for his part, offering to give up his own life as restitution for his offence, just as his father offered to produce him whenever he might be required.

This it was thought necessary to regard as a sort of honorable amend, and a satisfaction to justice. And it was considered that if we thus pardoned the offence, not only would the criminal receive his life from us, but, also, his father and companions would feel under great obligations. It was thought proper, however, to say to them as an explanation of our action, that, in view of the fact of the criminal's public assurance that all the other savages were in no respect accomplices, or to blame for the act, and had had no knowledge of it before its accomplishment, and in view of the fact that he had freely offered himself to death, it had been decided to restore him to his father, who should remain under obligations to produce him at any time. On these terms and on condition that he should in future render service to the French, his life was spared, that he and all the savages might continue friends and helpers of the French.

Thus it was decided to arrange the matter until the vessel should return from France, when, in accordance with the opinion of the captains and others, a definite and more authoritative settlement was to be concluded. In the mean time we promised them every favor and the preservation of their lives, saying to them, however, for our security, that they should leave some of their children as a kind of hostage, to which they very willingly acceded, and left at the settlement two in the hands of the holy fathers, who proceeded to teach them their letters, and in less than three months taught them the alphabet and how to make the letters.

From this it may be seen that they are capable of instruction and are easily taught, as Father Joseph can testify.

The vessels having safely arrived, Sieur du Pont Gravé, some others, and myself were informed how the affair had taken place, as has been narrated above, when we all decided that it was desirable to make the savages feel the enormity of this murder, but not to execute punishment upon them, for various good reasons hereafter to be mentioned.

As soon as our vessels had entered the harbor of Tadoussac, even on the morning of the next day, Sieur du Pont Gravé and myself set sail again, on a small barque of ten or twelve tons' burden. So also Sieur de la Mothe, together with Father Jean d'Albeau, a friar, and one of the clerks and agent of the merchants, named Loquin, embarked on a little shallop, and we set out together from Tadoussac. There remained on the vessel another friar, called Father Modeste,[1] together with the pilot and master, to take care of her. We arrived at Quebec, the place of our settlement, on the 27th of June following. Here we found Fathers Joseph, Paul, and Pacifique, the friars, and Sieur Hébert[2] with his family, together with the other members of the settlement. They were all well, and delighted at our return in good health like themselves, through the mercy of God.

The same day Sieur du Pont Gravé determined to go to Trois Rivières, where the merchants carried on their trading, and to take with him some merchandise, with the purpose of meeting Sieur des Chesnes, who was already there. He also took with him Loquin, as before mentioned. I stayed at our settlement some days, occupying myself with business relating to it; among other things in building a furnace for making an experiment with certain ashes, directions for which had been given me, and which are in truth of great value; but it requires labor, diligence, watchfulness and skill; and for the working of these ashes a sufficient number of men are needed who are acquainted with this art. This first experiment did not prove successful, and we postponed further trial to a more favorable opportunity.

I visited the cultivated lands, which I found planted with fine grain. The gardens contained all kinds of plants, cabbages, radishes, lettuce, purslain, sorrel, parsley, and other

---

[1] Frère Modeste Guines. See Sagard, *Histoire du Canada*, p. 40.

[2] Louis Hébert, an apothecary, who had been at Port Royal with Poutrincourt, removed in 1617 with his family from Paris to Quebec, where he was the first settler to live by the cultivation of the soil. He died at Quebec in 1627.

plants, squashes, cucumbers, melons, peas, beans and other vegetables, which were as fine and forward as in France. There were also the vines, which had been transplanted, already well advanced. In a word, you could see everything growing and flourishing. Aside from God, we are not to give the praise for this to the laborers or their skill, for it is probable that not much is due to them, but to the richness and excellence of the soil, which is naturally good and adapted for everything, as experience shows, and might be turned to good account, not only for purposes of tillage and the cultivation of fruit-trees and vines, but also for the nourishment and rearing of cattle and fowl, such as are common in France. But the thing lacking is zeal and affection for the welfare and service of the King.

I tarried some time at Quebec, in expectation of further intelligence, when there arrived a barque from Tadoussac, which had been sent by Sieur du Pont Gravé to get the men and merchandise remaining at that place on the before-mentioned large vessel. Leaving Quebec, I embarked with them for Trois Rivières, where the trading was going on, in order to see the savages and communicate with them, and ascertain what was taking place respecting the assassination above set forth, and what could be done to settle and smooth over the whole matter.

On the 5th of July following I set out from Quebec, together with Sieur de la Mothe, for Trois Rivières, both for engaging in traffic and to see the savages. We arrived at evening off Sainte Croix,[1] a place on the way so called. Here we saw a shallop coming straight to us, in which were some men from Sieurs du Pont Gravé and des Chesnes, and also some clerks and agents of the merchants. They asked me to despatch at once this shallop to Quebec for some merchandise remaining there, saying that a large number of savages had come for the purpose of making war.

This intelligence was very agreeable to us, and in order to satisfy them, on the morning of the next day I left my

---

[1] Now known as Point Platon.

barque and went on board a shallop in order to go more speedily to the savages, while the other, which had come from Trois Rivières, continued its course to Quebec.[1] We made such progress by rowing that we arrived at the before-mentioned place on the 7th of July at 3 o'clock in the afternoon. Upon landing, all the savages with whom I had been intimate in their country recognized me. They were awaiting me with impatience, and came up to me very happy and delighted to see me again, one after the other embracing me with demonstrations of great joy, I also receiving them in the same manner. In this agreeable way was spent the evening and remainder of this day, and on the next day the savages held a council among themselves, to ascertain from me whether I would again assist them, as I had done in the past and as I had promised them, in their wars against their enemies, by whom they are cruelly harassed and tortured.

Meanwhile on our part we took counsel together to determine what we should do in the matter of the murder of the two deceased, in order that justice might be done, and that they might be restrained from committing such an offence in future.

In regard to the assistance urgently requested by the savages for making war against their enemies, I replied that my disposition had not changed nor my courage abated, but that what prevented me from assisting them was that on the previous year, when the occasion and opportunity presented, they failed me when the time came; because when they had promised to return with a good number of warriors they did not do so, which caused me to withdraw without accomplishing much. Yet I told them the matter should be taken into consideration, but that for the present it was proper to deter-

---

[1] In the edition of 1627 the reading is: "I left my bark and went on board the said shallop to return to Quebec. Having arrived there, I had it loaded with various articles of merchandise from the store-houses of that settlement, of the sorts most desired by and most necessary to the savages. This done, I embarked next morning in a shallop, as one of a party of six, to engage in that trade, and we made such progress by rowing," etc.

mine what should be done in regard to the assassination of
the two unfortunate men, and that satisfaction must be had.
Upon this they left their council in seeming anger and vex-
ation about the matter, offering to kill the criminals, and proceed at once to their execution, if assent were given, and ac-
knowledging freely among themselves the enormity of the affair.

But we would not consent to this, postponing our assistance to another time, requiring them to return to us the next
year with a good number of men. I assured them, moreover,
that I would entreat the King to favor us with men, means,
and supplies to assist them and enable them to enjoy the rest
they longed for, and victory over their enemies. At this
they were greatly pleased, and thus we separated after they
had held two or three meetings on the subject, costing us
several hours of time. Two or three days after my arrival at
this place they proceeded to make merry, dance, and celebrate
many great banquets in view of the future war in which I
was to assist them.

Then I stated to Sieur du Pont Gravé what I thought about
this murder; that it was desirable to make a greater demand
upon them; that at present the savages would dare not only
to do the same thing again but what would be more injurious
to us; that I considered them people who were governed
by example; that they might accuse the French of being
wanting in courage; that if we said no more about the matter
they would infer that we were afraid of them: and that if we
should let them go so easily they would grow more insolent,
bold, and intolerable, and we should even thereby tempt
them to undertake greater and more pernicious designs.
Moreover I said that the other tribes of savages, who had or
should get knowledge of this act, and that it had been unre-
venged, or compromised by gifts and presents, as is their custom, would boast that killing a man is no great matter; since
the French make so little account of seeing their companions
killed by their neighbors, who drink, eat, and associate intimately with them, as may be seen.

But, on the other hand, in consideration of the various

2A

circumstances; namely, that the savages do not exercise reason, that they are hard to approach, are easily estranged, and are very ready to take vengeance, that, if we should force them to inflict punishment, there would be no security for those desirous of making explorations among them, we determined to settle this affair in a friendly manner, and pass over quietly what had occurred, leaving them to engage peaceably in their traffic with the clerks and agents of the merchants and others in charge.

Now there was with them a man named Estienne Brûlé, one of our interpreters, who had been living with them for eight years, as well to pass his time as to see the country and learn their language and mode of life. He is the one whom I had despatched with orders to go in the direction of the Entouhonorons, to Carantoüan, in order to bring with him the five hundred warriors they had promised to send to assist us in the war in which we were engaged against their enemies, a reference to which is made in the narrative of my previous book.[1]   I called this man, namely Estienne Brûlé, and asked him why he had not brought the assistance of the five hundred men, and what was the cause of the delay, and why he had not rendered me a report. Thereupon he gave me an account of the matter, a narrative of which it will not be out of place to give, as he is more to be pitied than blamed on account of the misfortunes which he experienced on this commission.

He proceeded to say that, after taking leave of me to go on his journey and execute his commission, he set out with the twelve savages whom I had given him for the purpose of showing the way, and to serve as an escort on account of the dangers which he might have to encounter. They were successful in reaching the place, Carantoüan, but not without exposing themselves to risk, since they had to pass through the territories of their enemies, and, in order to avoid any evil design, pursued a more secure route through thick and impenetrable forests, wood and brush, marshy bogs, frightful

[1] See p. 287.

and unfrequented places and wastes, all to avoid danger and a meeting with their enemies.

But, in spite of this great care, Brûlé and his savage companions, while crossing a plain, encountered some hostile savages, who were returning to their village and who were surprised and worsted by our savages, four of the enemy being killed on the spot and two taken prisoners, whom Brûlé and his companions took to Carantoüan, by the inhabitants of which place they were received with great affection, a cordial welcome, and good cheer, with the dances and banquets with which they are accustomed to entertain and honor strangers.

Some days were spent in this friendly reception; and, after Brûlé had told them his mission and explained to them the occasion of his journey, the savages of the place assembled in council to deliberate and resolve in regard to sending the five hundred warriors asked for by Brûlé.

When the council was ended and it was decided to send the men, orders were given to collect, prepare, and arm them, so as to go and join us where we were encamped before the fort and village of our enemies. This was only three short days' journey from Carantoüan, which was provided with more than eight hundred warriors, and strongly fortified, after the manner of those before described, which have high and strong palisades well bound and joined together, the quarters being constructed in a similar fashion.

After it had been resolved by the inhabitants of Carantoüan to send the five hundred men, these were very long in getting ready, although urged by Brûlé to make haste, who explained to them that if they delayed any longer they would not find us there. And in fact they did not succeed in arriving until two days after our departure from that place, which we were forced to abandon, since we were too weak and worn by the inclemency of the weather. This caused Brûlé, and the five hundred men whom he brought, to withdraw and return to their village of Carantoüan. After their return Brûlé was obliged to stay, and spend the rest of the autumn and all the winter, for lack of company and escort home. While awaiting, he busied himself in exploring the country and visiting the tribes and territories adjacent to that place, and in making a tour along a river [1] that debouches in the direction of Florida, where are many powerful and warlike nations, carrying on wars against each other. The climate there is very temperate, and there are great numbers of animals and abundance of small game. But to traverse and reach these regions requires patience, on account of the difficulties involved in passing the extensive wastes.

He continued his course along the river as far as the sea, and to islands and lands near them, which are inhabited by various tribes and large numbers of savages, who are well-disposed and love the French above all other nations. But those who know the Dutch complain severely of them, since they treated them very roughly. Among other things he observed that the winter was very temperate, that it snowed very rarely, and that when it did the snow was not a foot deep and melted immediately.

After traversing the country and observing what was noteworthy, he returned to the village of Carantoüan, in order to find an escort for returning to our settlement. After some stay at Carantoüan, five or six of the savages decided to make the journey with Brûlé. On the way they encountered a large number of their enemies, who charged upon Brûlé and his companions so violently that they caused them to break up and separate from each other, so that they were unable to rally: and Brûlé, who had kept apart in the hope of escaping, became so detached from the others that he could not return, nor find a road or sign in order to effect his retreat in any direction whatever. Thus he continued to wander through forest and wood for several days without eating, and almost despairing of his life from the pressure of hunger. At last he came upon a little footpath, which he determined to follow wherever it might lead, whether toward the enemy or not, preferring to expose himself to their hands trusting

[1] The Susquehanna.

in God rather than to die alone and in this wretched manner.
Besides he knew how to speak their language, which he thought
might afford him some assistance.

But he had not gone a long distance when he discovered
three savages loaded with fish repairing to their village. He
ran after them, and, as he approached, shouted at them, as
is their custom. At this they turned about, and filled with
fear were about to leave their burden and flee. But Brûlé
speaking to them reassured them, when they laid down their
bows and arrows in sign of peace, Brûlé on his part laying
down his arms. Moreover he was weak and feeble, not having eaten for three or four days. On coming up to them,
after he had told them of his misfortune and the miserable
condition to which he had been reduced, they smoked together, as they are accustomed to do with one another and
their acquaintances when they visit each other. They had
pity and compassion for him, offering him every assistance,
and conducting him to their village, where they entertained
him and gave him something to eat.

But as soon as the people of the place were informed that
an *Adoresetoüy* had arrived, for thus they call the French,
the name signifying *men of iron*, they came in a rush and in
great numbers to see Brûlé. They took him to the cabin of
one of the principal chiefs, where he was interrogated, and
asked who he was, whence he came, what circumstance had
driven and led him to this place, how he had lost his way, and
whether he did not belong to the French nation that made
war upon them. To this he replied that he belonged to a
better nation, that was desirous solely of their acquaintance
and friendship. Yet they would not believe this, but threw
themselves upon him, tore out his nails with their teeth,
burnt him with glowing firebrands, and tore out his beard,
hair by hair, though contrary to the will of the chief.

During this fit of passion, one of the savages observed an
Agnus Dei, which he had attached to his neck, and asked
what it was that he had thus attached to his neck, and was
on the point of seizing it and pulling it off. But Brûlé said

to him, with resolute words, If you take it and put me to death, you will find that immediately after you will suddenly die, and all those of your house. He paid no attention however to this, but continuing in his malicious purpose tried to seize the *Agnus Dei* and tear it from him, all of them together being desirous of putting him to death, but previously of making him suffer great pain and torture, such as they generally practise upon their enemies.

But God, showing him mercy, was pleased not to allow it, but in his providence caused the heavens to change suddenly from the serene and fair state they were in to darkness, and to become filled with great and thick clouds, upon which followed thunders and lightnings so violent and long continued that it was something strange and awful. This storm caused the savages such terror, it being not only unusual but unlike anything they had ever heard, that their attention was diverted and they forgot the evil purpose they had towards Brûlé, their prisoner. They accordingly left him without even unbinding him, as they did not dare to approach him. This gave the sufferer an opportunity to use gentle words, and he appealed to them and remonstrated with them on the harm they were doing him without cause, and set forth to them how our God was enraged at them for having so abused him.

The captain then approached Brûlé, unbound him, and took him to his house, where he took care of him and treated his wounds. After this there were no dances, banquets, or merry-makings to which Brûlé was not invited. So after remaining some time with these savages, he determined to proceed towards our settlement.

Taking leave of them, he promised to restore them to harmony with the French and their enemies, and cause them to swear friendship with each other, to which end he said he would return to them as soon as he could. Thence he went to the country and village of the Atinouaentans [1] where I

---

[1] The principal Huron tribe. Champlain employs different spellings. See p. 281, etc.

had already been; the savages at his departure having conducted him for a distance of four days' journey from their
village. Here Brûlé remained some time, when, resuming
his journey towards us, he came by way of the Mer Douce,
boating along its northern shores for some ten days, where
I had also gone when on my way to the war.

And if Brûlé had gone further on to explore these regions, as I had directed him to do, it would not have been a
mere rumor that we were preparing war with one another.
But this undertaking was reserved to another time, which he
promised me to continue and accomplish in a short period
with God's grace, and to conduct me there that I might obtain
fuller and more particular knowledge.

After he had made this recital, I gave him assurance that
his services would be recognized, and encouraged him to continue his good purpose until our return, when we should have
more abundant means to do that with which he would be satisfied. This is now the entire narrative and recital of his journey
from the time he left me to engage in the above-mentioned
explorations; and it afforded me pleasure in the prospect
thereby presented me of being better able to continue and
promote them.

With this purpose he took leave of me to return to the
savages, an intimate acquaintance with whom had been acquired by him in his journeys and explorations. I begged
him to continue with them until the next year, when I would
return with a good number of men, both to reward him for
his labors, and to assist as in the past the savages, his friends,
in their wars.[1]

Resuming the thread of my former discourse, I must note
that in my last and preceding voyages and explorations I
had passed through numerous and diverse tribes of savages
not known to the French nor to those of our settlement, with
whom I had made alliances and sworn friendship, on condi-

---

[1] In 1629 Brûlé turned traitor, and piloted the English up the river.
In the edition of 1632 Champlain speaks very severely of him, and omits
this account of his wanderings.

tion that they should come and trade with us, and that I
should assist them in their wars; for it must be understood
that there is not a single tribe living in peace, excepting the
Neutral Nation. According to their promise, there came
from the various tribes of savages recently discovered some
to trade in peltry, others to see the French and ascertain
what kind of treatment and welcome would be shown them.
This encouraged everybody, the French on the one hand to
show them cordiality and welcome, for they honored them with
some attentions and presents, which the agents of the merchants
gave to gratify them; on the other hand, it encouraged the
savages, who promised all the French to come and live in
future in friendship with them, all of them declaring that they
would deport themselves with such affection towards us that
we should have occasion to commend them, while we in like
manner were to assist them to the extent of our power in their
wars.

The trading having been concluded, and the savages having taken their leave and departed, we left Trois Rivières on
the 14th of July of this year. The next day we arrived at
our quarters at Quebec, where the barques were unloaded
of the merchandise which had remained over from the traffic
and which was put in the warehouse of the merchants at
that place.

Now Sieur de Pont Gravé went to Tadoussac with the
barques in order to load them and carry to the habitation the
provisions necessary to support those who were to remain
and winter there, and I determined while the barques were
thus engaged to continue there for some days in order to have
the necessary fortifications and repairs made.

At my departure from the settlement I took leave of the
holy fathers, Sieur de la Mothe, and all the others who were
to stay there, giving them to expect that I would return, God
assisting, with a good number of families to people the country. I embarked on the 26th of July, together with the
Fathers Paul and Pacifique, the latter having wintered here
once and the other having been here a year and a half, who

were to make a report of what they had seen in the country and of what could be done there.   We set out on the day above-mentioned from the settlement for Tadoussac, where we were to embark for France.   We arrived the next day and found our vessels ready to set sail.   We embarked, and left Tadoussac for France on the 13th of the month of July, 1618, and arrived at Honfleur on the 28th day of August, the wind having been favorable, and all being in good spirits.

INDEX

Abriou, succeeds his father, 114.
Acadia, search along the coast, 28; location, 49; mentioned, 66, 313; ways of spelling, 66 n.
Achelacy, St. Croix called, 140.
Adirondack Mountains, seen by Champlain, 162 n.
Advocate's Harbor, tides of, 36 n.
d'Albeau, *see* d'Olbeau.
Alexandria, position of, among the nations, 21–22.
Alfonse, Jean, describes Norumbega, 44 n.
Algonquins, dress, 95; physical characteristics, 95; weapons, 95; dwellings, 96; government, 96; religion, 96; Parkman's opinion of, 96 n.; character, 146; manner of life, 146; headquarters of, 146 n.; wars with the Iroquois, 149–166, 178–187, 287–296; character of, 164; Champlain's alliance with, 165 n.; return to their country, 167; presents gifts to Champlain, 167; Champlain goes to meet, 201; refusal to explore the Trois Rivières, 202; report concerning, 209; unite against the Iroquois, 210; promises, 211, 220; arrival, 217; ceremony, over the body of Outetoucos, 218; divisions of, 219; Champlain traffics with, 233; trouble with the Attigountans, 305–310.
Allen River, mill at, 107.
All-Isles Bay, Pont Gravé found at, 28.
Allumette Island, Champlain reaches, 279; location, 279 n.
Allumette Lake, Champlain visits, 245, 245 n.
Almouchiquois, 48 n.; de Monts visits, 56–68; country of, 56 n.; described, 61–63.

Alvert, sighted, 220.
American history, Champlain's connection with, 9.
Anadabijou, son of, 217.
Anassou, Champlain's alliance with, 77.
Andastes, engage in war against the Iroquois, 285, 285 n.
Androscoggin, river, 59 n.
Aneda, Indian captain, discovers the plant aneda, 60.
Aneda, plant used as a remedy for the scurvy, 53 n., 60.
L'Ange, accompanies Champlain, 232, 233, 258; gives information to Champlain, 256;
Angoulême, Lake, identified with St. Peters, 153 n.
Ann, Cape, sighted, 64 n.; named, 65, 65 n.; Indians of, 72–73; Champlain reaches, 76; Champlain proceeds to, 90, 90 n.
Annapolis, formerly a French fort, 35 n.; Poutrincourt's men at, 87, 87 n.
Annapolis Basin, 34 n.; Champlain at, 36.
Annapolis River, described, 35; former names, 35 n.
Antons, Sieur des, at St. Croix, 77.
Archangel, ship, 77 n.
Argall, Samuel, destroys St. Sauveur, 45 n., 339 n.
Argall's Bay, former name for Bay of Fundy, 30 n.
Argyll River, bay near, 86 n.
Armouchiquois, *see* Almouchiquois.
D'Arontal, Champlain entertained by, 297; accompanies Champlain, 332; departure 333.
Artichoke, Jerusalem, found by Champlain, 90 n.